# Artificial Intelligence

**Other TAB books by the author:**

No.  952  *Microprocessor Programming for Computer Hobbyists*

# Artificial Intelligence

## By Neill Graham

TAB BOOKS Inc.

BLUE RIDGE SUMMIT, PA. 17214

FIRST EDITION

FOURTH PRINTING

Copyright © 1979 by TAB BOOKS Inc.

Printed in the United States of America

Library of Congress Cataloging in Publication Data

Neill, Graham
    Artificial intelligence.

    Bibliography: p.
    Includes index.
    1. Artificial intelligence.    I. Title.
Q335.N44      001.53'5      78-26512
ISBN 0-8306-9835-3
ISBN 0-8306-1076-6 pbk.

Cover photo courtesy of Science News magazine.

# Foreword

Not too many years ago computer programming carried the aura of a Black Art, known only to a few mystical practitioners evoking their powers for a living. As computers slowly permeated our lives, workers in a multitude of fields found themselves involved with these wonders. And always there was the programmer performing his magic.

But as the manufacturers of integrated circuits developed increasingly complex functions in their microscopic wonders, computers soon followed that could rest on a desk, unlike the multiple racks of equipment they displaced. But what of the programmer? As this powerful and relatively inexpensive new generation of computers dotted the workplaces of the world, programming became a required skill for many of those in need of a computer.

And in the latest phase of the computer explosion, hobbyists are designing, building, and programming their own personal computers. What had once been the exclusive domain of professionals is today crowded with a host of semi-professional and amateur programmers. And this new breed soon realized the limitations of conventional programming. Computer applications today increasingly demand sophisticated programming techniques filtering down from universities and high-technology companies conducting research in Artificial Intelligence, the use of a computer to perform tasks that if performed by a human would require intelligence.

In one of the first applications of AI programming, the professionals set their computers to translating Russian into English. The launching of Sputnik I into Earth orbit in October 1957 led many to believe that the Russian scientists' knowledge of English placed our experts, most of whom didn't know Russian, at a disadvantage.

They could read our technical literature, but we couldn't read theirs. And soon computers were churning out translations of Russian about 80 percent complete. But obtaining the other 20 percent proved to be despairingly complex, so complex, in fact, that efforts virtually came to a halt. Again today, though, linguists and programmers work together, perfecting these computer translations of natural languages. Even hobbyists devote considerable efforts to natural language translations.

In another AI area, computerized chess playing has become so popular that annual World Computer Chess Championships take place. Computer vies against computer in a test of "intelligence." At present skilled human players can dominate a computer opponent. The computers lack sufficient long-range planning, the chess masters say. But it is likely that in the future more sophisticated AI techniques, combined with faster computers having larger memory capabilities, will master this shortcoming. Then the only relevant action will pit computer against computer.

Though the computer competes effectively against humans in games like chess, the gap remains wide in pattern recognition. This too is an area for AI practices. Discerning objects, perhaps to give a robot vision, requires very sophisticated programs. This facet of programming is yet in its infancy.

Pushing computers and their programs to maximum efficiency goes beyond a modern day application of the Puritan work ethic. In its essence the fascination seems to be in the simulation of life itself. Perhaps we have drawn from the writers of science fiction a longing for those future worlds, where mundane chores become the tasks of worker robots, where super powerful computer brains churn out solutions to problems as yet undreamed of. By looking to the stars, we may yet improve the lot of man here on Earth.

The author provides an introduction to this blossoming field. Whether your interests lie in intelligent game playing, natural language processing, robotics, math and science work, or in engineering aids, Artificial Intelligence will prove to be a powerful tool in your programming chest.

Neill Graham

# Contents

# Chapter 1
# What Is Artificial Intelligence?

Artificial Intelligence is the branch of computer science devoted to programming computers to carry out tasks that if carried out by human beings would require intelligence.

The reason for the qualification "if carried out by human beings" is this. When a computer has been programmed to carry out a certain task, people are tempted to deny that the task really requires intelligence after all, at least the way the computer does it. Endless arguments then ensure over what feats may or may not constitute intelligent behavior on the part of a computer. We can avoid most of the arguments by claiming only that we are trying to program computers to do tasks that would call for intelligence **in a person.** Whether or not you wish to call a computer that carries out such tasks "intelligent" is left up to you.

Like many other things in computer science, Artificial Intelligence is often known by its initials, AI.

## APPLICATIONS OF ARTIFICAL INTELLIGENCE

Some specific areas of interest to AI workers are:

- Problem Solving
- Natural Language Processing
- Perception and Pattern Recognition
- Information Storage and Retrieval
- Control of Robots
- Game Playing
- Automatic Programming
- Computational Logic

## Problem Solving

Most of the tasks we give to computers can be thought of as problems. In each case we wish the computer to carry out the operations necessary to achieve a given goal. For instance, we may have a file giving the hourly pay rate and the number of hours worked last week for each employee of a company. Our goal is then to get a paycheck printed for each worker. With the aid of a payroll program the computer achieves this goal and in doing so solves our problem.

Non-AI programs are designed to solve fairly limited classes of problems. A payroll program may be able to handle slight variations on the payroll problem, such as employees having different kinds and numbers of deductions, but no one would expect a payroll program to be able to solve a chess problem or chart a course to the moon for a spacecraft.

In contrast to these special-purpose programs, AI programs are designed to be as general purpose as possible. Such a general-purpose program, given a problem and the knowledge relevant to solving it, should be able to work out a method of solution much as a human would do.

Traditional computer science designs programs to solve specific problems, in each case following some step-by-step method provided by the programmer. AI tries to design programs that will, first, work out a step-by-step method for solving a given problem, and second, carry out the steps.

## Natural Language Processing

Currently, computers do not communicate very well with people. This is particularly true when the person is trying to give information or commands to the computer. (By using canned phrases computers can do a somewhat better job of passing information to people.)

Commands to computers must often be phrased in obscure codes written according to precise rules from which not the slightest deviation is allowed. Some popular programming languages are all-too-good examples of this problem. Anyone who has tried to teach such languages to beginner's knows how arbitrary and frustrating their many rules and restrictions seem to be to the uninitiated. But the best "horrible examples" of the problem are the job-control languages on large computers, which regularly confuse even experienced programmers.

If computers are to be widely used by nonspecialists, the computers must be able to communicate in natural langauges, such as English. And they should be able to communicate in speech as well as in writing.

In addition to having computers communicate easily with the people who use them, we would like to be able to give them language-oriented tasks, such as translating from one natural language to another, or have them find answers to questions in a textbook on the relevant subject.

## Perception and Pattern Recognition

For many applications a computer needs to perceive its surroundings through TV cameras, microphones, and other sensors. What's more, it needs to be able to recognize significant features, or patterns, in the environment it perceives.

Pattern recognition is a prerequisite to most other AI tasks. A problem-solving program, for instance, must be able to extract significant patterns from the problem situation and use these as clues to the solution. (For an example of such pattern-recognition-based probelm solving see any Sherlock Holmes story.)

## Information Storage and Retrieval

In this century there has been an information explosion in medicine, law, science, engineering and other fields. No worker in even one of these fields can possibly keep in his head all the information needed to do his job. He may even be unaware that the information he needs exists.

Computers can store large amounts of information. With current systems, however, you usually must describe the required information in considerable detail. You have to have a pretty good idea of what you are seeking in order to be able to tell the computer how to find it for you. How much more helpful it would be if you could describe your subject or the problem you are trying to solve (in a natural language, of course) and have the computer locate all the relevant information.

Information storage and retrieval is also needed for other AI tasks. A problem-solving program, for instance, needs full knowledge of the problem situation. It also needs to know the techniques and rules of thumb that have proved effective for solving similar problems in the past. AI workers classify the problem of making such information available under the heading *Representation of Knowledge*.

## Control of Robots

For some tasks, such as assembling machines in a factory, it isn't enough for the computer to know about its environment or even to be able to perceive it directly. The computer must be able to bring about changes in its environment, such as by picking up one part and attaching it to another. A computer with this capability is called a robot. (When the mechanism that does the manipulation is remote from the computer, the manipulating mechanism is often called a robot, and the remote computer is said to control the robot. By using time sharing one computer can control many robots.)

Part of the robot problem is mechanical: No one has yet designed a robot hand and arm as flexible and controllable as its human equivalent. This is a problem which mechanical and electrical engineers must solve before the computer scientists can even start to work.

But even given a robot with the appropriate appendages much work will still be needed to develop the computer programs that will send the detailed commands to those appendages.

## Game Playing

Ever since the exhibition of a fraudulent chess-playing machine in the late 18th century, people have been fascinated by the idea of building a machine (today, programming a computer) to play chess. Other games which computers have been programmed to play are checkers, cubic (3-D tic-tac-toe), dominoes, backgammon, and the Japanese game Go.

Game-playing programs are good exercises in artificial intelligence for the following reasons:

- The game board and the rules of the game are easy to represent inside the computer.
- In contrast to the ease of representing the rules, the problems of playing sophisticated games such as chess and go are very difficult. There is no trivial way in which the computer can calculate *the* correct move. The computer must approach the game in much the same way that a human player would.
- There are many human experts at these games, and they are only too delighted to criticize the performance of the computer. These criticisms will point up areas where the program needs improvement.
- For many games tournaments are regularly held, and the players are given ratings according to their performances in the tournaments. By entering a program in the tournaments, it can receive a rating too. In this way its performance can be directly compared with that of human experts.

## Automatic Programming

Writing and debugging a complex computer program is a time-consuming task. A large team of programmers may work for several years to produce a compiler or an operating system. And the result is seldom without flaws. Usually it will still contain bugs that plague users until the bugs have been laboriously found and eliminated. As a result computing currently suffers from a software "crisis."

One way out is to have the computer generate its own program from a statement of the problem to be solved. Such a program-writing program would be an extension of present-day compilers and report-program generators. These also produce programs, but they require us to describe the programs to be produced in much greater detail than we would prefer.

## Computational Logic

Sometimes we face the need to prove that one set of facts is a logical consequence of another. A prosecuting attorney, for instance, needs to prove from the evidence at hand that the defendant committed the illegal actions for which he was brought to trial. Computational logic is the art of programming a computer to make such deductions.

An obvious application is in mathematics. A mathematician starts with a small set of statements (called axioms) and deduces from them interesting consequences (called theorems). The mathematician guarantees that in any situation where the axioms are true, the theorems will also be true. Taking this guarantee at face value, we can apply the theorems in science and engineering without having to repeat the mathematician's deductions.

For instance, a computer recently helped to prove the long-outstanding four-color theorem of topology. In this case, however, the mathematicians planned the proof, and the computer just worked out the tedious details. We would like the computer to be able to plan the proof as well as to carry out the details.

Another application of computational logic would be to prove computer programs correct. This is an alternative to automatic programming. The human programmer would do the creative work of designing and writing the program. The computer would try to prove that the resulting program is correct; that is, it solves the problem it was designed to solve. If the computer succeeded, we could use the program with confidence. If the computer did not succeed, it could try to find out why the proof failed, perhaps pinpointing a bug in the program.

Other AI programs need computational logic, particularly those involved with information retrieval and representation of knowledge. Certain facts are stored in memory. Other facts are needed by the person or program working on a problem. The computer must try to deduce the needed facts from the available ones.

## WHY DO WE NEED SMARTER COMPUTERS?

The last section described a number of applications for computers that exhibit some aspects of human intelligence. Let us try to summarize why we really need such machines:

- Smarter computers can adapt themselves to their human users, instead of the other way around. Much of the criticism of computers arises because we often end up doing things the machine's way, instead of the machine doing things our way. Doing things our way includes speaking or writing to us in English or some other natural langauge.

- Robots can work in environments that are unsuited to people, such as on the floor of the ocean, in underground mines, or in outer space.

- Robots can do jobs that are tedious and repetitive, but which now require humans for their ability to perceive and manipulate their surroundings. Much production-line work falls into this category.

- Computers can store the large amounts of information that we need to do our jobs and conduct our personal lives. Depending upon the need, the computer can serve variously as a teacher, a librarian, a consultant, a reporter, or a mailman.

- In a complex world with complex problems, we need all the problem-solving ability we can get our hands on. Economics, energy, the environment, and foreign relations are just a few of the areas where smarter computers might provide helping hands to the humans who are working to get us out of some of the messes we seem to have gotten ourselves into.

- In attempting to imitate human intelligence, we can learn much about what we are trying to imitate. In fact, we can divide AI workers into two groups. Those in one group carefully imitate the methods of human intelligence, with as much interest in understanding those methods as in building smarter computers. The other group is interested only in achieving the results of human intelligence, regardless of the methods that must be used.

Science-fiction computers and robots, such as HAL in *2001: A Space Odyssey* and C-3PO in *Star Wars*, often have the broad, general-purpose intellectual powers of human beings. For the present these machines are likely to remain science fiction. So many aspects of human intelligence are still so poorly understood that it seems unlikely any sudden breakthrough will enable computers to exhibit human-like intelligence.

Fortunately, human-like intelligence is not needed for most of the applications that have been mentioned. A robot working in a warehouse, for instance, needs to be able to recognize and handle the items it is supposed to load, unload, and store. But it need not be able to discuss philosophy or to play chess. Conversely, a chess-playing program need not be able to perceive its environment directly, and its knowledge of the real world need not extend beyond the confines of the chess board.

Thus, while in pursuit of human-like intelligence in all its glory, AI research can begin to bear fruit at once by creating programs that exhibit some single aspect of human intelligence, perhaps in limited form. A few computer applications would fail to benefit from even a modest increase in the flexibility, responsiveness, or problem-solving ability of the programs. The techniques developed by artificial intelligence research are widely applicable, and belong in every programmer's "tool kit."

## ALGORITHMS

In non-AI programming, the programmer first develops a step-by-step method, or algorithm, for solving a certain class of problems. He then translates the steps of the algorithm into a particular programming language, and so obtains a program that will enable a computer to solve the same class of problems.

There are two difficulties with this approach:
1. There are some quite reasonable classes of problems for which mathematicians have proved that there is *no* algorithm that will solve every problem in a particular class.
2. Even if there is an algorithm that will solve every problem in a particular class, the algorithm may be practical only for the smallest examples of the problem, and so inefficient as to be out of the question for practically sized problems.

As an example of the first difficulty, consider the class of all computer programs written in some programming language, say

BASIC. It would be convenient to have an algorithm for examining one of these programs and determining whether it would eventually terminate or whether it would go into a nonterminating loop when the program was run. Alas, mathematicians have proven that no such algorithm exists. That is, no step-by-step method can be applied to any BASIC program to determine for every program whether or not that program will go into a nonterminating loop when it is run. The same result holds for programs written in any of the popular programming languages.

Even when an algorithm exists it may be impractical. To see why let us consider how the *time required to execute an algorithm* can depend on the *size of the problem being solved*.

Let us take addition and multiplication problems as examples. The algorithms for addition and multiplication will be the familiar ones that we learn in grade school. The size of the addition and multiplication problems will be measured by the number of digits in the values to be added or multiplied. Thus, if we are to add or multiply two 10-digit numbers, the size of the addition and multiplication problems will be 10.

Now consider the class of all two-number addition problems. It is clear that, using the method of addition we learned in school, the time required for an addition will be proportional to the number of digits in the two values to be added. It will take us twice as long, for instance, to add two 10-digit numbers as it would take us to add two 5-digit numbers.

Let us use the letter $n$ to denote the size of the problem, in this case the number of digits being added. Then the time required for executing the traditional addition algorithm is proportional to $n$.

In multiplication, we have to multiply every digit of one number by every digit of the other. The number of single-digit multiplications that we have to do is $n$ times $n$ or $n^2$. The time required to do all these multiplications is also proportional to $n^2$. It will take us four times as long to multiply two 10-digit numbers as to multiply two 5-digit numbers, since

$$10^2/5^2 = 100/25 = 4$$

As the size of the problems increases, then, the time required for multiplication will increase more rapidly than the time required for addition. In general, the way in which the time required to execute an algorithm varies with the size of the problem, $n$, will be different for different algorithms.

Mathematical expressions involving $n$, $n^2$, $n^3$, and so on are called *polynomials*. Algorithms whose running times are proportional to $n$, or $n^2$, or $n^3$, and so on are said to run in *polynomial time*. Algorithms that run in polynomial time are considered to be practical.

Some algorithms, however, have running times that are proportional to expressions such as $2^n$, $n!$ ($n$ factorial, the product of all the integers from 1 through $n$), and $n^n$. Such algorithms are said to run in *exponential time*. As Table 1-1 shows, the exponential expressions increase much more rapidly with $n$ than do the polynomial ones.

Algorithms which run in exponential time are considered to be impractical. Such an algorithm can be successfully applied only to the smallest members of a class or problems. As the size of the problem increases, the running time increases so fast that even modestly sized problems would require thousands of hours of computer time. And large problems would require thousands of years (or more) of computer time.

## PRINCIPLES OF ARTIFICIAL INTELLIGENCE PROGRAMMING

Now, for many important classes of problems of the kind that human beings face every day, the best known algorithms run in exponential time. And for many of these classes of problems mathematicians believe that *all* algorithms must run in exponential time.

How is it, then, that human beings can often cope with a class of problems even though there is no algorithm that will solve every problem in the class, or if one exists, it runs in exponential time? There seem to be three reasons:

1. An algorithm is guaranteed to work for every problem in a class. Human methods need only to apply to "reasonable"

Table 1-1. Polynomial vs Exponential Increase

| Size | Polynomials | | | Exponentials | | |
|---|---|---|---|---|---|---|
| $n$ | $n$ | $n^2$ | $n^3$ | $2^n$ | $n!$ | $n^n$ |
| 1 | 1 | 1 | 1 | 2 | 1 | 1 |
| 2 | 2 | 4 | 8 | 4 | 2 | 4 |
| 3 | 3 | 9 | 27 | 8 | 6 | 27 |
| 4 | 4 | 16 | 64 | 16 | 24 | 256 |
| 5 | 5 | 25 | 125 | 32 | 120 | 3,125 |
| 6 | 6 | 36 | 216 | 64 | 720 | 46,656 |
| 7 | 7 | 49 | 343 | 128 | 5,040 | 823,543 |
| 8 | 8 | 64 | 512 | 256 | 40,320 | 16,777,216 |
| 9 | 9 | 81 | 729 | 512 | 362,880 | $3.9 \times 10^8$ |
| 10 | 10 | 100 | 1000 | 1024 | 3,628,800 | $10^{10}$ |
| . | . | . | . | . | . | . |
| . | . | . | . | . | . | . |
| . | . | . | . | . | . | . |
| 20 | 20 | 400 | 8000 | 1,048,576 | $2.4 \times 10^{18}$ | $1.0 \times 10^{26}$ |

problems or those likely to be encountered in practice. For instance, humans can analyze computer programs with reasonable success, but anyone asked to analyze a 1000 page BASIC program would certainly protest the assignment as being unreasonable.

2. Algorithms are required to be infallible. Humans are allowed occasional failures and mistakes. A human is willing to use a method that works most of the time or even only occasionally, turning to some other method when the one in question fails.

3. Humans do not always insist on finding the exact or the best possible solution to a problem. Frequently an approximate solution is good enough for the job at hand, and to try to do better would be a waste of time.

These seem to be a list of failings of human beings as compared to algorithms, but in practice, human beings are spectacularly more successful than algorithms in solving the large majority of practical problems. In a typical case there will be an algorithm guaranteed in theory to solve all problems in a class, but the algorithm will run in exponential time and so cannot be applied to problems of practical size. Usually, however, a human—using fallible, approximate, quick-and-dirty techniques—can come up with workable (if not the theoretical-best) solutions to problems of practical size.

Instead of trying to construct algorithms guaranteed to solve large classes of problems, then, AI workers concentrate on the more fallible but paradoxically more successful techniques employed by humans, although AI doesn't spurn algorithms when practical ones exist for the problem at hand. The rest of this section will describe some of these techniques, the basis of most current AI research.

### Search

One way that human beings go about solving problems is trial-and-error search. Possible candidates for a solution are examined, one after another, until one that will work is found.

Examining every possible candidate for a solution without considering in advance which candidates are most likely to work is known as *blind*, or *brute-force, search*.

Blind search is not the answer to solving large or complex problems. For reasons that we will see in a later chapter, blind-search algorithms inevitably run in exponential time. The reason for this usually turns out to be that to carry out a complete search we must examine the elements of the problem in every possible combination. As the size of the problem increases, the number of possible combinations grows enormously. This effect is often called a *combinatorial explosion*.

## Heuristic Search

Combinatorial explosion can be avoided if we have some hints or rules of thumb that will guide the search in the right direction. By following the hints we can avoid examining every possible candidate for a solution, confining ourselves to those most likely to work.

The word *heuristic* comes from a Greek word that means "serving to discover." A heuristic is any hint or rule of thumb that helps us discover a solution to a problem. A search guided by heuristics is called a *heuristic search*.

Human beings use heuristics extensively. Sometimes we think of these explicitly as rules of thumb, as for instance, the rule for loosening the lid of a jar by running warm water over the lid. In other cases the heuristics simply make up our knowledge of the right way to do a particular job. We "know" how to do the job and do not think of ourselves as following any particular rules, but we would regard strangely anyone who tried to do the job without observing those unstated rules.

Proverbs are good examples of heuristics. Consider the following selection:

- A stitch in time saves nine.
- A bird in the hand is worth two in the bush.
- Look before you leap.
- If at first you don't succeed, try, try again.

Notice the features that these proverbs (and all heuristics) have in common.

Each proverb applies to a very specific situation. The situations in which it would be helpful to remember that "A stitch in time saves nine" are quite different from those in which it would help to recall that "A bird in the hand is worth two in the bush."

Each proverb is good advice. That is, each is certainly worth considering in the appropriate situation.

On the other hand no proverb is guaranteed to always yield desirable results. For each proverb quoted it is not hard to think of a situation to which the proverb would apply, but in which it should not be followed. For instance it is of no help to "try, try again" if the task we are attempting is an impossible one.

All heuristics share these features: they apply to specific situations, and their advice is certainly worth considering. But unlike algorithms, heuristics carry no guarantees of success. They are simply things which are worth trying, but which may or may not work in any particular situation.

Heuristic search is the principal problem-solving technique of artificial intelligence.

## Pattern Recognition

Since each heuristic applies only to a specific situation, we need some way of looking at a problem situation and determining which heuristics might be helpful. The problem solver must look for *patterns* in problem situations and from these patterns determine which heuristics are applicable.

Many of the rules found in how-to books, for instance, have the form: *If* a certain situation occurs, *then* do the following. The "certain situation" is the pattern. The thing to do is the heuristic to be applied when the corresponding pattern is found.

Often a master of a skill and a well-educated novice both know the same heuristics. But the master can immediately see the patterns that suggest which heuristic is most likely to work, while the novice must try one rule after another until he either gives up or stumbles on one that will work.

## Planning

Another way to avoid combinatorial explosions is to first devise a plan for solving a problem and then to consider only those candidate solutions which are consistent with the plan.

Suppose, for instance, you are to drive from one city to another distant one. You do not wish to bother consulting a map while driving. On the other hand, road signs do not tell you how to get to the distant destination, but only how to get from one city to another nearby one.

The solution is to plan your trip. Before starting out you consult a map. Using the heuristic that the cities you go through should lie roughly on a straight line from your starting point to your destination, you make a list of the cities you should pass through. This plan is easily followed while driving by using the road signs to direct you from one city to the next one on the list. It greatly reduces the number of possible paths from your starting point to your destination that you will have to worry about while driving. When leaving a particular city, for instance, you have only to worry about those that the road signs tell you go to the next city on your list, instead of having to consider every road leaving the city.

A plan, then, greatly reduces the number of alternatives that must be considered at each stage of a search, and so reduces the likelihood of combinatorial explosion.

A good way to use heuristics is to use them to suggest plans. The problem solver will start by looking for patterns associated with particular heuristics in the problem situation. The heuristic associated with a pattern will recommend a particular plan for solving the problem. Once a recommended plan has been tentatively adopted, the problem solver takes each step of the plan as a new problem and applies the same techniques to it.

Since heuristics are fallible, of course, the first plan recommended may turn out to be unworkable; the problem solver must be prepared to abandon a bad plan and start out afresh. On the other hand if he tries to start out afresh too many times, a combinatorial explosion is sure to result.

## Representation of Knowledge

Before a computer can even start to work on a problem the details of the problem must be represented, or coded, inside the computer.

Even more important, heuristics and plans for solving the problem, as well as the patterns that recommend these, must be stored inside the computer. And the information must be stored in such a way that it is readily accessible. The computer must be able to go quickly from a pattern in the problem situation to the particular plans or rules of thumb that it suggests.

Humans, with experience, seem to be able to do this almost automatically. A chess expert examining a chess position will see at once many patterns that suggest possible lines of play. A novice looking at the same position will see only the simplest relationships. A math teacher looking at an algebraic expression will probably see at once several ways to transform it into a required form, but the student will complain, in all honesty, that he "doesn't know where to begin."

Notice that each of the various AI techniques makes use of the others. Problem solving calls for pattern recognition and representation of knowledge. Recognizing patterns can involve solving problems (finding relevant patterns is usually a problem!) and representation of knowledge (for the patterns to be found) must be stored conveniently in memory. Retrieving appropriate information from memory involves both problem solving and pattern recognition. It seems impossible to advance in any one of these areas without advancing in all of them.

# Chapter 2
# Problem Strategy

The previous chapter pointed out that Artificial Intelligence programs are *problem-solving programs*. The natural place to begin our study of AI, then, is with problems. What features, for instance, do most problems have in common? Can we discuss these features in a general way that is independent of the details of any particular problem? And how can we represent these features inside a computer in such a way that they can easily be manipulated by problem-solving programs?

## STATES, OPERATIONS, AND GOALS

The three most important features common to all problems are *states*, *operators*, and *goals*. We can understand these features best by seeing how they occur in a particular problem. We will use the well-known Missionaries and Cannibals problem for our example.

On the bank of a river are three missionaries, three cannibals, and a boat. The missionaries wish to use the boat to get the entire party across the river. Unfortunately, there are two problems...

1. The boat will carry two people at most. Both the missionaries and the cannibals can operate the boat, however; so the boat can carry one missionary, or one cannibal, or two missionaries, or two cannibals, or one missionary and one cannibal.

2. If on either bank of the river the cannibals outnumber the missionaries, the cannibals will eat the outnumbered missionaries.

The missionaries wish to plan a series of boat trips that will transport the entire party across the river without any missionaries being devoured. We assume the cannibals will cooperate in carrying out the plan, perhaps because they do not realize that it is designed to cheat them out of an easy meal.

## States

As we start to work out the solution to the problem, mentally moving cannibals and missionaries back and forth from bank to bank, we will constantly be concerned with three things:

1. How many missionaries are there on each bank?
2. How many cannibals are there on each bank?
3. On which bank is the boat?

These three pieces of information describe the current *state* of our problem-solving efforts. How many missionaries and cannibals have we gotten across the river, how many remain to be transported, where is the boat, and who is available to operate it?

We can also think of a certain "universe," or "world," being associated with each problem. The state is simply the current state of affairs in this world. It may be a purely hypothetical state of affairs, of course, if the problem solver is merely thinking through the solution to the problem before taking any actions in the real world.

For toy problems, of course, the world will be a toy world. The Missionaries and Cannibals world encompasses only the three missionaries, the three cannibals, the boat, and the river. But if the problem solver were a robot trying to cope with the real world, the state would be the state of the real world, or at least the part of it which is of current concern to the robot.

In a problem we're always given the *initial state* of the problem world. For the Missionaries and Cannibals problem the initial state is with all the missionaries, all the cannibals, and the boat on one bank of the river, say the left bank. The object of the problem is to change the initial state into one having some given characteristics.

It is often useful to consider all the possible states of a problem world. Let us do this for the Missionaries and Cannibals.

To describe a particular state, we must give the number of missionaries and cannibals on each bank, as well as the position of the boat. The description of the initial state looks like this:

|  | Left Bank | Right Bank |
|---|---|---|
| Missionaries | 3 | 0 |
| Cannibals | 3 | 0 |
| Boat | Yes | No |

If we send one missionary and one cannibal across the river in the boat, we get this state:

|  | Left Bank | Right Bank |
|---|---|---|
| Missionaries | 2 | 1 |
| Cannibals | 2 | 1 |
| Boat | No | Yes |

Actually, we are giving more than is necessary. The number of missionaries on the left and the right bank must add up to three; the same must be true for the number of cannibals; and the boat must be on one bank or the other. Thus, if we give the situation on one bank, say the left, we will also know what the situation on the other bank must be. We can specify the initial state by:

|  | Left Bank |
|---|---|
| Missionaries | 3 |
| Cannibals | 3 |
| Boat | Yes |

and the one that results from sending across a missionary and a cannibal by:

|  | Left Bank |
|---|---|
| Missionaries | 2 |
| Cannibals | 2 |
| Boat | No |

How many possible states of the Missionaries and Cannibals world are there? We can have 0, 1, 2, or 3 missionaries on the left bank, with the remainder on the right bank. Thus we have four possibilities for dividing up the missionaries between the two banks. We also have four possibilities for the cannibals. And the boat can be on either bank, which gives us two more possibillities. The number of possible states, then, is $4 \times 4 \times 2$, which equals 32.

Table 2-1 shows all 32 possible states. For convenience the situations on both banks are given, although only the left-bank information is strictly necessary.

But wait! Some of the states in the table have more cannibals than missionaries on one bank or the other, a situation sure to put missionary on the menu. Obviously these cannot be legal states.

## Table 2-1. The 32 Possible Missionaries and Cannibals States

| Left Bank | | | Right Bank | | |
| --- | --- | --- | --- | --- | --- |
| M | C | Boat | M | C | Boat |
| 0 | 0 | Yes | 3 | 3 | No |
| 0 | 1 | Yes | 3 | 2 | No |
| 0 | 2 | Yes | 3 | 1 | No |
| 0 | 3 | Yes | 3 | 0 | No |
| 1 | 0 | Yes | 2 | 3* | No |
| 1 | 1 | Yes | 2 | 2 | No |
| 1 | 2* | Yes | 2 | 1 | No |
| 1 | 3* | Yes | 2 | 0 | No |
| 2 | 0 | Yes | 1 | 3* | No |
| 2 | 1 | Yes | 1 | 2* | No |
| 2 | 2 | Yes | 1 | 1 | No |
| 2 | 3* | Yes | 1 | 0 | No |
| 3 | 0 | Yes | 0 | 3 | No |
| 3 | 1 | Yes | 0 | 2 | No |
| 3 | 2 | Yes | 0 | 1 | No |
| 3 | 3 | Yes | 0 | 0 | No |
| 0 | 0 | No | 3 | 3 | Yes |
| 0 | 1 | No | 3 | 2 | Yes |
| 0 | 2 | No | 3 | 1 | Yes |
| 0 | 3 | No | 3 | 0 | Yes |
| 1 | 0 | No | 2 | 3* | Yes |
| 1 | 1 | No | 2 | 2 | Yes |
| 1 | 2* | No | 2 | 1 | Yes |
| 1 | 3* | No | 2 | 0 | Yes |
| 2 | 0 | No | 1 | 3* | Yes |
| 2 | 1 | No | 1 | 2* | Yes |
| 2 | 2 | No | 1 | 1 | Yes |
| 2 | 3* | No | 1 | 0 | Yes |
| 3 | 0 | No | 0 | 3 | Yes |
| 3 | 1 | No | 0 | 2 | Yes |
| 3 | 2 | No | 0 | 1 | Yes |
| 3 | 3 | No | 0 | 0 | Yes |

*illegal state

A little thought shows that the allowed states are of two types:

1. There are an equal number of missionaries and cannibals on each bank.
2. There are three missionaries on one bank and none on the other. The cannibals can be divided between the banks in any way whatever, since on one bank the missionaries can never be outnumbered, and on the other there are no missionaries to eat.

If we check the 32 states in the table we find that 20 of them satisfy one of the above two conditions. Table 2-2 lists the 20 legal states, but four of these states are still questionable in that they can never be reached from the initial state. These states are:

| Left Bank | | | Right Bank | | |
|---|---|---|---|---|---|
| Missionaries | Cannibals | Boat | Missionaries | Cannibals | Boat |
| 3 | 3 | No | 0 | 0 | Yes |
| 0 | 0 | Yes | 3 | 3 | No |
| 3 | 0 | Yes | 0 | 3 | No |
| 0 | 3 | No | 3 | 0 | Yes |

That the first two of these states cannot be reached is obvious. The boat cannot possibly be on a bank where there are no people, since someone had to be in the boat to operate it when it went to the bank in question.

Table 2-2. The 20 Legal Missionaries and Cannibals States

| Left Bank | | | Right Bank | | |
|---|---|---|---|---|---|
| M | C | Boat | M | C | Boat |
| 0 | 0 | Yes* | 3 | 3 | No |
| 0 | 1 | Yes | 3 | 2 | No |
| 0 | 2 | Yes | 3 | 1 | No |
| 0 | 3 | Yes | 3 | 0 | No |
| 1 | 1 | Yes | 2 | 2 | No |
| 2 | 2 | Yes | 1 | 1 | No |
| 3 | 0 | Yes* | 0 | 3 | No |
| 3 | 1 | Yes | 0 | 2 | No |
| 3 | 2 | Yes | 0 | 1 | No |
| 3 | 3 | Yes | 0 | 0 | No |
| 0 | 0 | No | 3 | 3 | Yes |
| 0 | 1 | No | 3 | 2 | Yes |
| 0 | 2 | No | 3 | 1 | Yes |
| 0 | 3 | No* | 3 | 0 | Yes |
| 1 | 1 | No | 2 | 2 | Yes |
| 2 | 2 | No | 1 | 1 | Yes |
| 3 | 0 | No | 0 | 3 | Yes |
| 3 | 1 | No | 0 | 2 | Yes |
| 3 | 2 | No | 0 | 1 | Yes |
| 3 | 3 | No* | 0 | 0 | Yes |

*cannot be reached from starting state

**Table 2-3. The 16 Attainable Missionaries and Cannibals States**

| Left Bank | | | Right Bank | | |
|---|---|---|---|---|---|
| M | C | Boat | M | C | Boat |
| 0 | 1 | Yes | 3 | 2 | No |
| 0 | 2 | Yes | 3 | 1 | No |
| 0 | 3 | Yes | 3 | 0 | No |
| 1 | 1 | Yes | 2 | 2 | No |
| 2 | 2 | Yes | 1 | 1 | No |
| 3 | 1 | Yes | 0 | 2 | No |
| 3 | 2 | Yes | 0 | 1 | No |
| 3 | 3 | Yes | 0 | 0 | No |
| 0 | 0 | No | 3 | 3 | Yes |
| 0 | 1 | No | 3 | 2 | Yes |
| 0 | 2 | No | 3 | 1 | Yes |
| 1 | 1 | No | 2 | 2 | Yes |
| 2 | 2 | No | 1 | 1 | Yes |
| 3 | 0 | No | 0 | 3 | Yes |
| 3 | 1 | No | 0 | 2 | Yes |
| 3 | 2 | No | 0 | 1 | Yes |

The reason why the last two states are unreachable is slightly trickier. Since the boat is on the bank with the missionaries, the last boat trip must have been made by a missionary who carried over the last of the three cannibals and then returned. Except, in fact, he did not return. When he reached his destination there were three cannibals and one missionary present, and the missionary was promptly eaten.

Table 2-3 shows the 16 legal states that are reachable from the initial state.

## Operations and Operators

When we solve a problem we carry out a series of operations on the initial state to change it into some other, more desirable state.

Normally there are restrictions, or *constraints*, on the allowable operations. Isaac Asimov's Three Laws of Robotics are constraints on the operations a robot can carry out in solving its problems. (Killing a human, for instance, is not a permissible operation.)

For the Missionaries and Cannibals problem the operations consist of using the boat to move the missionaries and the cannibals back and forth across the river. We cannot, however, make arbitrary changes in the number of missionaries and cannibals on each bank or in the location of the boat. The changes we may make are limited by the following four constraints:

1. Missionaries and cannibals can only cross the river by using the boat, and the boat requires at least one person to operate it. Therefore, there must always be a decrease in the number of people on the bank which the boat leaves and an increase in the number on the one at which it arrives.
2. Since the boat holds two people at most, no more than this number may be transferred in a single operation.
3. No more missionaries or cannibals may be transferred than are actually present on the bank which has the boat.
4. The transfer must not result in an illegal state in which cannibals outnumber missionaries on one bank or the other.

An *operator* is a detailed prescription for the change in state corresponding to a valid operation. The operator consists of a *condition* part and an *action* part. The operator may only be applied to those states for which the condition holds. The condition part restricts the applicability of the operator. The action part describes the changes to be made in a state to which the operator is applied.

The condition parts of the operators embody the constraints on the permissible operations.

For the Missionaries and Cannibals problem we will give each operator a descriptive name which describes its effect. Here is an operator. "Transfer one missionary and one cannibal from left bank to right bank":

| **Condition** | **Action** |
|---|---|
| The boat is on the left bank; there are at least one missionary and one cannibal on the left bank; and the number of missionaries and the number of cannibals on the left bank is equal. | Move the boat from the left bank to the right bank; decrease the number of missionaries and the number of cannibals on the left bank by one each; increase the number of missionaries and the number of cannibals on the right bank by one each. |

Here is another operator which moves a single cannibal from the left bank to the right. "Transfer one cannibal from left bank to right bank":

| Condition | Action |
|---|---|
| The boat is on the left bank; there are either zero missionaries or three missionaries on the left bank; and there is at least one cannibal on the left bank. | Move the boat from the left bank to the right bank; decrease the number of cannibals on the left bank by one; increase the number of cannibals on the right bank by one. |

The condition assures, among other things, that no operator will yield an illegal state. The operator "Transfer one missionary and one cannibal from left bank to right bank" can be applied to a state only if the number of cannibals equals the number of missionaries on both the left and the right banks. The action does not change this condition, so it still holds after the operator has been applied. Hence the resulting state is legal.

Table 2-4 gives the descriptive names of all the operators for the Missionaries and Cannibals problem. The actions of these operators follow at once from their descriptive names. You may find it interesting to think of the condition needed for each operator so that:

- The operator may be reasonably applied to the state in question and
- The result will be a legal state. The first part of the condition is easy; the second requires more thought.

## Goals

The goals of a problem are the states we are trying to achieve by starting with the initial state and applying operators.

Sometimes there is a single goal state. In the Missionaries and Cannibals problem, for instance, we wish to reach the following state:

| | Left Bank | Right Bank |
|---|---|---|
| Missionaries | 0 | 3 |
| Cannibals | 0 | 3 |
| Boat | No | Yes |

On the other hand a goal state may be any state for which a given condition holds. The condition may hold for many states, and each of these will be an acceptable goal. If the problem is to win a chess game, for instance, any state (chess position) in which the opponent is checkmated is a satisfactory goal.

1. Transfer 1 missionary from left bank to right bank
2. Transfer 1 cannibal from left bank to right bank
3. Transfer 1 missionary and 1 cannibal from left bank to right bank
4. Transfer 2 missionaries from left bank to right bank
5. Transfer 2 cannibals from left bank to right bank

6. Transfer 1 missionary from right bank to left bank
7. Transfer 1 cannibal from right bank to left bank
8. Transfer 1 missionary and 1 cannibal from right bank to left bank
9. Transfer 2 missionaries from right bank to left bank
10. Transfer 2 cannibals from right bank to left bank

## Solution

A solution to a problem is a sequence of operators such that, if we start with the initial state and apply the operators one after another, the resulting state will be a goal state. In displaying a solution the intermediate states resulting from the application of each operator are also usually shown.

Table 2-5 shows a solution to the Missionaries and Cannibals' problem. There are several other solutions that differ in only minor ways from this one.

## STATE GRAPHS

In thinking about a problem it is often helpful to concentrate on the relationships between the states and the operators, while ignoring the detailed structure of each. State graphs are very useful for thinking about problems at this level.

### Graph Terminology

The word graph is used with two meanings in mathematics. The graphs we are talking about here are not those used to plot mathematical functions or experimental data. Instead, they are diagrams made up of points connected by lines. The word network would be a good synonym for graph as we are going to use it.

Figure 2-1 illustrates the basic terminology of graphs. The points are called *nodes*. For ease of labeling the nodes are often drawn as circles rather than geometrical points. The lines connecting the nodes are called *arcs*. If the arcs have arrows on them the graph is a *directed graph*. The only kinds of graphs we will talk about in this book will be directed graphs. If the arcs have labels on them the graph is a *labeled graph*. A labeled graph is also called a *colored graph*, since we can think of all arcs with the same label being drawn with the same color, but of arcs with different labels being drawn with different colors.

We say that an arc goes from node A to node B if it joins the two nodes and if the arrow points at node B. We say that A is the *predecessor* of B, and B is the successor of A. A *path* through the graph is a series of nodes such that each node is the predecessor of the following node in the series.

## State Graphs

In a state graph, nodes correspond to states and arc labels to operators. One node corresponds to the initial state and one or more nodes correspond to goal states. A solution to the problem is a path connecting the node corresponding to the initial state to one corresponding to a goal state.

As was the case with states, operators, and goals, we can best understand state graphs by looking at a specific example. For our example we will take the so-called Tower of Hanoi problem, illustrated in Fig. 2-2. At A we have three pegs, numbered 1, 2, and 3. On peg 1 are a number of disks, each one smaller than the one below it. The problem is to move all the disks from peg 1 to peg 3. The constraint is that we may never stack a larger disk above a smaller one. On each peg the largest disk must always be on the bottom, the next largest just above it, and so on.

The complexity of the solution of the Tower of Hanoi problem depends on the number of disks involved. Since we are looking for a small problem for which we can easily draw the state graph, we will use only two disks.

Figure 2-2b illustrates the two-disk problem. Let A be the smaller disk and B the larger one; then we can describe the state of the Tower of Hanoi world by specifying which peg disk A is on and which peg disk B is on. If A and B are on the same peg we do not have

### Table 2-5. A Missionaries and Cannibals Solution

| Solution | States | | | | | |
|---|---|---|---|---|---|---|
| | Left Bank | | | Right Bank | | |
| | M | C | B | M | C | B |
| Initial positions | 3 | 3 | Y | 0 | 0 | N |
| Transfer 1 missionary and 1 cannibal from left bank to right bank | 2 | 2 | N | 1 | 1 | Y |
| Transfer 1 missionary from right bank to left bank | 3 | 2 | Y | 0 | 1 | N |
| Transfer 2 cannibals from left bank to right bank | 3 | 0 | N | 0 | 3 | Y |
| Transfer 1 cannibal from right bank to left bank | 3 | 1 | Y | 0 | 2 | N |
| Transfer 2 missionaries from left bank to right bank | 1 | 1 | N | 2 | 2 | Y |
| Transfer 1 missionary and 1 cannibal from right bank to left bank | 2 | 2 | Y | 1 | 1 | N |
| Transfer 2 missionaries from left bank to right bank | 0 | 2 | N | 3 | 1 | Y |
| Transfer 1 cannibal from right bank to left bank | 0 | 3 | Y | 3 | 0 | N |
| Transfer 2 cannibals from left bank to right bank | 0 | 1 | N | 3 | 2 | Y |
| Transfer 1 missionary from right bank to left bank | 1 | 1 | Y | 2 | 2 | N |
| Transfer 1 missionary and 1 cannibal from left bank to right bank | 0 | 0 | N | 3 | 3 | Y |

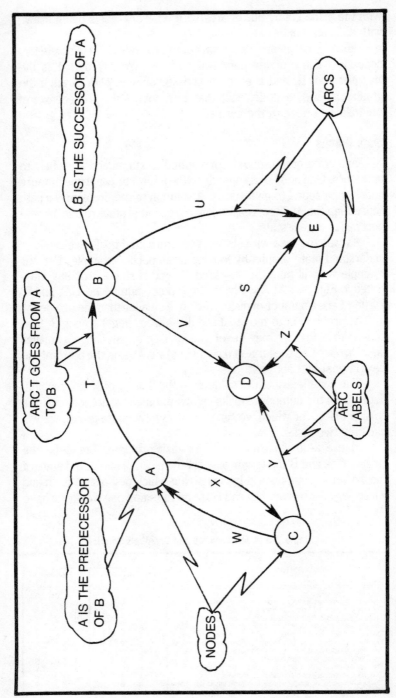

Fig. 2-1. The basic terminology of graphs.

34

to worry about what order they are in, for the larger disk must always be on the bottom and the smaller disk on top.

We can describe any state using a pair of numbers, such as (32) or (13). The first number tells which peg A is on; the second tells which peg B is on. Thus (13) is the state in which A is on peg 1 and B is on peg 3. In state (33), both A and B are on peg 3. Naturally they are in the required order, with B on the bottom and A on top.

A and B can each be on peg 1, peg 2, and peg 3. Thus there are 3 × 3, or 9, possible states of the Tower of Hanoi world. Any pair of numbers, such as (31) or (22), describes a state, provided that each number is in the range from 1 to 3. All combinations of allowable numbers are permitted; none are excluded, as in the Missionaries and Cannibals' problem. Figure 2-3 shows all nine states and their descriptions.

The initial state is (11), the goal state is (33).

Each operation consists of moving a disk from one peg to another. The operator changes one of the numbers in the state description to reflect the disk having been moved. As usual, the operators cannot change the numbers arbitrarily. There are constraints:

1. Only one disk can be moved at a time. Therefore the operator can change either the first number of a pair or the second, but not both.

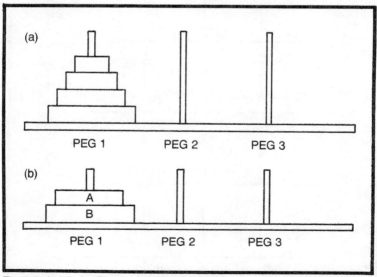

Fig. 2-2. At (a), the Tower of Hanoi disk-transfer problem, and (b) a two-disk version.

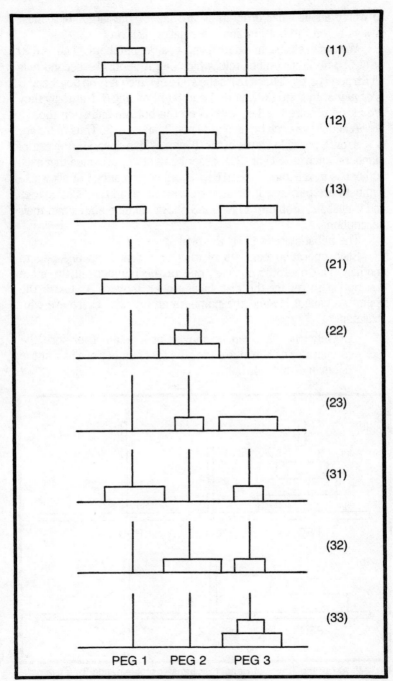

(11)

(12)

(13)

(21)

(22)

(23)

(31)

(32)

(33)

PEG 1    PEG 2    PEG 3

Fig. 2-3. The nine states of the Tower of Hanoi world.

2. If both A and B are on the same peg we can only move the top disk, which is of course A. Therefore with states (11), (22), and (33), only the first number, corresponding to A, can be changed.

3. And B can never be placed on top of A. Therefore the second number of a pair cannot be changed so that it becomes equal to the first. In other words we cannot change (21) to (22), since A is already on peg 2, and placing B on top of it would violate the rules. (We assume that we cannot take A off, put B on, and then put A back.)

We will write operators in the following way: A: 3—2 means move A from peg 3 to peg 2; B: 1—2 means move B from peg 1 to peg 2, and so on. Table 2-6 shows the 12 operators for the Tower of Hanoi problem.

Of the above constraints, constraint 1 is automatically satisfied, since each operator moves only one disk. But constraints 2 and 3 prevent every operator from being applied to every state. For instance, B: 2—3 cannot be applied to (22) because of constraint 2, and B: 3—2 cannot be applied to (23) because of constraint 3.

Finally, B: 1—2, for instance, can only be applied to those states in which B is on peg 1. We cannot move B from peg 1 if it is not already there.

**The Tower of Hanoi State Graph.** Figure 2-4 shows the state graph for the Tower of Hanoi problem.

Each of the nine nodes of the graph corresponds to one of the nine states of the Tower of Hanoi world. Every node is labeled with the corresponding state description.

Each of the 24 arcs corresponds to one of the 12 operators.

Note that some pairs of nodes are not directly joined by any arc. This is a result of the constraints, which prevent some states from being changed into others in a single operation. (If the constraints were absent the problem would be nonexistent, since we could change the initial state to the goal state with a single operation.)

The initial state and the goal state are marked on the graph.

**Table 2-6. The 12 Tower of Hanoi Operators**

| | |
|---|---|
| A: 1—2 | B: 1—2 |
| A: 1—3 | B: 1—3 |
| A: 2—1 | B: 2—1 |
| A: 2—3 | B: 2—3 |
| A: 3—1 | B: 3—1 |
| A: 3—2 | B: 3—2 |

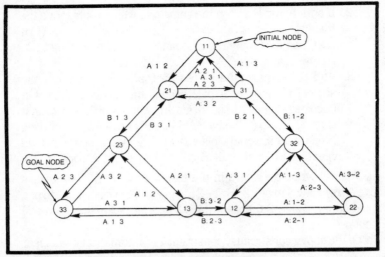

Fig. 2-4. State graph for the Tower of Hanoi problem.

A solution is any path which starts at the initial state and ends at the goal state. There are many solutions to the Tower of Hanoi problem, three of which are shown in Fig. 2-5. When more than one solution is possible we must use some criterion to select the "best" one. Often the best solution is the one that requires the fewest operations to change the initial state into the goal state.

Solving a problem, then, is equivalent to finding a path through a graph from the initial node to a goal node. This problem is the same as that of finding one's way through a maze. All problems are maze problems when viewed in terms of graphs.

**Implicit Graphs.** The graph we have just examined is *explicit*. That is, we could draw the entire graph on a sheet of paper or store it in a computer's memory.

This is not always possible. In the original Tower of Hanoi problem, for instance, there are 64 disks. This means that there are $3^{64}$ or about $3 \times 10^{30}$—3 followed by 30 zeros—states. No way can a graph with this many nodes be drawn on a sheet of paper or stored inside a computer.

Fortunately, we often do not need the entire graph. Given any node, we are mainly interested in its *immediate successors*, those nodes to which the original one is joined by arcs. In terms of states, an immediate successor is any state that can be obtained from the original state by applying a single operator. By applying all permissible operators to a state, we can generate all its immediate successors.

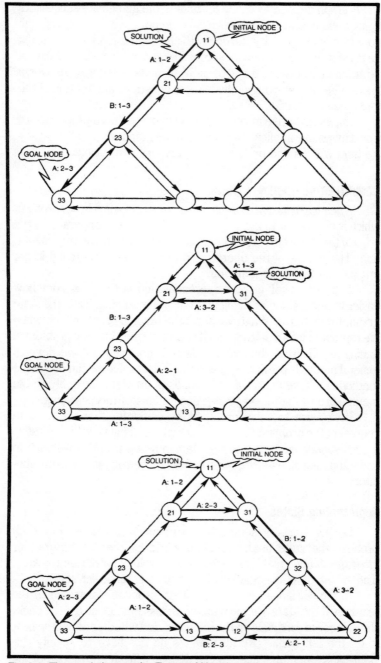

Fig. 2-5. Three solutions to the Tower of Hanoi problem. Each is a path in the state graph from the initial node to the goal node.

A graph defined by a rule for finding the immediate successors of any node is said to be *implicit*. We do not have the entire graph stored anywhere, but by starting with one node and repeatedly using the rule for finding immediate successors, we can construct a part of the graph that can be reached by paths from the starting node. Doing this for different starting nodes we can construct any portion of the graph that we need.

Graphs that arise in connection with complicated problems are almost invariably implicit. How much of the graph we can store at any one time will depend on how much memory is available.

## COMPUTER REPRESENTATIONS

When we *represent* a problem we construct some other problem which is equivalent to the original. To every state or operator in the original there is a corresponding state or operator in the representation. The effects of the operators on the states correspond in the original and the representation.

The reason for using a representation is that it is somehow easier to understand or manipulate than the original. Take the state graph, for instance. Whatever form the original problem had, when we represent it as a state graph it is transformed into the problem of finding a path from the initial node to a goal node. If we develop general methods for finding paths through graphs we can use those methods to solve many different kinds of problems by applying the methods to the state-graph representations of the problems.

If we wish to solve problems by computer then we need to represent the problems inside the computer. That is, we must set up a correspondence between the elements of a problem we wish to solve and the values-stored-in-memory that a computer can manipulate.

### Representing States

Let us start by seeing how to represent states. For each problem the state of the problem world has certain *features*, or *attributes*. These features have different values for different states. The values of all the features determines a particular state.

In the Missionaries and Cannibals' problem, for instance, the features of the state are the number of missionaries on the left bank, the number of cannibals on the left bank, and whether or not the boat is on the left bank. (Recall that we do not have to specify the right-bank situation since we can deduce it from knowledge of the situation on the left bank.)

Now, higher-level languages such as BASIC and FORTRAN provide for *variables*. These variables have *values* which can change as program execution proceeds. We can use one variable for each feature, or attribute, of the state. A particular assignment of values to these variables will determine a particular state.

For instance, we could let M be the number of missionaries on the left bank, and C the number of cannibals. We could let B have the value 1 if the boat was on the left bank and 0 if it was on the right bank. Then the values

| Variable | Value |
|----------|-------|
| M | 3 |
| C | 1 |
| B | 1 |

designate the state in which there are three missionaries on the left bank (and none on the right), one cannibal on the left bank (and two on the right), and the boat is on the left bank.

We can move the missionaries and cannibals around by changing the values of the variables. This is done with assignment statements. In the notation of BASIC, the statements

10 LET M = M-2
20 LET B = 0

will move two missionaries from the left bank to the right bank. The resulting state will be

| Variable | Value |
|----------|-------|
| M | 1 |
| C | 1 |
| B | 0 |

One problem that comes up is that it is just as easy to represent an illegal state as a legal one. Both

| Variable | Value | | Variable | Value |
|----------|-------|-----|----------|-------|
| M | 5 | | M | 1 |
| C | 100 | and | C | 2 |
| B | 3 | | B | 1 |

are illegal. The first state is illegal because the values are not meaningful for the problem at hand. The second is illegal because it represents a situation in which missionaries would be devoured.

In most programming languages there is no way to restrict the values a variable can have so as to assure that those values describe a legal state. Thus we must make sure that whenever the values of the variables are changed, the new values will describe a legal state. In other words, the burden of seeing that state descriptions are legal falls on the *operators*, rather than the state variables.

Finally, let us represent the state for the Tower of Hanoi problem. The two features of the state are the number of the peg on which disk A is placed and the number of the peg on which disk B is placed. We can use two state variables, A and B, whose values designate the pegs holding disks A and B. The values

| Variable | Value |
|:--------:|:-----:|
| A | 2 |
| B | 3 |

describe the state in which disk A is on peg 2 and disk B is on peg 3.

## Representing Operators

As we have seen an operator consists of a *condition* part and an *action* part.

The action part changes the state by changing the values of the state variables. It is easily represented with assignment statements. The action part of the operator "Move one missionary and one cannibal from the left bank to the right bank," for instance, would be represented in BASIC by

$$10 \text{ LET } M = M\text{-}1$$
$$20 \text{ LET } C = C\text{-}1$$
$$30 \text{ LET } B = 0$$

The condition part allows an operator to be applied to a particular state only if carrying out the action part on that state will yield another legal state. For instance, the action just given could not be

Table 2-7. Comparing the Value of Variables

| Condition | Meaning |
|-----------|---------|
| X x Y | The value of X equals the value of Y. |
| X< Y | The value of X is less than the value of Y. |
| X > Y | The value of X is greater than the value of Y. |
| X<= Y | The value of X is less than or equal to the value of Y. |
| X>= Y | The value of X is greater than or equal to the value of Y. |
| X <> Y | The value of X is not equal to the value of Y. |

## Table 2-8. The 10 Missionaries and Cannibals Operators

| Condition | Action |
|---|---|
| 1.    B = 1<br>AND (  (M = 3 AND C = 2)<br>     OR (M = 1 AND C = 1)) | LET M = M-1<br>Let B = 0 |
| 2.    B = 1<br>AND C ≥ 1<br>AND (M = 0 OR M = 3) | LET C = C-1<br>LET B = 0 |
| 3.    B = 1<br>AND C ≥ 1<br>AND M = C | LET M = M-1<br>LET C = C-1<br>LET B = 0 |
| 4.    B = 1<br>AND ( (M = 3 AND C = 1)<br>    OR  (M = 2 AND C = 2)) | LET M = M − 2<br>LET B = 0 |
| 5.    B = 1<br>AND C ≥ 2<br>AND (M = 0 OR M = 3) | LET C = C-2<br>LET B = 0 |
| 6.    B = 0<br>AND (  (M = 0 AND C = 1)<br>    OR  (M = 2 AND C = 2)) | LET M = M+1<br>LET B = 1 |
| 7.    B = 0<br>AND C ·. 2<br>AND (M = 0 OR M = 3) | LET C = C+1<br>LET B = 1 |
| 8.    B = 0<br>AND C ≤ 2<br>AND M = C | LET M = M+1<br>LET C = C+1<br>LET B = 1 |
| 9.    B = 0<br>AND (  (M = 0 AND C = 2)<br>    OR  (M = 1 AND C = 1)) | LET M = M+2<br>LET B = 1 |
| 10.   B = 0<br>AND C ≤ 1<br>AND (M = 0 OR M = 3) | LET C = C+2<br>LET B = 1 |

carried out on a state in which the value of C was 0, since the result would be an illegal state, with C having the value −1.

For stating conditions, we assume that we have at least the facilities of the better versions of BASIC. Thus we can compare the values of variables as in Table 2-7. The simple conditions there can be combined with AND, OR, and NOT to yield more-complex conditions. For instance

(B = 1) AND (C >= 1) AND ( (M = 0) OR (M = 3) )

describes a state in which the value of B is 1; the value of C is greater than or equal to 1; and the value of M is equal to 0 or 3.

In programs these conditions are used in conditional statements such as the IF statement in BASIC. The following statements, for instance, will set the variable F to 1 if the above condition is true, and to 0 otherwise:

```
10 LET F = 0
20 IF (B = 1) AND (C >= 1) AND
   (M = 0) OR (M = 3) THEN LET F = 1
```

Variables such as F whose values reflect the results of checking conditions are often used in AI programming. Such variables are called *flags*.

Table 2-8 shows all 10 operators for the Missionaries and Cannibals' problem. The conditions and actions are stated using the notation just described. Indentation has been used to make the conditions more readable. Without indentation, the condition for operator 1 would be written:

B = 0 AND ( (M = 0 AND C = 1) OR (M = 2 AND C = 2) )

The descriptive names of the operators are not repeated in this table. Instead, the same numbering is used as in Table 2-4, where the descriptive names are given. It would be instructive to check each operator to see why the action will yield a legal state only if the condition holds.

# Chapter 3
# State-Graph Search

One way to try solving a problem is to start out with the initial state and explore the state graph in hopes of finding a path leading to a goal state. We call this exploration a *state-graph search*; it is also called *state-space search*, state-space being another name for the state graph.

## SEARCH TREES

Figure 3-1 shows a *maze problem*. The object is to find a path through the maze from the starting point to the specified finishing point.

The maze is, of course, a graph, and is in fact its own state graph. As shown in Fig. 3-2, mazes drawn in more traditional ways are easily translated into state-graph form. From the last chapter we know we can construct a state graph for any problem, so we can, if we wish, think of any problem as a maze problem.

Now suppose we begin at the starting node and set out to find our way through the maze. What situation do we face? Several paths lead from the starting node to other nodes. If we follow one of these paths to the next node we find the same situation again: a number of paths leading to other nodes.

In short, we are faced with a *repeated-branching* situation. Whenever the path we are following encounters a node, it branches into a number of different paths. When, in turn, each of those branches encounters a node, the branching is repeated, and so on. A repeated branching situation is best represented by using a *tree*.

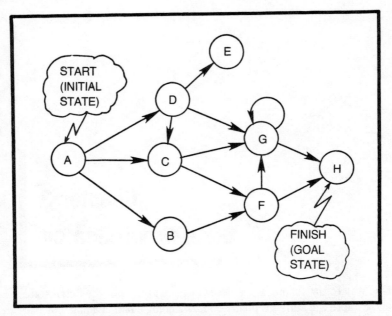

Fig. 3-1. A maze problem. The problem is to find a path from the starting point to the specified finishing point. A maze drawn in this way is its own state graph.

## Trees

As shown in Fig. 3-3, a tree in computer science is similar to a natural tree except that it is drawn upside down, with its root at the top and its leaves at the bottom.

Technically, a tree is a directed graph in which each node has at most one predecessor. Exactly one node has no predecessor, and this node is called the *root*. A node having no successor is called a *leaf*. The arcs are called *branches*. Although the tree is a directed graph, the arrows are usually omitted, since they would always point in the top-to-bottom direction.

Each node in a tree can be assigned a level. The root is on level 0. The successors of the root are on level 1. The successors of the successors of the root are on level 2, and so on. In AI the level number of a node is often called its *depth*. The root of a tree has a depth of 0, its successors a depth of 1, and so on. Thinking of the levels as representing depth, we say that the root is on the topmost level, the successors of the root are on the next lowest level, and so on.

The successors of a node are its *children*. Their common predecessor is their *parent*. Children having the same parent are *siblings*, or *twins*.

A *subtree* is a tree which is a part of another, larger tree. If we take any node of a tree together with its children, its children's children, and so on, we will have a subtree. The node we started with will be the root of the subtree.

## Search Trees

A search tree shows which paths in a state graph have currently been explored. When the search begins the search tree consists of a

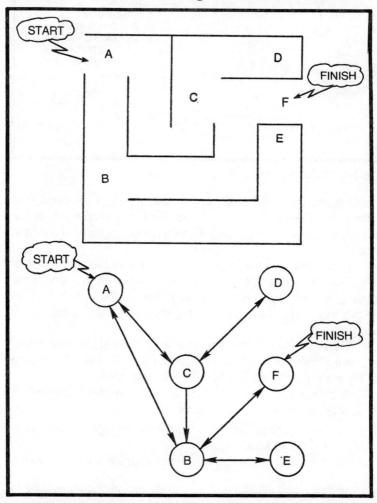

Fig. 3-2. Mazes drawn in conventional ways are also easily converted into state graphs. (An arc with arrows at both ends is an abbreviation for two directed arcs going in opposite directions between the same two nodes; such arcs represent the fact that a corridor can be traversed in either direction.)

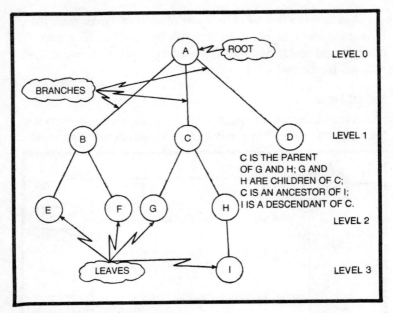

Fig. 3-3. Tree terminology.

single node, the initial node of the state graph. The search tree grows as various paths are explored. When the search is over the search tree shows every path that has been explored during the search.

Figure 3-4 shows a possible search tree for the state graph of Fig. 3-1. The nodes of the search tree correspond to nodes of the state graph and states of the problem world. The branches of the search tree correspond to arcs of the state graph and operators for the problem.

The root of the search tree is the initial node of the state graph. A path in the search tree from the root to a leaf corresponds to a path in the state graph that has already been explored.

A leaf is a node from which no arcs have yet been followed. A node may be a leaf for four reasons:

1. The corresponding node in the state graph is a dead end, having no arcs leaving it.
2. The node is a goal node. When a goal is found the search terminates.
3. The arcs leaving the node have already been followed. It may be possible to reach a node in the state graph from the initial node in more than one way, hence that node may occur more than once in the search tree. If the arcs leaving

a node were followed up when that node was first encountered, no reason exists to follow them again on subsequent encounters.

4. At its current stage the search has simply not gotten around to following the arcs leaving the node in question.

A path from the root to a goal node (a leaf) constitutes a solution to the problem.

There are several different strategies for searching state graphs. The strategies may explore different paths; when they explore the same paths, though, they usually do not explore them in the same order. The exact manner in which a search tree "grows" will depend on the search strategy being used.

Let us look at the growth process more closely. Usually the state graph is given only implicitly. We do not have the entire state graph stored away anywhere. But by applying all possible operators to a given state, we can generate all the successors of a given node. In the search tree we can generate all the children of a given node. We say that a node is *expanded* when its children are generated, adding to a tree. A search tree grows by expanding nodes, as shown in Fig. 3-5.

It is helpful to classify the nodes of a search tree as either *open* or *closed*. An open node has not yet been examined for possible expansion. A closed node has already been examined. It was expanded unless it was a goal node, or a dead end, or the corresponding state graph node had already been expanded elsewhere in the search tree. In Fig. 3-5 open nodes are unshaded, closed nodes are shaded.

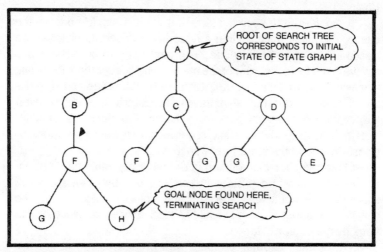

Fig. 3-4. A search tree based on the state graph Fig. 3-1.

49

An open node is always a leaf of the search tree. A closed node is usually not a leaf. It may be a leaf, however, if for one of the reasons given it is not to be expanded.

All searches proceed by expanding open nodes. The particular search strategy being used determines the order in which the open nodes will be expanded.

## BREADTH-FIRST SEARCH

In *breadth-first search* the nodes of the search tree are examined level by level. No node on one level is examined until every node on the next highest level has been examined.

Figure 3-6 illustrates breadth-first search. We begin with the initial node, which is open. This node is expanded, generating level 1 nodes. Each level 1 node is now examined; those which are expanded create level 2 nodes. When all the level 1 nodes have been examined, we move on to the level 2 nodes. The process continues until a goal node is found or until no more open nodes remain.

If the open node being examined corresponds to a state-graph node which has already been encountered, then the open node is closed without being expanded.

A breadth-first search can be managed using a data structure called a *queue*. A queue has the properties of a waiting line. Nodes are added to the rear of the queue and are removed from the front.

Details on how data structures such as queues, stacks, trees, and graphs can be represented inside a computer can be found in my book *Microprocessor Programming for Computer Hobbyists,* TAB Books, 1977.

A breadth-first search starts out with a single node in the queue, the initial node. When a node is expanded its children are placed at the end of the queue. The next node to be examined is always taken from the front of the queue. The queue, then, is the line in which open nodes await their turns to be exmained and closed.

The most important advantage of breadth-first search is that it always finds the *shortest* path from the initial node to a goal node. This path is the solution that requires the fewest operations to transform the initial state into a goal state.

Often the shortest solution is the most desirable one, but not always. In real-world problems *costs* are usually associated with applying each operator. The shortest solution may not be the cheapest solution, for it may call for much more expensive operations than a longer solution.

We can see another problem with breadth-first search if we imagine we are exploring some area of the country by car. Suppose

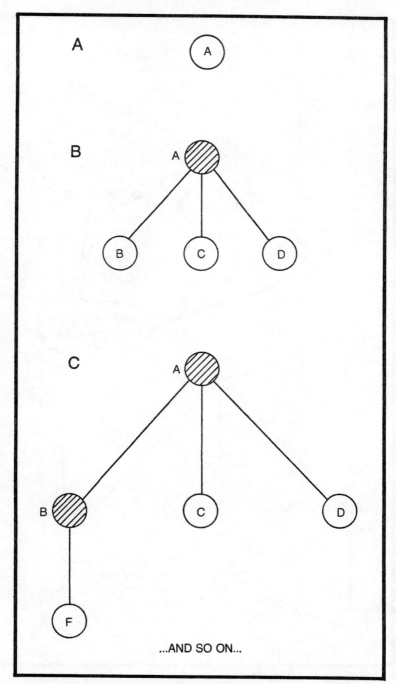

...AND SO ON...

Fig. 3-5. A search tree grows by expanding nodes.

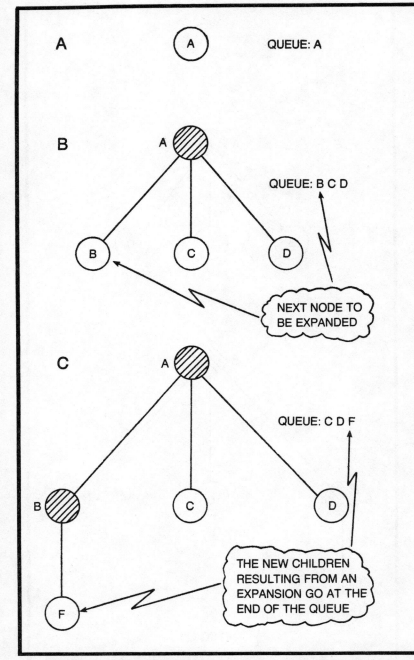

Fig. 3-6. Breadth-first search. The front of the queue is on the left, the rear on the right.

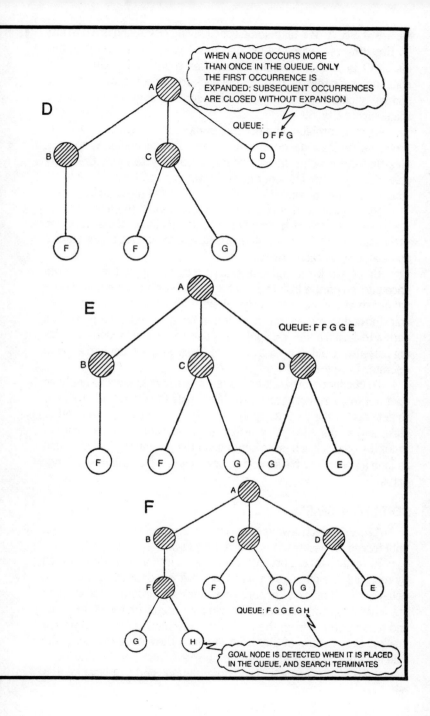

53

we are at city A. We take some road leaving city A and drive to city B. Breadth-first search would demand that we continue by driving back to city A then set out on another road leaving city A. But common sense tells us that driving back to city A is a waste of time and we should continue by following some previously unexplored road leaving city B.

A similar problem can occur in computer search. In real-world problems the state description may be extremely complex, so complex that there is insufficient room in memory to store the many state descriptions. The operators, however, may be much simpler, since each operator may affect only a small part of the complex state.

The answer to this programming problem is to store just one state description, which would be, at the beginning, the description of the initial state. The search tree is stored by storing the operators associated with each branch.

As we work through the search tree we apply the operators encountered on the branches to the single state description. When we arrive at any node the original state description will have been transformed into the state description for that node. To go from a parent to a child node, we apply the operator on the branch connecting parent to child. To go from child to parent, we apply the same operator in reverse.

To conduct a breadth-first search, we would have to apply an operator to go from a parent to a child, apply the operator in reverse to get back to the parent, apply another operator to get to another child, and so on. Always returning to the parent seems a waste of time. It would seem best to continue in the parent-to-child direction as long as possible, backtracking only when we can find no further paths.

## DEPTH-FIRST SEARCH

A search which always continues in the parent-to-child direction until forced to backtrack is called a *depth-first* search.

We can change a breadth-first search into a depth-first search by replacing the queue by a *stack*. A stack is a data structure which behaves like a stack of papers or a stack of cards on a table. The stack has a top and a bottom. We can place items on top of the stack and remove items from the top. Items are always removed from a stack in the reverse of the order in which they were put on. If the rule for a queue is "first come, first served," or "first in, first out," then the rule for a stack is "last come, first served," or "last in, first out."

54

Figure 3-7 illustrates a depth-first search. We start with the initial node on the stack. When we expand a node we place its children on top of the stack. The next node to be examined is taken from the top of the stack.

If the node currently being examined is expanded, its children are placed on top of the stack. The next node examined will be taken from the top of the stack, so we move forward from parent to child. If the node currently being examined is not expanded, the next node taken from the top of the stack will be either on the same level as or on a higher level than the current node. In moving to the new node we will backtrack, either staying on the same level or moving back to a higher one instead of moving forward in the parent-to-child direction.

A node examined in a depth-first search may fail to be expanded for the same reasons as in breadth-first search: the node is a goal node; the node is a dead end; or a node corresponding to the same state has been expanded elsewhere in the search tree.

But in depth-first search we have another reason for not expanding a node. For many problems the state graph contains an infinite number of states, or some number such as $10^{100}$, which is so large as to be practically infinite. For such a graph a depth-first search could travel in the parent-child direction forever, or nearly forever, without ever backtracking. Usually however, if a search does not find a goal node within some reasonable distance from the starting state, we would like for it to backtrack, trying some alternate path instead of continually getting further and further away from the initial state.

For a depth-first search, then, we usually specify a *depth bound*, or a maximum depth, for the search tree. When a node is examined it is not expanded if its depth is equal to the depth bound. Backtracking takes place instead. As shown in Fig. 3-8, this forces the search tree to spread out instead of letting it explore a few paths (perhaps only one path) to great depths.

Depth-first search minimizes backtracking. It is best used in situations such as the one described in the last section, where backtracking involved complex, time consuming calculations.

The solution which depth-first search finds may not be the shortest solution. The solution found, however, can have a length no greater than the depth-bound. A small depth bound forces the search to look only for short solutions. But no solution may be found at all if all solutions have lengths greater than the depth bound. A larger depth bound will allow longer solutions to be found, and will increase the chance of *some* solution being found.

STATE GRAPH FOR DEPTH-FIRST SEARCH EXAMPLE:

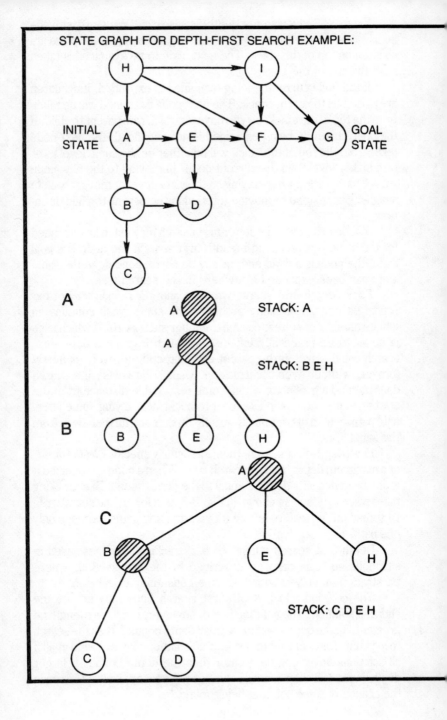

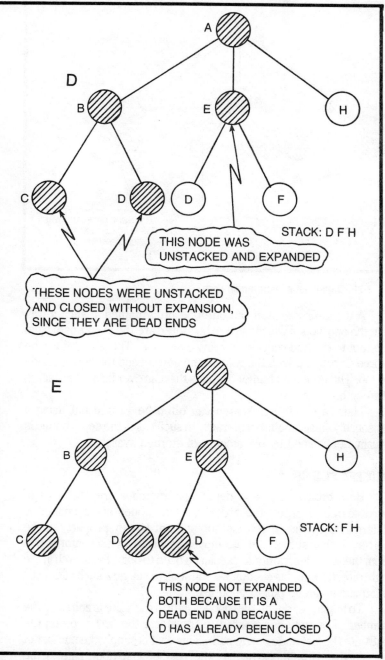

Fig. 3-7. Depth-first search. The top of the stack is on the left, the bottom on the right.

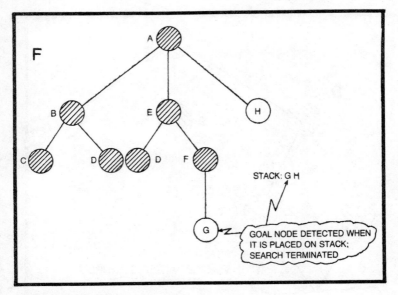

Fig. 3-7F. Depth-first search terminated.

A depth-first search can often be programmed in such a way that the only nodes which have to be stored are those on a path from the root to the node currently being examined. These nodes can be stored on a stack, with the root on the bottom and the current node on top. The greatest number of nodes that can ever be on the stack is the depth bound plus 1.

Thus, a depth-first search can often be carried out using a reasonably small amount of storage. In such cases the depth bound is usually determined by the amount of storage available.

## ORDERED SEARCH

Both breadth-first and depth-first searches are examples of blind search. That is, the order in which nodes are examined is determined by the search method and not by any property of the corresponding states. No attempt is made to extract information from the state descriptions that can be used to point the search in the right direction. In this section we will start to see how such additional information can be put to good use.

To begin, we define the *cost* of a path in the state graph to be the number of operations required to transform the first node on the path into the last node on the path. This cost is simply the number of arcs in the path. In particular, the cost of a solution path is the number of operations required to transform the initial state into the

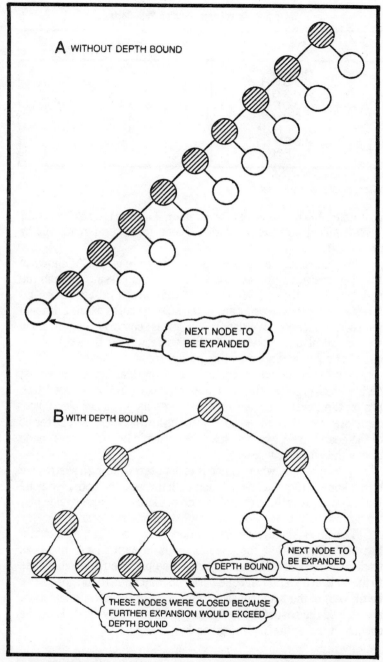

**A** WITHOUT DEPTH BOUND

NEXT NODE TO BE EXPANDED

**B** WITH DEPTH BOUND

NEXT NODE TO BE EXPANDED

DEPTH BOUND

THESE NODES WERE CLOSED BECAUSE FURTHER EXPANSION WOULD EXCEED DEPTH BOUND

Fig. 3-8. The depth bound forces a search tree to spread out instead of following one path to very great depths.

**Table 3-1. Calculating Solution-Path Costs**

| Solution* | Cost† |
|---|---|
| A D G H | 3 |
| A D G G H | 4 |
| A D C G H | 4 |
| A D C F G H | 5 |
| A C G H | 3 |
| A C F H | 3 |
| A B F G H | 4 |
| A B F H | 3 |

*Nodes passed through
†Number of arcs traversed

goal state. Again, this is just the number of arcs in the solution path. Table 3-1 illustrates the calculation of costs for several solution paths of Fig. 3-1.

Now consider a particular node in the state graph. As shown in Fig. 3-9, there may be several solution paths passing through the node. Each of those solution paths will have a cost. We are interested in the *lowest cost* of any of the solution paths passing through the node in question. We denote this lowest cost by $f$. For any node we can calculate a value for $f$; that value will be the cost of the cheapest solution whose path passes through the node.

Now, suppose we are searching in the state graph and must decide which of several possible nodes to go to next. The node which lies on the lowest cost solution path seems a reasonable choice; therefore, we will go to the node with the lowest value for $f$. In terms of the search tree, we will select for examination that open node having the smallest value of $f$.

Unfortunately, when a node is encountered during a search, we do not know if there is any solution path through the node, let alone the lowest-cost path. Although we do not know the exact value of $f$, we can *estimate* that value and use it to guide the search.

To help estimate $f$, we break it down into two parts, as shown in Fig. 3-10. The lowest-cost-solution path through a given node can itself be broken down into two parts—one part from the initial node to the node in question and one part from that node to the goal. Let $g$ be the cost of the path from the initial node to the node in question, and let $h$ be the cost of the path from that node to the goal. Then the cost, $f$, of the entire path is given by:

$$f = g + h$$

We can calculate $g$ exactly for every node in the search tree. As shown in Fig. 3-11, for a particular node in the search tree there is a

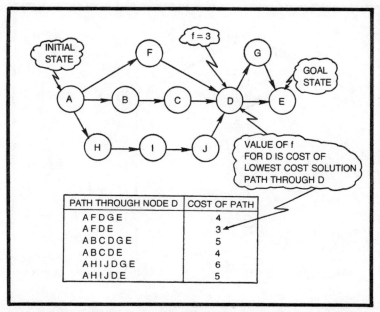

| PATH THROUGH NODE D | COST OF PATH |
|---|---|
| A F D G E | 4 |
| A F D E | 3 |
| A B C D G E | 5 |
| A B C D E | 4 |
| A H I J D G E | 6 |
| A H I J D E | 5 |

Fig. 3-9. The value of f for a given node is the cost of the lowest cost solution path passing through that node.

unique path from the root of the tree to that node. This path in the search tree corresponds to a path in the state graph connecting the initial node to the corresponding state-graph node. The cost of this

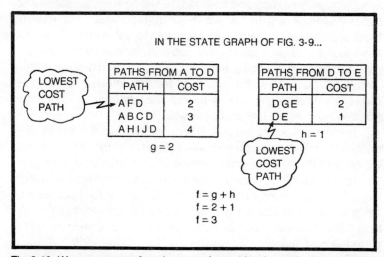

IN THE STATE GRAPH OF FIG. 3-9...

| PATHS FROM A TO D | |
|---|---|
| PATH | COST |
| A F D | 2 |
| A B C D | 3 |
| A H I J D | 4 |

g = 2

| PATHS FROM D TO E | |
|---|---|
| PATH | COST |
| D G E | 2 |
| D E | 1 |

h = 1

$$f = g + h$$
$$f = 2 + 1$$
$$f = 3$$

Fig. 3-10. We can express f as the sum of g and h, where g is the cost of the cheapest path from the initial node to the node in question, and h is the cost of the cheapest path from the node to a goal node.

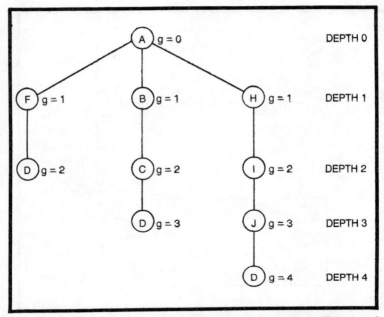

Fig. 3-11. We can calculate g exactly for every node in a search tree. The value of g is simply the depth of the node.

path from the root to the node is the value of $g$ for the search-tree node. This value $g$ is just equal to the depth of the node.

Now, since a given state-graph node can usually be reached in several ways from the initial node, there will be several search-tree nodes corresponding to the same state-graph node. For each of these search-tree nodes we can calculate the value of $g$. We do not know that any of the root-to-node paths in the search tree correspond to the *shortest*, initial node-to-node path in the state graph. Therefore, the values of $g$ calculated for the different search-tree nodes are *estimates* of the value for the state-graph node, the smallest value being the best estimate.

In carrying out our search, then, we will use the values of $g$ calculated for search-graph nodes as estimates of the values of $g$ for the corresponding state-graph nodes. Figure 3-12 illustrates this.

In contrast to $g$, there is no way to estimate $h$ from the search tree. We will be mostly interested in estimating $h$ for open nodes. Since an open node has not yet been expanded, the search tree tells us nothing whatever about the paths leaving the open node and going on to the goal node.

The only thing we have to help us estimate $h$ is the state description itself. We study the state description and try to guess how many operations will be needed to transform this state into a goal state. That guess is our estimate of $h$.

Table 3-2 and Fig. 3-13 show ways of estimating $h$ for the two problems that we examined in the last chapter.

For the Missionaries and Cannibals problem the number of missionaries and cannibals still on the left bank is an estimate of the amount of work that remains to be done. It takes two boat trips, one across and one back, to take one person across the river and then bring the boat back to pick up another person. Therefore, two times the number of persons on the left bank is an estimate of the number of operations necessary to move those persons across the river, and so reach a goal state. We can use this as our estimate of $h$. This is only a rough estimate, since it ignores all the juggling of missionaries and cannibals needed to assure that no missionaries are eaten.

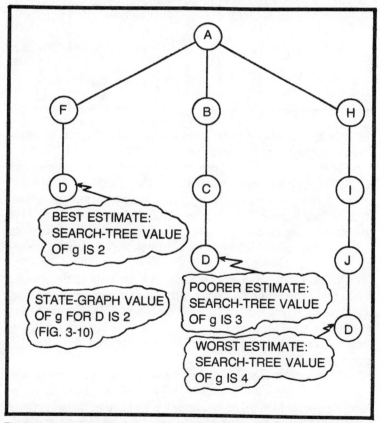

Fig. 3-12. The values of **g** calculated for search tree nodes corresponding to a given state are estimates of the value of **g** for the corresponding state-graph node.

**Table 3-2. Estimating h for the Tower of Hanoi Problem**

| Left Bank | | | Right Bank | | | Estimate Of h |
|---|---|---|---|---|---|---|
| M | C | B | M | C | B | |
| 0 | 1 | Yes | 3 | 2 | No | 2 |
| 0 | 2 | Yes | 3 | 1 | No | 4 |
| 0 | 3 | Yes | 3 | 0 | No | 6 |
| 1 | 1 | Yes | 2 | 2 | No | 4 |
| 2 | 2 | Yes | 1 | 1 | No | 8 |
| 3 | 1 | Yes | 0 | 2 | No | 8 |
| 3 | 2 | Yes | 0 | 1 | No | 10 |
| 3 | 3 | Yes | 0 | 0 | No | 12 |
| 0 | 0 | No | 3 | 3 | Yes | 0 |
| 0 | 1 | No | 3 | 2 | Yes | 2 |
| 0 | 2 | No | 3 | 1 | Yes | 4 |
| 1 | 1 | No | 2 | 2 | Yes | 4 |
| 2 | 2 | No | 1 | 1 | Yes | 8 |
| 3 | 0 | No | 0 | 3 | Yes | 6 |
| 3 | 1 | No | 0 | 2 | Yes | 8 |
| 3 | 2 | No | 0 | 1 | Yes | 10 |

Nevertheless, it will keep the search focused on the task at hand, which is getting people across the river.

For the Tower of Hanoi problem we can focus our attention on peg 3 and ignore whatever manipulations must be done on the other two pegs. We can then easily determine the number of operations involving peg 3 alone that are needed to reach the goal state. This number we take as our estimate of $h$. It is an underestimate, of course, since we have ignored manipulations on pegs 1 and 2 entirely.

Obviously, the method of estimating $h$ depends on the specific details of a particular problem. We cannot devise any general method of estimating $h$ that will work for all problems. For each particular problem we must study the features of the state description to see which ones will give us some clue as to how far the state at hand is from a goal state.

The information which we extract from the state description and use to estimate $h$ is called *heuristic information*, since it aids us in discovering a solution to the problem. We said earlier that a heuristic was a rule of thumb for solving a problem. A method for estimating $h$ can be thought of as a rule of thumb for deciding how close a given state is to a goal state.

Like all heuristic methods, the estimation of $h$ is subject to error. That is, our rule of thumb may erroneously estimate a higher value of $h$ for a state closer to the goal and a lower value for some other state further away. When this happens the function $g$ comes in handy. If a bad value of $h$ sends us on a wild goose chase, then increasing values of $g$ along the wild-goose-chase path will quickly force us to backtrack and try alternate paths, even though this may mean going to nodes which do not have the lowest value for $h$.

The function which estimates $h$ is often called an *evaluation function*, since it evaluates a given state by estimating the cost of transforming that state into a goal state. We will return to evaluation functions when we take up game-playing programs, in which evaluation functions play a fundamental role.

Now let us see how to carry out a search guided by the estimated values of $f$, $g$, and $h$. Such a search is called an *ordered search*, since the estimated value of $f$ determines the order in which open nodes are examined and closed.

Figure 3-14 shows an ordered search. In this Fig. 3-15 and the following discussion, the letters $f$, $g$, and $h$ stand for the *estimated values* of $f$, $g$, and $h$, though we will not always say so.

We start the search with the initial node of the state graph, which becomes the root of the search tree. The value of $g$ for the root is 0. We compute $h$ using whatever rule of thumb we have devised. The value of $f$ is the value of $g + h$. Since the value of $g$ is 0, the value of $f$ is just the value of $h$.

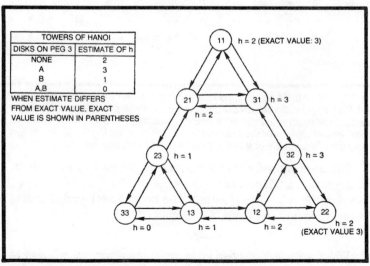

Fig. 3-13. Estimating h for the Tower of Hanoi problem.

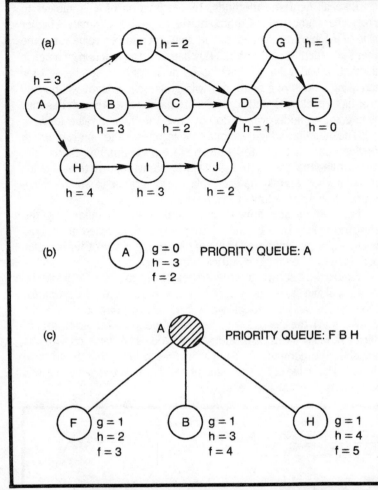

Fig. 3-14. An ordered search: the node with the lowest value of f is expanded next. Part (a) gives the values of h used; because of the simplicity of the problem these are the exact values; in more realistic problems the exact value would not be known and some heuristic estimate (as in Table 3-2 and Fig. 3-13) would have to be used. The values of g calculated for the search tree are used.

When we expand a node we calculate f for each of its children. We can easily calculate g, since the value of g for a child is always 1 more than the value for the parent. The value of h is calculated using the rule of thumb. As usual, f is calculated using

$$f = g + h$$

When we select an open node for examination, we will always select the one with the smallest value for f. If several open nodes

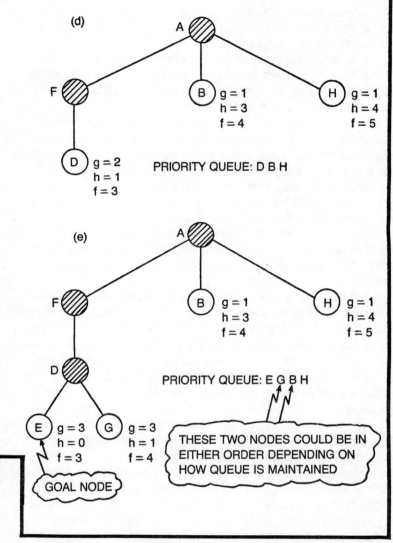

have the same value for $f$, any may be chosen, except that if one of the nodes is a goal node, it should be chosen.

Except for the calculations of $f$, ordered search is similar to breadth-first and depth-first search. The queue or stack is replaced with a list on which open nodes are ordered according to their values of $f$, the nodes with the smaller values being near the beginning of the list, and those with the larger values being near the end. Then the first node on the list will be the one with the smallest value of $f$. And this is the one that will be selected for examination next.

When a node is expanded each of its children is placed on the list. Each child is inserted in its proper position according to its value for $f$ so as to keep the list in order.

A list like this is sometimes called a *priority queue*, since regardless of the order in which items are added, the next one removed will be the one with the highest priority. In our case "highest priority" means smallest value for $f$.

If the node removed from the priority queue for examination is a goal node, the search terminates. If it is a dead end it is closed without being expanded. If the node does not correspond to the same rate as any other node in the search tree, it will be expanded.

If the node being examined corresponds to the same state as some other node in the search tree, the steps we must take are a bit more complicated than for breath-first or depth-first search.

If the value of $g$ for the node being examined is greater than or equal to the value of $g$ for some other node corresponding to the same state, the node being examined is closed without being expanded.

But suppose that the value of $g$ for the node being examined is less than its value for any other node corresponding to the same state. If no other node corresponding to the same state has been expanded, the node being examined is expanded. If one of the other nodes corresponding to the same state has already been expanded, its children are taken from it and attached to the node being examined, as shown in Fig. 3-15. The value of $g$ must now be recomputed for all the descendants of the node being examined.

The purpose of these somewhat complicated manipulations is to assure that of all the nodes corresponding to the same state, the one with the lowest value of $g$, will be expanded. (This value of $g$ will be the best estimate of the cost of the shortest path from the initial state to the state in question.) If we expand a node and then find another node corresponding to the same state and with a lower value of $g$, we must restructure the tree so that it is the newly found node which is expanded.

The outstanding feature of ordered search is that detailed information about the states, in the form of the estimate of $h$, is used to guide search toward a goal. The effect of $g$ is similar to that of the depth bound in depth-first search: it prevents the search program from following a fruitless path too far.

For simplicity we have assumed that the cost of applying an operator is the same for every operator. But ordered search can be

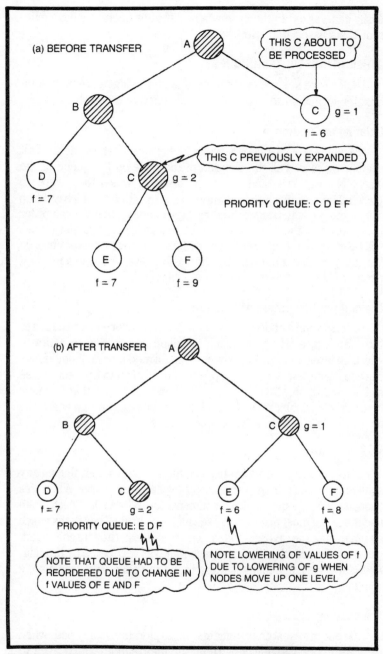

Fig. 3-15. If after a node has been expanded, a node corresponding to the same state and with a lower value of **g** is found, the children of the expanded node are transferred to the newly found one.

easily generalized to the case where different operators have different costs associated with them.

## OTHER HEURISTIC TECHNIQUES

There are several other techniques for using heuristic rule-of-thumb information to improve the efficiency of a search.

### Ordering of Children

When we expanded a node in breadth-first or depth-first search, we placed all the children of the node on the queue or the stack. Nothing was said about the *order* in which they were so placed. If we can use heuristic information to estimate which children can be most easily transformed into goal nodes, then we can order the children on the stack or queue so that the more promising ones will be examined first. Since this ordering is done only for children belonging to the same parent, the basic breath-first or depth-first nature of the search method is not changed.

### Limiting the Generation of Children

So far when a node was expanded, all its children were added to the search tree. By again using heuristic information to estimate which children can most easily be transformed into goal nodes, we can add only a few of the more promising children to the search tree and discard the rest. Of course, we should not forget that heuristic methods are fallible, and we could discard a node through which the best or even the only solution had to pass.

### Tree Pruning

After a search program has run for a while without finding any solution, the search tree will fill up available memory. When this happens we can use heuristic information to decide which open nodes are the most promising. We can then "prune" any paths which do not lead to the favored nodes. The search can they be continued, with the tree growing into the space that was recovered by pruning. As before, we could inadvertently prune the only paths leading to a solution.

### Termination

Depth-first search terminates the exploration of any path when the depth bound is reached. Heuristic information can be used to allow seemingly promising paths to be pursued more deeply than seemingly unpromising ones.

# Chapter 4
# Subproblems, Subgoals, and Plans

Many problems are too complex for the state-graph search methods of the last chapter. The state graphs for these problems are very large (perhaps even infinite). There are no heuristics powerful enough to guide the search to a solution without having to explore a very large part of the state graph. Problems like this cannot be solved with state-graph search using reasonable amounts of computer memory and computer time. Some more-powerful approach is needed.

Such a complex problem can be tackled by breaking it down into two or more *subproblems* such that:

- The subproblems are easier to solve than the original problem.
- If all the subproblems are solved then the original problem will be solved.

In everyday life we automatically break problems down in this way without thinking about it. Suppose our problem is to paint a room. We automatically break this down into the subproblems of procuring the paint, obtaining a ladder, covering the furniture, painting the ceiling, and painting the walls.

Notice that the order in which some of the subproblems are solved is important. We must procure the paint before painting the ceiling or the walls. We must cover the furniture before painting the ceiling, and so on. On the other hand it does not matter whether we procure the paint first or the ladder first.

Some subproblems can be broken down further into still simpler subproblems. Procuring the paint, for instance, can be broken down into driving to the paint store, selecting the paint, paying for it, and driving back home again.

## SUBGOALS AND PLANS

One way of breaking a problem down into subproblems is to introduce *subgoals*, or intermediate goals, and between the initial state and the goal state. The original problem of going from the initial state to the goal state is replaced by the problems of going from the initial state to the first subgoal, from the first subgoal to the second subgoal, and so on. The final subproblem is that of going from the last subgoal to the goal state.

The sequence of subgoals constitutes a *plan* for solving the original problem. The plan is carried out by solving each of the subproblems.

This is illustrated in Fig. 4-1. The problem is to get from the initial state A to the goal state B. We plan the solution by introducing the subgoals X and Y. The plan is to go from A to X, from X to Y, and from Y to B. Each step of the plan is a subproblem, and when all the subproblems have been solved, the plan will have been realized.

Notice that this is like planning a trip from city A to city B. We plan to go through cities X and Y along the way. We realize the plan by working out the details of how to get from city A to city X, and so on.

Why are the problems of going from A to X, from X to Y, and so on simpler than the original problem of going from A to B? There are several possible reasons, not all of which are obvious from the state graph:

1. X is closer to A than it is to B. If we started at A searching for X, we would have to search a smaller portion of the state graph before reaching our goal than we would if we were searching for B. The same remarks would apply to finding Y starting at X and finding B starting at Y.
2. There may be powerful heuristics that will quickly guide a search from A to X or from X to Y or from Y to B. No such heuristics may exist for getting directly from A to B.
3. We may know from previous experience with the problem world how to get from A to X, from X to Y, or from Y to B. Once we have planned the solution the problem is solved, since we already know how to carry out each step of the plan. Even if we only knew how to carry out one step, say going from X to Y, the problem would still be substantially simplified.

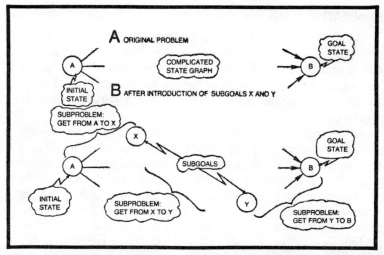

Fig. 4-1. X and Y are subgoals, or intermediate goals, lying between the initial state A and the goal B. We plan to reach B by going from A to X, from X to Y, and then from Y to B.

Another approach to planning is to determine a *key operator*. This is an operator that must be applied at some point in solving the problem. For instance, suppose the problem is to travel from city 1 to city 2. The two cities are separated by a river. There is only one bridge across the river. Clearly "Cross the bridge" is a key operator.

Given a key operator we plan as follows:

1. Transform the initial state into a state to which the key operator can be applied. This is a state for which the condition part of the key operator is true.
2. Apply the key operator.
3. Transform the state which results from applying the key operator into the goals state.

Now we know how to solve subproblem 2, since we know what the key operator is, and need only apply it. Problems 1 and 3, however, may still be too complex to solve directly, and may have to be broken down into still simpler subproblems.

For the problem of getting from city 1 to city 2 the key-operator method yields the following reasonable plan:

1. Travel from city 1 to the bridge.
2. Cross the bridge.
3. Travel from the other side of the bridge to city 2.

73

## FORMULATING PLANS

How can a computer program formulate a plan to solve a problem? This is a current research problem in AI, and one that is by no means fully solved. In this section we will look at some of the planning methods that have been used in AI programs. All of these are experimental, and much further research will be needed to perfect them.

If we could draw the entire state graph of a problem on a piece of paper and then look at it, we would have little trouble in identifying key operators and reasonable subgoals. Unfortunately, (a) a computer cannot take in the state graph in a single glance the way a person can, and (b) for most real-world problems the state graph is too large to draw on a piece of paper or store in memory. Therefore the overall structure of the state graph is of little help in planning. Instead, we must concentrate on the detailed structure of the states and operators.

### Difference Reduction

One of the oldest AI planning techniques focuses on the *differences* between the initial state and the goal state. It then tries to find an operator that will reduce the difference between the initial state and the goal state and thus bring the initial state closer to the goal.

A difference is any feature of the state description that has different values for the initial state and the goal state. Often the goal states are specified by giving some condition that they must satisfy. In that case a difference is any feature of the initial state whose value prevents the initial state from satisfying the goal condition.

To illustrate the use of differences, consider the problem shown in Fig. 4-2. A room contains table A, table B, a box, and a robot. The box is sitting on table A. The problem for the robot is to move the box from table A to table B.

The features of the state are the position of the robot, the position of the box, and whether or not the robot is holding the box. The initial state is the one shown in Fig. 4-2. The goal state is any state in which the box is on table B.

The operators for this problem will be commands we can give to the robot. We assume the robot can obey the following commands:

- GO TO. The robot goes to the designated position. The positions of interest are beside table A and beside table B.
- PICK UP BOX. The robot picks up the box from the table the robot is standing beside. This operator can only be applied if the robot is not already holding something and if it is standing beside a table containing the box.

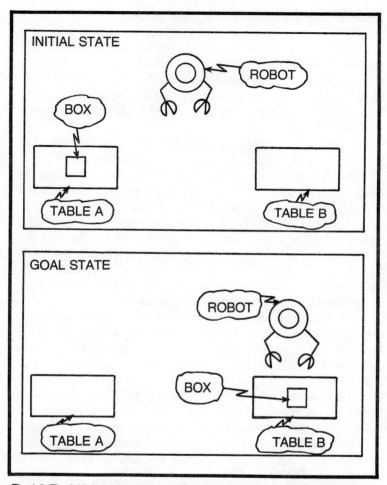

Fig. 4-2. The initial state and the goal state for a robot-control problem. The robot is to move the box from table A to table B.

- SET DOWN BOX. The robot sets the box down on the table the robot is standing beside. This operator can be applied only if the robot has a box in its hands and is standing beside an empty table.

We begin by asking why the initial state is not a goal state. The reason is that in the initial state the box is not on table B. We look for an operator that will place the box on table B.

SET DOWN BOX is such an operator. In order for SET DOWN BOX to be applied, the robot must have the box in its hands and must be standing next to a table. The operator could be applied if the robot

75

were standing next to either table, but to produce the desired result the robot must be standing next to table B.

Therefore, we break the original problem down into two subproblems (Fig. 4-3a). The first subproblem is to change the initial state into one in which the robot is standing by table B with the box in its hands. The second subproblem is to set the box down on table B. The second subproblem is trivially solved by applying the operator SET DOWN BOX.

We now turn to the first subproblem. In its goal state the robot is standing beside table B with the box in its hands.

For this subproblem there are two differences between the initial state and the goal state. In the initial state the robot (1) is not beside table B and (2) does not have the box in its hands.

Let us work on difference 1. The operator GO TO table B will move the robot to table B. Our plan is now as shown in Fig. 4-3b. We first get the box into the robot's hands. Then we apply the operators GO TO table B and SET DOWN BOX. Note: it is important for the planner to realize that applying the operator GO TO table B will not change the fact that the robot is holding the box.

The subproblem to be solved now is to change the initial state to one in which the robot is holding the box. The operator PICK UP BOX will do this. But this operator can only be applied if the robot is empty handed beside table A. Our plan is now the one shown in Fig. 4-3c.

The remaining subproblem is to get the robot empty handed to table A. In the initial state the robot is empty handed, but is not at table A. The operator GO TO table A eliminates this difference.

Thus we finally end up with the plan shown in Fig. 4-3d. Our orders to the robot are: GO TO table A; PICK UP BOX; GO TO table B; SET DOWN BOX.

Notice that in solving this problem we started with the goal state and worked back to the initial state. For obvious reasons this technique is known as working backwards.

For simple problems like the one in the example, difference reduction works well. For more complicated problems it is often defeated by one of several difficulties:

- The initial state and the goal state may be so different that their differences contain few clues as to how to get from one to another. Suppose our problem is to build a house. We would have a hard time deducing the techniques of architecture and carpentry by comparing stacks of lumber and brick with a finished house.

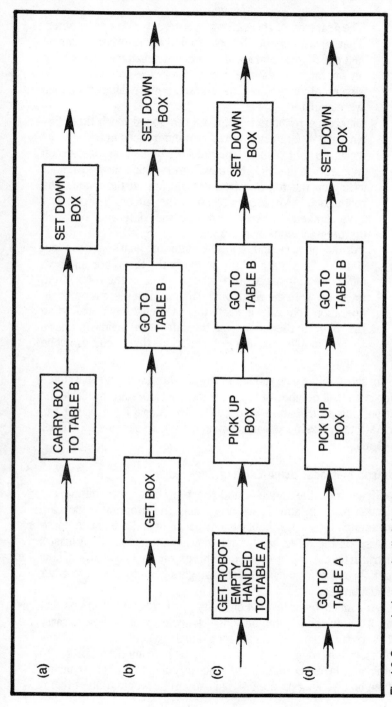

Fig. 4-3. Successively more detailed plans for solving the robot control problem.

77

- The features of the state may interact with one another. That is, we may not be able to find operators that change just one feature and leave all others unchanged. In applying an operator to eliminate one difference we may change several other features and so create more differences than we eliminated.
- Difference reduction programs can spend much time discovering operators that reduce differences in trivial ways which do not lead to solutions. Not long ago a cartoon appeared in the SIGART newsletter which showed a robot sitting in the top of a tree and staring at the moon. The robot said, "My goal is to go to the moon. Therefore, I have climbed this tree to reduce the difference between my present state and my goal."
- For the moon-bound robot the initial and goal states are too similar. The state of the world with the robot on earth differs in only one feature (the position of the robot) from the state with the robot on the moon. But there is no single operation that will eliminate this difference by transporting the robot to the moon. And the difference yields no clue as to the complex sequence of operations that would in fact be required.

In short, difference reduction works when initial and final states differ in a small number of features and operators are available for manipulating each feature individually. But there is no way it can generate the *ideas* necessary to plan complex solutions to difficult problems.

## Heuristic Methods: Using Existing Knowledge

If we give the moon-bound-robot problem to a difference-reduction problem solver, we are asking the program to develop from scratch the entire theory and practice of space flight. A space scientist, on the other hand, could quickly come up with at least a rough plan for the trip by drawing on his extensive knowledge of how to get objects of various sizes and weights from the earth to other celestial bodies.

At a much lower level of difficulty (for humans), programs that control robots need "common sense" knowledge about how to carry out everyday actions. A human, for example, would not have to think at all about how to move a box from one table to another. If asked to explain why he did certain things (such as going to the table containing the box, picking up the box, and so on) he would protest that it was just "common sense" that those things had to be done to move the box. A difference-reduction problem solver must go through a tedious chain of reasoning before it can guide a robot through the same task.

How to incorporate existing knowledge into problem-solving programs is still very much a topic for research. The final answers are far from in. We will present here one idea that has been suggested and which seems promising, but which still needs much further testing and elaboration.

The idea is to incorporate knowledge in heuristics, which we remember, are just rules of thumb. Each heuristic contains a *condition* and one or more *plans*.

The condition part functions like the condition part of an operator in that it determines when the heuristic can be applied. Instead of just referring to the initial state, however, the condition may refer to all elements of the problem: initial state, goal states, and available operators.

The plan part contains a list of plans which can be recommended when the condition in the condition part holds. The plans can be presented in various ways: as sequences of subgoals, as key operators, or as lists of subproblems into which the original problem can be decomposed.

As always, heuristics are fallible, so a recommended plan may not work—that is, one or more of its subproblems cannot be solved. In that case the program can try another plan from the list in the plan part of the heuristic. If the list is exhausted the program can try other heuristics whose conditions hold for the problem at hand. If all such heuristics are exhausted then the program cannot solve the problem.

We can think of the condition part of the heuristic as holding when certain *patterns* are present in the problem. A heuristic, then, looks for certain patterns in the problem, and if they are found, recommends certain plans that should have a chance of working. Recognizing patterns is itself an important problem to which a later chapter will be devoted.

The importance of formulating and carrying out plans cannot be overemphasized. Computer chess, for instance, is the one area in which the performance of AI programs have been subjected to extensive criticism by human experts. And the invariable comment has been that while the program often handles the details of play well, particularly when defending against immediate threats, its frequent aimless moves show that it has no overall plan for bringing about a victory.

## SEARCHING AND/OR TREES

When we try to solve a problem by breaking it down into subproblems, and breaking down those subproblems into still other subproblems, and so on, we are searching for a solution using *problem reduction*. In this section we will look at some of the details of managing a problem-reduction search.

Like the state-graph search described in chapter 3, a problem-reduction search can best be understood in terms of search trees.

The nodes of the problem-reduction search tree are problems. The root of the tree is the original problem. All the other nodes are subproblems. The children of a node are the subproblems to which the parent has been reduced. Expanding a node reduces the problem corresponding to the parent to the subproblems corresponding to the children.

The leaves of the search tree are of three types:

1. The problem corresponding to the leaf can be solved without further reduction into subproblems. Such a problem is called a *primitive problem*. The leaf node is said to be *solved*.
2. The problem corresponding to the leaf node cannot be solved or further reduced into subproblems. The leaf node is said to be *unsolvable*. An unsolvable node corresponds to a dead end in state-graph search. The search program can proceed no further along the path leading to the unsolvable node, but must backtrack and try some other path.
3. At this stage of the search the leaf node has not yet been examined for possible expansion.

There are two ways of reducing a problem into subproblems and, consequently, two ways of expanding a node. These are illustrated in Fig. 4-4.

### The AND Expansion

The problem is solved only if *all* its subproblems are solved. This is the kind of problem reduction we have mainly discussed so far. As shown in Fig. 4-4a the AND expansion is designated by a circular arc across the branches leading to the children. Figure 4-5a shows an AND tree, which uses only AND expansions. In an AND tree the problem corresponding to the root is solved only if *all* the leaf nodes are solved.

### The OR Expansion

The problem is solved if any one of its subproblems is solved. The subproblems are *alternatives* to the original problem, and solv-

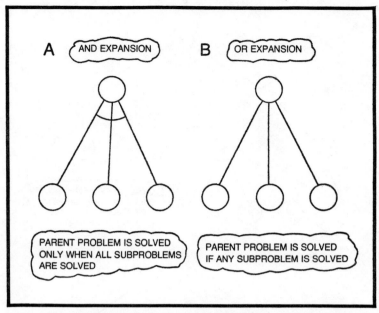

Fig. 4-4. The AND expansion and the OR expansion. The arc below the node designates an AND expansion.

ing any one of them solves the original problem. Figure 4-4b shows an OR expansion and Fig. 4-5b shows an OR tree. In an OR tree the problem corresponding to the root is solved if *any one* of the leaf nodes is solved.

The OR tree corresponds most closely to the trees used in state-graph search. (Remember that in state-graph search the branches leading from a parent to its children represent *alternative* paths to be explored.) A solved leaf node in the OR tree corresponds to a goal node in the state-graph tree, and an unsolvable leaf node corresponds to a dead end.

Usually, instead of a pure AND tree or pure OR tree we will have an AND/OR tree, as shown in Fig. 4-5c. An AND expansion introduces a set of subproblems, all of which must be solved to solve the parent problem. The subproblems constitute a plan for solving the parent problem. An OR expansion introduces a set of alternative plans for solving the parent problem. If any one of the plans can be carried out, the parent problem is solved.

Figure 4-6 shows the search tree for the robot-control problem of Fig. 4-2. This is a pure AND tree, since the problem was so simple we could go directly to the solution without having to consider alternative plans.

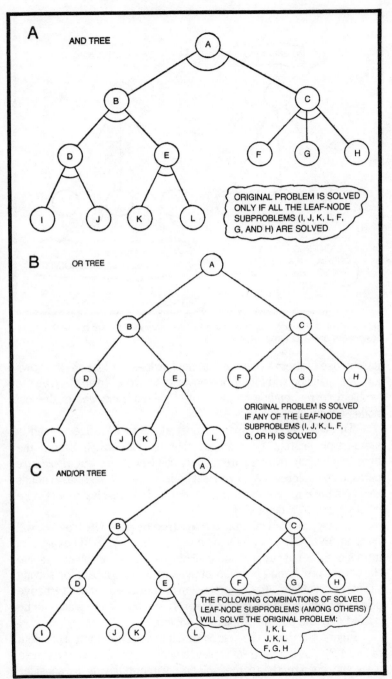

Fig. 4-5. An AND tree, an OR tree, and an AND/OR tree.

AND/OR trees can be searched using breadth-first, depth-first, or ordered search. The details are similar to those for state graphs, and we will not go over them again here. More details can be found in the book by Nilsson, listed in the bibliography.

The same subproblem can occur in the expansions of several different problems. This means that several different nodes in the search tree will correspond to the same subproblem. This is analogous to the situation for state-graph search trees where several different search tree nodes correspond to the same state-graph node. The two situations are handled in similar ways.

There is one feature of problem-reduction search which is completely different from the corresponding feature of state-graph search. This is determining when the problem is solved and the search can be terminated.

In state-graph search the search is terminated when a goal node is found. In problem-reduction search, if we were searching a pure OR tree, we could stop as soon as we found a solved node. But for an AND/OR tree the procedure is more complicated.

Figure 4-7 illustrates how to determine whether or not an AND/OR tree search can terminate. We start with the leaves of the search tree. Those leaves corresponding to problems with known solutions are marked *s* for *solved*. Those corresponding to problems which cannot be solved are marked *u* for *unsolvable*. The remaining unmarked leaves are nodes which have not yet been expanded.

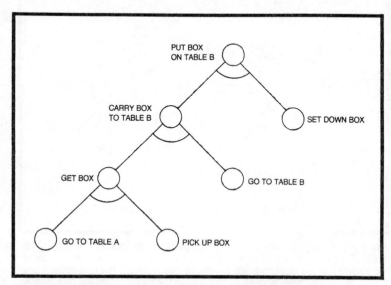

Fig. 4-6. The search tree for the robot-control problem of Fig. 4-2.

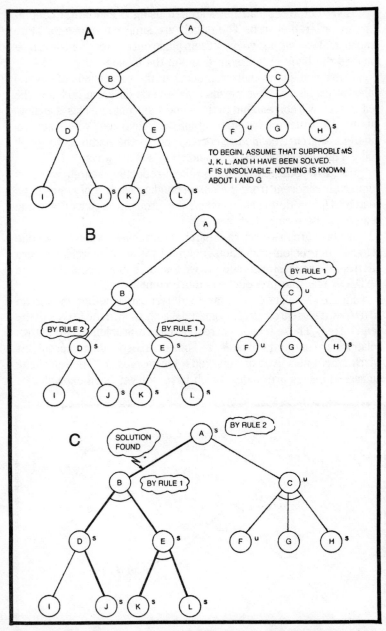

Fig. 4-7. Determining whether the problem corresponding to the root of an AND/OR tree has been solved or has been declared unsolvable. Nodes marked **s** are solved; those marked **u** are unsolvable. We assume the leaf nodes have been marked and work from leaves to root. In the last diagram the heavy lines show the solution that was found.

84

We now work upward, level by level, from the leaves to the root, marking nodes with *u* or *s* or leaving them unmarked. The rules for marking the nodes are as follows:

1. *The node has an AND expansion.* If all the children of the node are marked *s*, mark the node *s*. If any children are marked *u*, mark the node *u*. Otherwise leave the node unmarked.

2. *The node has an OR expansion.* If any of the children of the node are marked *s*, mark the node *s*. If all the children are marked *u*, mark the node *u*. Otherwise leave the node unmarked.

We start with the leaves and work upward to the root, always marking the children of a node before marking that node. If the procedure marks the root *s*, the original problem is solved. If the root is marked *u*, the original problem cannot be solved, and the problem-solving program must report failure. If the root is not marked either *s* or *u*, the search should continue.

During the search, whenever a leaf node is examined and discovered to be either solved or unsolvable, the above procedure should be carried out to see if the root node can be marked solved or unsolvable. The markings need be recomputed only for those nodes lying on the path from the root to the leaf.

We will return to AND/OR trees when we take up game-playing programs.

# Chapter 5
# Hierarchical Plans
# and Procedural Nets

In Chapter 1 we mentioned the combinatorial explosion that can occur when we attempt to explore a continually branching path. Both state-graph search and problem-reduction search can be formulated in terms of search trees, and so both are subject to the combinatorial explosion.

Let us look for a moment at the extent of the explosion. Suppose that every node has seven children (seven was the branching factor used in an early chess program). This means that in state-graph search there are seven arcs leaving each node in the state graph, and in problem-reduction search each problem or subproblem is broken down into seven subproblems.

At the root of the tree there is only one path to explore, and every time we go to the next level, the number of paths to be explored is multiplied by seven. Table 5-1 gives the number of paths to be explored on levels 0 through 10.

Searching nearly 300 million paths in any reasonable time is at the current limits of computer technology. And a few more levels would put us beyond anything likely to be developed in the foreseeable future.

What are needed, of course, are heuristics that will limit the number of children generated for each node. However, it is difficult to find *local* heuristics—those which only take into account the situation at a single node—that are sufficiently limiting. As in the example of Chapter 1, the road signs that direct us from city to city (local heuristics) are useless in directing us to a distant destination, unless we know in advance what cities we have to go through to get there.

## HIERARCHICAL PLANNING

A human problem solver usually avoids combinatorial explosion by formulating a plan for solving the problem before plunging into the

**Table 5-1. Combinatorial Explosion**

| Search Tree Level | Paths to be Explored |
|---|---|
| 0 | 1 |
| 1 | 7 |
| 2 | 49 |
| 3 | 343 |
| 4 | 2,401 |
| 5 | 16,807 |
| 6 | 117,649 |
| 7 | 823,543 |
| 8 | 5,764,801 |
| 9 | 40,353,607 |
| 10 | 282,475,249 |

details. At each step of the solution he explores only the few paths (perhaps only one) consistent with the plan.

A detailed plan for solving a problem does not come all at once. Usually, one starts with a general idea and then refines it several times, adding more details on each refinement until arriving at a detailed plan. Some may be familiar with the technique of *structured programming*, in which the idea for a program is systematically developed into the program by repeated stepwise refinement.

This approach to planning is called *hierarchical*, since it generates an entire *hierarchy* of plans, with the roughest plan at the top of the hierarchy and the most detailed one at the bottom. As shown in Fig. 5-1, the steps in the plans form an AND tree. Each level of the tree corresponds to a particular refinement of the original plan.

When a plan has been refined, we should not discard the less detailed plans that gave rise to it. We should, in fact, keep the entire tree of Fig. 5-1. If it turns out that a step in the detailed plan cannot be carried through, we need not abandon the entire plan. Instead, we go back to the parent of the troublesome step and try to refine it in some way. Thus, we can often work around a difficulty without having to abandon the entire plan and start from scratch.

Some programs must not only think up plans, but also see to it that the plans are carried out in the real world. Typical examples of such programs are:

- A robot-control program
- A program that gives a human step-by-step instructions for carrying out a certain task
- A game-playing program

We say that such programs must *monitor the execution* of their plans.

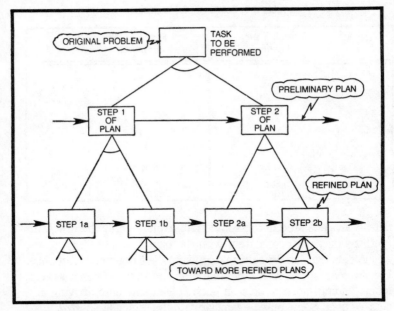

Fig. 5-1. A hierarchy of plans. Each level of the tree is a plan which is a refinement of the next highest level.

Now even if a plan is well thought out, unanticipated difficulties can arise when the plan is executed. The robot may find an unexpected obstacle in its path; the human may report that he cannot carry out a particular instruction; an opponent may make an unexpected move. Again, one can try refining the parent or some other ancestor of the troublesome step instead of throwing away the entire plan.

Another way of looking at the matter is that all the ancestors of a given step in the most detailed plan represent knowledge of why that step was chosen. If trouble arises with that step, this knowledge can be used to choose a reasonable alternative, with as little modification to the rest of the plan as possible.

In this chapter we will introduce a method of hierarchical planning developed by Earl D. Sacerdoti. Readers interested in more details should refer to Sacerdoti's book, *A Structure for Plans and Behavior* (see bibliography), which contains a wealth of ideas on formulating and executing plans.

## PROCEDURAL NETS

Sacerdoti represents each level of refinement of a plan by a *procedural network* or *procedural net*. (The word *network* is synonymous with *graph*.)

To see what procedural nets are and how they are used, let us look at a particular problem. We will use a robot-control problem. As with our previous robot-control problem, the task in question is trivial for humans, but most emphatically, not trivial for robots.

Figure 5-2a shows the problem situation. A robot is in a room with three boxes, a small A, a medium-size box B, and a large box C. The boxes are stacked as shown. The robot is to put all the boxes in a single stack, as shown in Fig. 5-2b. Naturally the large box must be on the bottom, the medium-sized one in the middle, and the small one on top, since otherwise, the pile would topple over.

We assume the robot can lift a box and set it on the floor or on any other box. We also assume that all the boxes are heavy so that the robot will not attempt to handle more than one at a time.

The robot-control program must examine the problem and come up with a rough plan for solving it. We will not go into any detail here about how patterns in the problem are recognized and how these are associated with plans. In later chapters we will see some ideas for doing these things. At present it is far from clear which idea is best.

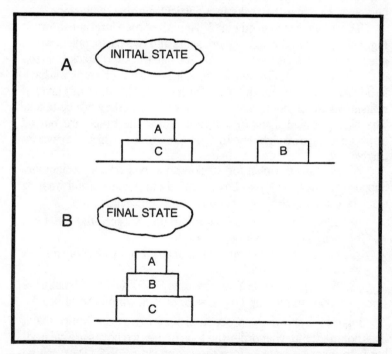

Fig. 5-2. A robot-control problem. The robot is to place all three boxes in a single stack. If the stack is not to topple over, A must go on top, B in the middle, and C on the bottom.

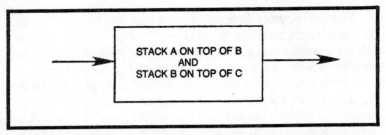

Fig. 5-3. The initial plan is to stack A on B and to stack B on C. The order in which the two operations will be performed is left unspecified.

We assume the problem solver recognizes that A must go on B and B must go on C if the stack is to be stable. As shown in Fig. 5-3, then, the initial plan is to stack A on B and B on C. For the present we do not worry about the order in which these two operations have to be carried out.

Figure 5-3 is the simplest possible procedural net. It contains a single node which specifies the single step in a one-step plan.

When we have two tasks to carry out, an obvious plan is to carry out each of the tasks separately. We still do not wish to commit ourselves to doing the tasks in a particular order, however.

Therefore, we expand Fig. 5-3 into the procedural net shown in Fig. 5-4. The path through the net splits into two parts, one of which goes through "Stack A on top of B" and one through "Stack B on top of C." We use the AND-node arc to indicate that both steps will have to be taken to carry out the plan. On the other hand, at this level of refinement we do not specify the order in which they will be taken. The plan is called a *nonlinear plan*, since the steps are not all arranged along a straight line to show the order in which they will be carried out.

We now need a plan for stacking one box on top of another. Suppose we have any two boxes, call them X and Y, and want to stack box X on box Y. We need to do three things:

1.  Clear everything off the top of box X, since the robot can only pick up one box at a time.
2.  Clear everything off the top of box Y to make room for box X.
3.  Set box X on box Y. We assume SET X ON Y will cause the robot to pick up box X and set it down on top of box Y.

Figure 5-5 shows the procedural net for this plan. Notice that it does not matter in what order the tops of the two boxes are cleared, but both must be clear before the command SET X ON Y can be issued.

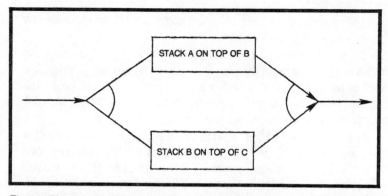

Fig. 5-4. This procedural net has two parallel branches. The operations in both branches must be carried out, but the order in which they will be carried out is left unspecified.

Now we refine the plan of Fig. 5-4 by using the box-stacking plan of Fig. 5-5. Figure 5-5 is used twice, in fact, once with A and B in place of X and Y, and once with B and C in place of X and Y. Figure 5-6a shows the result.

Notice that in Fig. 5-6a three of the nodes are drawn as ovals rather than rectangles. These are called *phantom nodes*. The reasons they are phantoms is that the subgoals they are supposed to achieve are already true in the initial state. Specifically, in the initial state the tops of both A and B are clear, so "Clear A" and "Clear B" are phantom nodes.

Phantom nodes are never expanded into greater detail at lower levels. On the other hand they *are* left in the plan to show what assumptions are being made about the initial state. Beyond the fact

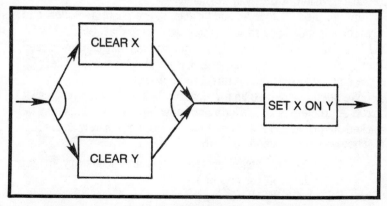

Fig. 5-5. A plan for stacking box X on box Y. It is immaterial whether the top of X or the top of Y is cleared first.

91

that they are not expanded, phantom nodes are treated just like any other node during planning.

Now we come to a crucial feature of hierarchical planning. At each level of refinement the plan is examined to see if any difficulties need to be corrected or whether any improvements can be made. Saceroti calls this step *criticism*. The first two levels of our plan did not require any criticism, but the current one does.

The comments in Fig. 5-6a reveal a problem. In the top half of the plan "SET A ON B" places A on top of B. The phantom node "Clear B" says that we are assuming B to be clear for the bottom half of the plan. If we tried to do the top half first and then the bottom half, B would not be clear when we got to the bottom half; thus SET B ON C could not be performed. (If "Clear B" were a real node rather than a phantom node, the bottom half of the plan would *undo* the work of "SET A ON B." Regardless of whether "Clear B" is phantom or real, we have a problem.)

To fix the problem, we must make sure that the bottom half of Fig. 5-6a will be executed before "SET A ON B." Figure 5-6b shows the corrected plan. Notice that instead of saying that the bottom half had to be executed before the entire bottom half, we have changed the ordering by the smallest amount possible to assure that "Clear B" will always come before "SET A ON B."

The plan in Fig. 5-6b can be improved still more. When the bottom half of the plan finishes executing, B will be clear, since it was clear just before "SET B ON C" was executed, and "SET B ON C" does not put anything on top of B. Therefore, "Clear B" in the top half of the plan is redundant and can be eliminated. Figure 5-6c shows the final revision of the plan at this level.

In Fig. 5-6c, "Clear A" and "Clear B" are phantom nodes, and so will be expanded no further. We are assuming that "SET A ON B" and "SET B ON C" are primitive operations that can be passed directly to the robot, so no expansion is needed for these. "Clear C" is the only node that needs further expansion.

We need a general plan for clearing the top of some box, call it box X. A problem is that we do not know how many boxes may be stacked on top of X. But assume that the box immediately above X is Y. Then we can proceed as follows:

- Clear Y. Do whatever operations are necessary to get everything off the top of Y.
- SET Y ON FLOOR.

Figure 5-7 shows the procedural net for this plan. Note that the definition of Clear itself contains a Clear operation, so Clear is

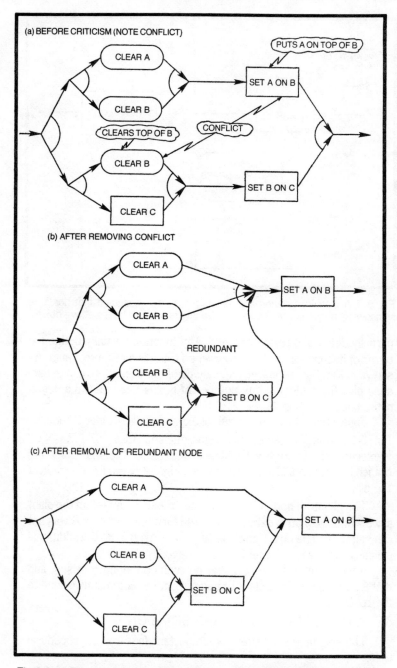

Fig. 5-6. (a) Fig. 5-4 after expanding "Stack A on top of B" and "Stack B on top of C" using the plan of Fig. 5-5. (b) Part a after criticism has resolved the conflict between "SET A ON B" and "Clear B." (c) Part b after criticism has eliminated a redundant "Clear B."

93

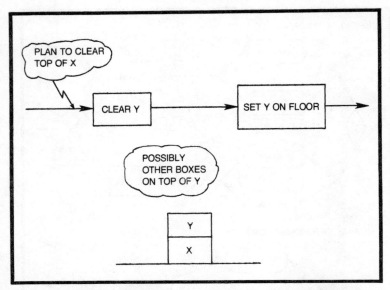

Fig. 5-7. A plan for clearing the top of box X. It is assumed that box Y is immediately above box X. There may be any number of boxes above box Y.

partially defined in terms of itself. Any function partially defined in terms of itself is said to be *recursive*, so Clear is a recursive plan. As shown in Fig. 5-8, repeated expansions of the Clear step can generate a plan for removing any number of boxes from on top a designated one.

Figure 5-9a shows the result of expanding the "Clear C" node in Fig. 5-6c. This plan can benefit from criticism. After "SET B ON C" is executed the top of A will still be clear, so the "Clear A" in the top branch is redundant. Removing it gives Fig. 5-9b, our final version of the plan.

The phantom nodes "Clear A" and "Clear B" are left in the plan, since when the plan is executed it could turn out that A or B was not clear after all. The phantom nodes would be used to do the additional planning necessary to meet this contingency.

If we assume, however, that no such contingency arises, and that A and B are indeed clear to begin with, the commands issued to the robot will be:

SET A ON FLOOR; SET B ON C; SET A ON B.

This example illustrates two important features of procedural nets:

1. When a plan is generated, it is often unclear what will be the best order in which to carry out some of the steps. Pro-

94

cedural nets allow this order to be left unspecified until some later time when the correct ordering does become clear. This may not take place until the plan is actually executed.

2. At each level of refinement we use heuristics, which Sacerdoti calls *critics*, to eliminate errors and redundancies, and to make improvements. Critics often specify the order of execution for steps whose order was originally left unspecified.

These are not the only interesting features of procedural nets. Other ones will be brought out in the chapters on "Representation of Knowledge" and "Natural Language Processing."

## MONITORING EXECUTION

Programs that control robots or other machinery, instruct humans, or play games must not only devise plans but see that those plans are carried out. Procedural nets are particularly appropriate for this *execution monitoring* for two reasons:

1. Planning and execution are interchangeable. If a plan is made, and then some obstacle to the plan is discovered during execution, we can return to the planning phase to plan a way around the obstacle, then continue execution with the modified procedural net. If frequent obstacles are

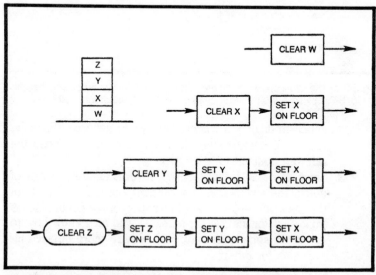

Fig. 5-8. By repeatedly expanding the "Clear" node, the plan of Fig. 5-7 can be used to clear any number of boxes from on top of the designated one.

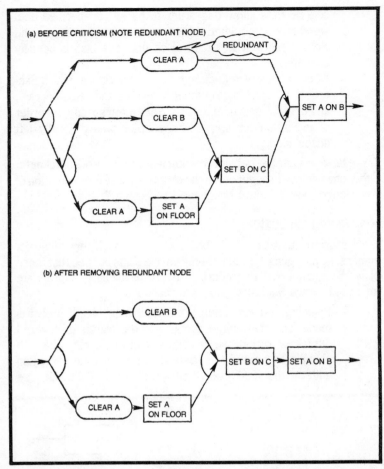

Fig. 5-9. a) The result of expanding the "Clear C" node in Fig. 5-6c using the plan of Fig. 5-7. b) Part a after criticism has eliminated a redundant "Clear A."

anticipated, only a rough plan can be generated initially, each step being refined just before execution when the relevant obstacles are known.

2. Since the plan is available at several different levels of detail, the instructions for carrying out different parts of the plan can be given at different levels of detail. This is important for instructing humans, who may know how to carry out some parts but may require more detailed instruction for others.

Let us look at some of the details of applying procedural nets to the three problem areas mentioned at the start of this section.

## Control of Robots

All instructions to a robot must be given at a uniform level of detail. That is, all must be stated in terms of the commands which the robot mechanism can carry out.

Ultimately, the commands given to the robot must be extremely detailed: the robot will be told to move one hand so many centimeters in a certain direction, or to bring its hands together until pressure sensors show they are grasping a box.

It seems useless to plan these detailed actions in advance, since what is to be done will depend on the second-by-second information gathered by the robot's sensors. Exactly where is the robot located in relation to the next box it is supposed to pick up? Where are the robot's hands in relation to the box it is supposed to grasp? If an object to be moved turns out to have an awkward shape, what is the best way to grasp it?

Therefore, it seems that preliminary planning for a robot should be carried out to about the level of detail shown in our examples: "Pick up box," "Set down box," "Set box A on box B." Finer details are best planned just before the robot is ready to carry them out, when all the information necessary to planning is available from the machine's sensors. This is an example of where being able to alternate planning and execution comes in handy.

We may also need to plan at execution time if some unexpected obstacle is found in the robot's environment, or if there is a mechanical malfunction in the robot itself.

Suppose, for instance, that when the robot set out to execute the box-stacking plan developed in the last section, it unexpectedly found a box Q on top of box A, as shown in Fig. 5-10a. It would have to return to the planning phase and replace the phantom node "Clear A" with a real node, as shown in Fig. 5-10b. Expanding that node, as in Fig. 5-10c, would update the original plan to work in the new situation.

What will be done if some part of the robot malfunctions will depend on the circumstances. An industrial robot would probably be replaced by another robot and scheduled for repair. But if the robot were exploring another planet, to which it had been sent at fantastic expense, then every effort would surely be made to plan a way to get around the malfunction and complete as much of the remainder of the mission as possible.

A robot-control computer will certainly have stored in memory a large repertoire of plans for frequently carried out actions. These could be recalled when needed, and would not have to be redeveloped each time the corresponding actions had to be carried out.

The robot could learn by storing newly developed plans. In each case the entire hierarchy would be stored, rather than just the most detailed levels. As usual, the higher levels would be used to aid in any replanning needed during execution.

Somewhat more difficult to implement would be a scheme for breaking the plans down into parts and classifying the parts so that the plan for an action learned in connection with one task could be extracted and inserted into the plan for another task.

## Instructing Humans

The main difference between instructing humans and instructing robots is that the level of detail needed will vary from person to person and even from one step of the plan to another. A person might be quite familiar with one step of a plan, having carried out the required action many times before, and would not want to be bothered with detailed instructions. But the next step might be unfamiliar, and the detailed guidance would be welcome.

One solution is for the program to initially issue its instructions using a fairly high level, unrefined version of the plan. For each step the human could request more details. When this request was made, the program would move down to the next more refined level for the step in question. If some step on this level proved puzzling, the program could move down another level, and so on.

A human might not know how to carry out some needed operation or may carry it out incorrectly. A person assembling a piece of machinery, for instance, might install a part backwards. The original plan would have to be modified so as to get the person out of his difficulties.

## Game Playing

As far as I know, nothing like procedural nets has ever been used for game playing. But this certainly seems to be a possible area of application for them, particularly since the most common criticism of chess programs is that the program obviously has no long-range plan for winning.

The interesting thing about a game plan is that it will have to evolve as the game progresses, since the plan for the final attack that leads to victory will be based on the strengths of the player's position and the weaknesses of the opponent's.

The game program would start off with a fairly high-level, general plan for playing the game. The first step of this plan would be expanded. The expansion would be based on general-purpose rules

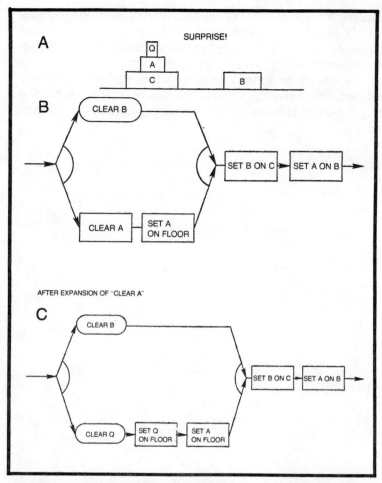

Fig. 5-10. When attempting to execute the plan of Fig. 5-9b, the robot discovered the situation of part a, with box Q unexpectedly on top of box A. The plan had to be modified by changing "Clear A" from a phantom node to a real one, and expanding it, as shown in parts b and c.

for the opening, such as the chess rules for developing pieces and controlling the center. Or standard openings may be drawn from memory, as is often done in chess programs.

As play proceeds, the program will study the game board for "openings," for patterns that would suggest profitable lines of attack or defense. These would be used to modify the plan for the as-yet-unplayed part of the game. The modifications would be made on as low a level as possible to keep the program on its currently planned course to the extent possible. This would also help to keep it from aimlessly trying first one thing and then another and then something else. Of course, if the opponent makes a completely unanticipated move, all previous planning may become worthless, and the program would have to start planning from scratch again.

Because of the uncertainty of the opponent's moves, planning and execution monitoring would be much more closely intermingled in a game-playing program than in any of the others we have discussed.

# Chapter 6
# Game Playing
# Programs: Tree Search

In this chapter and the next we will be interested in programs that play difficult games, such as checkers or chess, against humans or other programs. Programs that turn the computer into a sophisticated gameboard on which humans can play against each other (or play solitaire) belong more to the area of system simulation than to artificial intelligence.

## GAME TREES

Suppose two persons or machines are playing a game. Let us call one of these the player and the other one the opponent. We will always look at the game from the player's point of view. Thus we will say the game is won if the player wins and the opponent loses, and is lost if the player loses and the opponent wins.

Now suppose it is the player's turn to move. In most game positions he will have a number of choices for his next move. For each move the player makes, the opponent has a choice of replies. For each move the player makes and each replay the opponent makes, the player has a choice of counterreplies. Obviously, we have the same branching situation already encountered in problem solving.

In fact, we can imagine a game as a maze with one entrance (the starting position) and a number of exits. Some of the exits are labeled "win," some "lose," and some "draw" (Fig. 6-1). At the entrance the player chooses which path to follow (makes the first move). At the first fork in the path the opponent chooses which path will be followed (makes the second move). The player and the opponent continue to take turns choosing which path will be followed, the player always trying to direct them to a win exit, the opponent trying

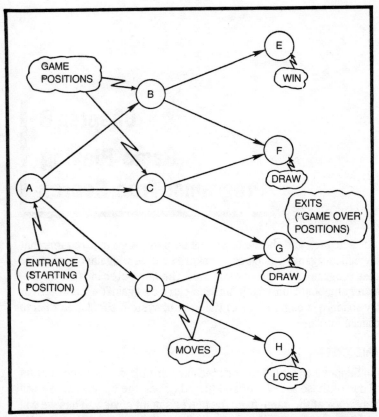

Fig. 6-1. We can think of a game as a maze with an entrance corresponding to the starting position and exists labeled "win," "lose," and "draw."

to direct them to a lose exit. Sometimes their efforts will cancel out and they will end up at a draw exit. Or they may just continue to wander in the maze until a draw is declared when it bcomes clear they are wandering in circles.

Thus playing a game is similar to solving a problem by finding a path in a state graph from initial state to a goal state. But there is one big difference. In a state-graph search only one player can always choose which arc to follow next. In a game the player can only make half the choices; the opponent gets to make the other half. The player still has to reach the goal (a winning position), but with the added burden that every other move the opponent gets the opportunity to detour him away from the goal.

For any game, we can construct a *game tree* analogous to the search trees used in state-graph and problem-reduction search. As shown in Fig. 6-2, the nodes in the game tree correspond to board positions, the branches to moves. The root corresponds to the starting position, and the leaves to positions in which the game is over (no legal moves can be made). In a position corresponding to a leaf the game may be won, lost, or drawn.

By a "position" we mean all the information that would have to be recorded if the game were adjourned with plans to resume it late. Typically, this would include the locations of the playing pieces on the game board and an indication of whether the player or the opponent has the next move.

In AI literature the term "half move," or "ply," is sometimes used for a move by the player or the opponent, a "fill move" being the player's (half) move and the opponent's reply. This terminology probably comes from the method of recording chess games, where a move by white and the reply by black are recorded on the same line and given a single move number. Nevertheless, in ordinary usage a "move" means a move by the player *or* a move by the opponent, not a move-reply combination. This is the usage we will follow in this book.

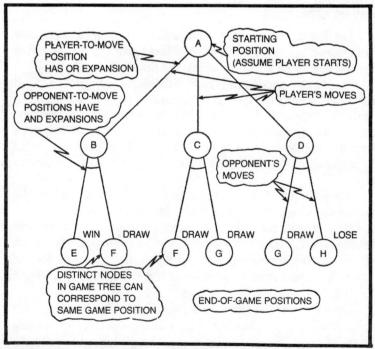

Fig. 6-2. The nodes in a game tree correspond to board positions. The root corresponds to the starting position, and the leaves to positions in which the game is over. The branches correspond to moves.

The game tree is an AND/OR tree instead of the pure OR tree used in state-graph search.

The reason is this: When it is the player's turn to move, he *has a choice* of which move to make. If *at least one of the moves* leads to a position in which the player is guaranteed to win, the player can choose that move and be assured of winning. Thus a node corresponding to a position in which it is the player's turn to move has an OR expansion.

When it is the opponent's turn to move, the player *has no choice*. The choice is the opponent's. The player is guaranteed a win only if *all the moves* the opponent can make lead to positions in which the player is guaranteed a win. Thus a node corresponding to a position in which it is the opponent's turn has an AND expansion.

The game tree for a sophisticated game is so vast ($10^{120}$ nodes for chess) that it can never be stored in a computer or exhaustively searched in any reasonable time. Nevertheless, it will be instructive to continue thinking about the complete game tree for a while and then see how our ideas have to be modified to keep the search tree down to a reasonable size.

## PLAYING STRATEGIES

Let us suppose we have constructed the complete game tree for the game in question. We wish to find a strategy for the player that will guarantee a win or, at least, a draw.

We start by marking each node of the game tree $w$ (for "win"), $d$ (for "draw"), or $l$ (for "lose"). If the current game position corresponds to a node marked $w$, a strategy exists that will guarantee the player a win. If the node is marked $d$, the player can at best get a draw, unless the opponent makes a mistake. If the node is marked $l$ the player will surely lose, unless the opponent makes an incorrect move.

The procedure for labeling the nodes $w$, $d$, or $l$ is precisely the one used in Chapter 4 to label nodes *solved* or *unsolvable*.

We start with the leaf nodes, which correspond to the terminal positions in which the game is over. The rules of the game determine whether such a terminal position is a win, draw, or loss for the player. We accordingly mark each leaf node $w$, $d$, or $l$, as shown in Fig. 6-3.

Now we work up from the leaves to the root, marking each node according to the markings of its children. The rules for marking the nodes are:

- *Player's turn to move (node with OR expansion).* If at least one of the children of the node is marked $w$, then mark the node $w$. If all the children are marked $l$, then mark the node $l$. Otherwise, mark the node $d$.

- *Opponent's turn to move (node with AND expansion).* If all the children of the node are marked $w$, then mark the node $w$. If at least one of the children is marked $l$, mark the node $l$. Otherwise, mark the node $d$.

The marking of the root node shows the best the player can achieve if the opponent makes no mistakes. If the root is marked $w$, the player can always force a win. If it is marked $l$, the opponent can always force a loss. If it is marked $d$, the player can at best obtain a draw in the game if the opponent makes no mistakes.

Games in which the root is marked $w$ or $l$, and which are simple enough to analyze, are the basis of many "sucker bets." Either the person who moves first (root marked $w$) or the person who moves second (root marked $l$) is guaranteed a win, provided the correct strategy is followed. The gambler knows which player is guaranteed a win and the strategy required to bring the win about. The sucker, by definition, knows neither.

The strategy for the player is the following: If any move leads to a position whose node is marked $w$, make that move. If all moves lead to positions whose nodes are marked $l$, then resign. Otherwise, move to a position whose node is marked $d$.

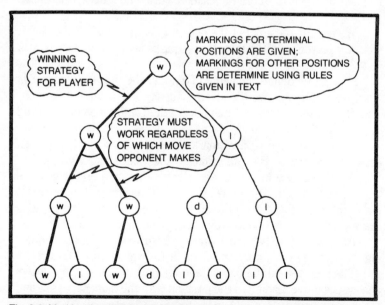

Fig. 6-3. Marking the nodes of a game tree **w** (win), **l** (lose), or **d** (draw). We mark the leaves first, then work upwards toward the root.

The strategy for the opponent is just the opposite: If any move leads to a position whose node is marked $l$, make that move. In all moves lead to positions whose nodes are marked $w$, then resign. Otherwise, move to a position whose node is marked $d$.

When there is more than one way to move to a node marked $l$ or a node marked $d$, the player's strategy does not say which move to make. In practice the player wants to choose the $w$-node that leads to the simplest play, and so reduce the chances of making a mistake that will lose him the advantage. For the same reason the player should choose the $d$-node that leads to the most complicated play, in hopes the opponent will make a mistake that lets the player regain the advantage. It is a deficiency of the discussion so far that no distinction is made between nodes that are all marked $w$ or all marked $d$.

## THE MINIMAX METHOD

Now let us look at another method for marking the nodes of a game tree, called the *minimax* method. The minimax method has the advantage that it can easily be generalized to situations where the complete game is impractically large and only a part of the game tree is available.

Suppose money is riding on the outcome of the game. For convenience let the stake be $1. If the player wins he will get $1. If he loses he will lose $1. In the case of a draw no money will change hands.

We will call the amount the player wins the *payoff*. If the player wins, the playoff is 1; if he loses it is $-1$; in case of a draw the payoff is 0.

Now let us define the *value* of a node, the payoff the player is guaranteed if he follows the strategy described in the last section. Therefore, the payoff is 1 for a node marked $w$, 0 for a node marked $d$, and $-1$ for a node marked $l$.

We do not have to first mark the nodes $w$, $d$, or $l$, and then assign them values. We can calculate the values directly.

As before, we know for each leaf node whether the game is won, drawn, or lost. Therefore, we start by assigning 1 to those leaf nodes in which the game is won, 0 to those in which the game is drawn, and $-1$ to those in which the game is lost.

Again as before, we work upward from leaves to root, computing the value of each node in terms of the values of its children.

The idea behind the computation is that the player will always choose the move leading to the position with the highest payoff, and the opponent will always choose the move leading to the position with the lowest payoff (since the opponent wins what the player loses). More specifically, we have the following rules for calculating the value of a node:

- *Player's turn to move (node with OR expansion).* The value of the node is the *maximum* of the values of its children.
- *Opponent's turn to move (node with AND expansion).* The value of the node is the *minimum* of the values of the children.

Figure 6-4 illustrates the calculation of values for nodes using the minimax method. Compare it with Fig. 6-3 and see that the minimax method is equivalent to the *w-d-l* labeling procedure.

In discussing the minimax method, the player and the opponent are sometimes referred to as *Max* and *Min*. Max, the player, always chooses the move leading to the node with maximum value. Min, the opponent, always chooses the move leading to the node with minimum value.

So far the minimax method has simply given us another, equivalent, way of labeling the nodes of a game tree. But the minimax method uses numbers rather than the arbitrary labels *w*, *d*, and *l*. This means we can easily generalize it so that the values of nodes are not restricted to 1, 0, and $-1$.

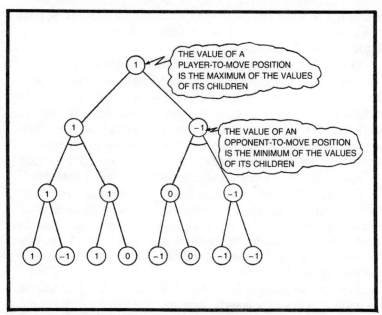

Fig. 6-4. Assigning values to nodes in a game tree using the minimax method.

## TERMINAL POSITIONS AND STATIC EVALUATION FUNCTIONS

We now at last have to face the fact that for games of interest such as chess we cannot construct the complete game tree. We cannot even construct a substantial portion of it. The best we can do is construct a very small portion of the tree around the position of current interest.

Therefore, the root of our tree will no longer be the starting position of the game, but will be the position currently facing the player. We have no interest in parts of the tree referring to the part of the game already played, but only in those referring to the part which has yet to be played.

The leaves of the tree will no longer represent positions in which the game has been won, drawn, or lost. Instead, they represent the furthest points to which the lines of play could be explored in the available time and with the available memory for storing the tree.

Let us continue to call a position corresponding to a leaf node a *terminal position*. What are the criteria for a terminal position? Or in other words, when is it safe to break off exploring a particular line of play?

We intend to assign values to the terminal positions, reflecting the worth of each position to the player. We will then apply the minimax technique to these values. A terminal position thus has to be one whose value can be reliably estimated by considering such things as the number and type of men each side has and their distribution on the playing board.

Here is an example of a position which could not be reliably evaluated in that way and so is not a good terminal position. Suppose the game is checkers and it is the player's turn to move. The only available move is one of those multiple jumps checkers is famous for, which will destroy the opponent's forces at a single stroke. Obviously, it would be meaningless to try to evaluate this position in terms of the distribution of forces on both sides, since after the next (multiple) move the opponent's situation will be changed drastically.

This is an extreme example. Less extremely, no position in which the side to move could jump would make a good terminal position, nor would one in which a king was about to be made. In either case the nature of the position is going to be substantially different after the next move, and an evaluation based on the current position may not be worth very much.

In short, we distinguish between "live" and "dead" positions. A live position is one in which the next move is likely to bring about some significant change in the relative strengths of the two sides. A dead position is one in which no available move will bring about such a change. Which positions should be considered live and which ones dead will depend on the criteria used to evaluate a position.

A terminal position, then, should be a dead position. Occasionally, time or memory limitations may force breaking off investigation of a line of play at a live position. But when these limitations do not intervene, each line of play will be pursued to a dead position.

Specifically, the game-playing program will have a procedure TERMINAL (POSITION, DEPTH) which will determine whether or not a particular node in the tree is a leaf node. As the items in parentheses show, TERMINAL will base its decision on the details of the corresponding position and the depth of the node.

Normally, TERMINAL weighs the "liveliness" of the position, the chance that some interesting change will take place in the next move or so, against the depth of the node. A typical strategy would be the following:

- If DEPTH is less than 3, the position is not terminal. Every line of play is explored to at least depth 3.
- If DEPTH is 3 through 10, the position is terminal if it is dead and not terminal if it is live. In this range of depths we follow a line of play until a dead position is found, then break off. Often, the definition of a live position is narrowed as the depth increases. At depth 3 any feature of the position suggesting that interesting play will be forthcoming in a few moves would be enough to render the position live. At depth 10 only the possibility of some drastic change on the next move—say the capture of an important piece—would be enough to render the position live.
- If DEPTH is 11 the position is terminal. Exploration is cut off at depth 11 regardless of the live or dead status of the position to insure that time and memory will remain to explore other lines of play.

Depth cutoffs (such as 3, 10, and 11) must usually be chosen by experiment for a particular program so that the program will look far enough ahead for good play but will not waste too much of its time and memory exploring uninteresting lines of play. Choosing such values is knows as *turning* the program.

Given a terminal position, we need some way to estimate the value of the position to the player so the minimax technique can be used to find the player's best move. A game-playing program, then, will have a procedure TERMINAL-VALUE(POSITION) which estimates the value of the position to the player. This is called a *static evaluation function*, since the evaluation is based on the static distribution of pieces on the board rather than on the dynamic exploration of the consequences of possible moves.

We can still think of the value of a position as the payoff the player would be guaranteed in that position. In the terminal positions, however, the game is not (usually) either won, drawn, or lost, so it would not be fair to assign the entire stake to one player or the other, or to divide it evenly between them. Instead, we may suppose that when the terminal position in question was reached, the game had to be suspended, say because the player or the opponent had business elsewhere. A disinterested expert is asked to decide how the stake should be divided based on the relative strengths of the two sides' positions. The amount that the player wins by this decision is the value of the position. The procedure TERMINAL—VALUE must try to emulate the considerations of the disinterested expert. (Compare this evaluation function, which estimates the value of a position to the player, with the one in chapter 3, which estimated the cost of reaching a goal.)

TERMINAL—VALUE must base its estimate on the features of the game position. Some features of importance for board games such as chess and checkers are:

- *Material.* This is the advantage in the number of playing pieces, or "men." The relative values of the different pieces must be taken into account. In checkers, for instance, the relative values of a king and an ordinary man are three and two (one should be willing to trade 3 men for 2 kings). Thus in evaluating a position we could assign each side 3 points for each king and 2 points for each man.

- *Mobility.* Mobility is the number of squares to which a man can be moved. Beyond this, definitions of mobility vary. Sometimes, any legal move will count toward mobility. Sometimes, the move will be counted only if the man is not exposed to immediate capture afterwards. Sometimes, only moves into the other side's territory are counted.

- *Control of Critical Squares.* In most games there are critical squares, the control of which is of strategic importance. Often the critical squares are those in the center of the board. We can give each side points according to the number of critical squares controlled.

- *Specific Patterns.* For each game there are certain patterns of playing pieces considered to be of strategic importance. Each side is assigned points for each pattern in its position.

For each of these features we work out an advantage, which is the number of points assigned to the player minus the number assigned to the opponent for the feature in question.

In the simplest case each advantage is multiplied by a number, depending on its relative importance, and then the results are added together to get the value of the position. A more sophisticated procedure is to use a table which gives the value of the position for each combination of values of advantages. The table allows the interaction of different features to be taken into account. (Perhaps one feature is important only if another feature is present.) This kind of interaction cannot be taken into account when we simply add together values calculated for each feature.

Let us look at a very simple evaluation function for checkers. It will have three terms:

1. $k$ = king advantage
   = number of player's kings – number of opponent's kings
2. $m$ = man advantage
   = number of player's men – number of opponent's men
3. $mb$ = mobility advantage
   = player's mobility – opponent's mobility.

By a "man" we mean a checker other than a king. Each side's mobility is the number of squares it can move a man to without exposing it to capture.

We must now decide on the relative importance of king advantage, man advantage, and mobility advantage. Checkers lore tells us that the relative values of kings and men are 3 to 2. Suppose we decide that each man is four times as important as an extra square of mobility. Then the evaluation function would be

$$value = 6k + 4m + mb$$

Finding the correct number to multiply each feature advantage is again a matter of tuning.

If a position is encountered in which the game is won, drawn, or lost, this position is treated as a special case. The game-won position is assigned a large positive number as its value. The negative of this value is assigned to a game-lost position. A game-drawn position gets the usual value of 0. The exact value assigned to game-won positions is not important as long as it is larger than any value the evaluation-function calculation would yield for a position in which the game was not won.

Notice that the evaluation function is defined in such a way that if the player and the opponent were to suddenly change sides, the

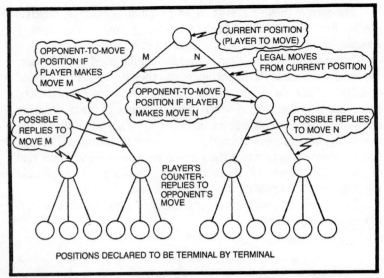

Fig. 6-5. The partial game tree used to find the best move from the current position. The root of the tree corresponds to the current position; its leaves correspond to positions declared to be terminal by the procedure TERMINAL.

player taking over the opponent's men and vice versa, then the value of the position would simply change its algebraic sign. Put another way, a position with a value of, say, 100 from the player's point of view would have a value of −100 from the opponent's point of view.

## DEPTH-FIRST-MINIMAX EVALUATION

We now return to the player contemplating the current game position and trying to decide which move to make next. We assume that we have a procedure for generating all the legal moves in any position and also the positions that will result from making any of those moves. We also assume that we have the procedure TERMINAL and TERMINAL—VALUE described in the last section. We wish to determine what move the player should make.

We construct the partial game tree shown in Fig. 6-5 by starting with the current position, expanding it, then expanding its children, and so on. But before expanding any node we test it with the procedure TERMINAL. If the node is declared to be terminal it is not expanded. Otherwise it is. Note that DEPTH used by TERMINAL is the depth in this tree whose root is the current position nd not the depth in the complete game tree whose root is the starting position.

Continuing this process until no more nodes can be expanded, we end up with a tree whose root corresponds to the current position and whose leaves correspond to positions that have been declared terminal by TERMINAL.

For each leaf node we can apply TERMINAL—VALUE to the corresponding position and calculate a value for the node.

By applying the minimax technique, we assign a value to each node in the tree. As before, the value of a node in which the player is to move will be the *maximum* of the values of its children, and the value of a node in which the opponent is to move will be the *minimum* of the values of its children. Figure 6-6 illustrates this calculation. Because of the way they are calculated, values assigned to nonleaf nodes are often called *backed-up values*.

The best move for the player is the one that leads to the position having the highest backed-up value.

After the opponent's next move a new tree will be constructed from the then current position, and the process will be repeated. Thus each partial game tree is used to decide just one move. The only values actually used are the backed-up values assigned to the children of the root, which correspond to positions to which the player has the option of moving.

Actually, we do not have to store the entire game tree in memory at one time. Using a procedure known as *depth-first-*

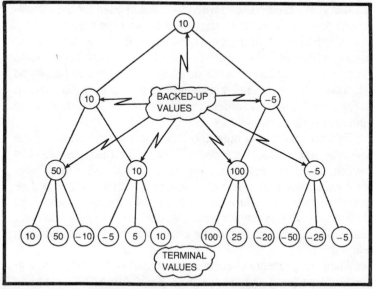

Fig. 6-6. Assigning values to nodes in the partial game tree using the minimax technique. The values of the leaves are calculated using the procedure TERMINAL—VALUE. These values are backed up to the other nodes, using the minimax technique.

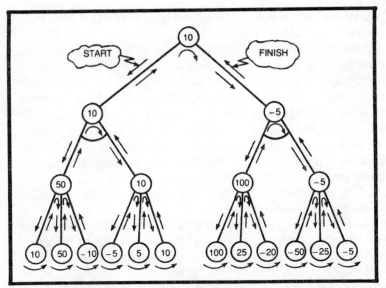

Fig. 6-7. The path through the partial game tree taken by the depth-first-minimax procedure.

*minimax evaluation,* we can compute the values of the children of the of the root while never storing more than a small part of the tree in memory. We create nodes when they are needed for the calculation and destroy them when they have served their purpose.

As with all depth-first procedures, depth-first-minimax starts at the root and moves in the parent-to-child direction until it encounters a terminal position. It then backs up until it finds another unexplored path, follows that path until it encounters a terminal position, and so on. Figure 6-7 shows the order in which the nodes are visited by the depth-first-minimax procedure.

This procedure can build the tree and evaluate nodes at the same time. As the procedure works downward in the parent-to-child direction, nodes are expanded. As shown in Fig. 6-8, when a node is first expanded, only one child is created. Other children will be created when the procedure backs up and visits this node again. The only children kept in memory are the ones on the path currently being explored and those holding values which have not yet been backed up.

When the procedure reaches a terminal node (which it recognizes by applying the procedure TERMINAL), it applies TERMINAL—VALUE to the corresponding position and assigns the calculated value to the node. The procedure then backs up the parent of the terminal node.

114

As mentioned, when the procedure revisits a node during backup, it normally continues the expansion of that node by creating a new child and then moves on to the newly created child. But eventually, all the children of a node will have been created (all the legal moves from the corresponding position will have been explored). When such a node is revisted the procedure computes the backed-up value for that node from the values of the children, taking either their maximum or minimum, depending on which side is to move. The children are no longer needed and are eliminated. The procedure then backs up to the parent of the node that has just been assigned a value and continues as before.

We can eliminate the need for storing any children of a node other than the one on the path currently being explored. As shown in Fig. 6-9, we assign a partially backed-up value to each node. This value is given an initial value when a node is created and is updated every time the node is revisited. At any time, the partially backed-up value for a node will be the maximum or the minimum (depending on who is to move) of the values of all children that have been evaluated so far. When all a node's children have been evaluated, its partially backed-up value will be the maximum or the minimum of the values of all its children, which will be just the value of the node.

For a node in which the player is to move, the partially backed-up value is initially given a large negative value. When the node is revisited, the value of the child just evaluated is compared with the

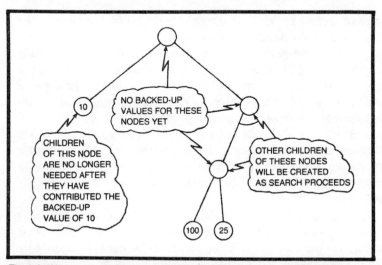

Fig. 6-8. We may save memory in the depth-first-minimax procedure by creating nodes only when they are needed and abandoning them when they are no longer needed.

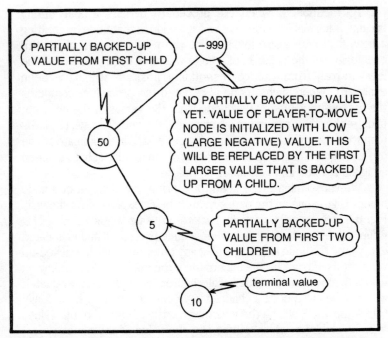

Fig. 6-9. We can reduce the number of nodes that have to be stored even further by maintaining a partially backed-up value for each node. Whenever a new child of a node is evaluated, the partially backed-up value of the node is updated (if necessary).

current partially backed-up value, and the larger of the two becomes the new partially backed-up value.

For a node in which the opponent is to move, the partially backed-up value is initially given a large positive value. When the node is revisited, the value of the child just evaluated is compared with the current partially backed-up value, and the smaller of the two becomes the new partially backed-up value.

As Fig. 6-9 shows, the only nodes we need to store at any one time are those on a path from the root to the node currently being processed. These can be most conveniently stored on a stack, with the root at the bottom of the stack and the node currently being processed on top.

Although we can get by with storing only the part of the tree from the root to the current node, we do not guarantee that this is always the best approach. Some programs do store the entire tree so that a previously explored line of play can be revisited and explored further if it turns out to be more promising than those lines explored afterwards. On the other hand, when memory is limited the thought of storing as few nodes at a time as possible is very attractive.

## THE ALPHA-BETA PROCEDURE

In a depth-first-minimax evaluation we can show that certain parts of the tree will not affect any values of interest, and so need not be explored at all. The technique for identifying those parts of the tree that can be ignored is, for historical reasons, known as the *alpha-beta procedure*.

Consider the situation shown in Fig. 6-10a. The partially backed-up value for a node in which the player is to move is 10. The partially backed-up value for the child currently being evaluated is 5. Now since the child is a node in which the opponent has the move, further exploration can only lower its value, since the opponent always moves to the position having the minimum value. Whatever the final value of the child is, it will always be 5 or less.

On the other hand, the partially backed-up value of the node itself is 10. Since the player is to move, only values of children larger than 10 could change the partially backed-up value.

The conclusion is that we need not further explore the child or any of its descendents. Further exploration would at most reduce

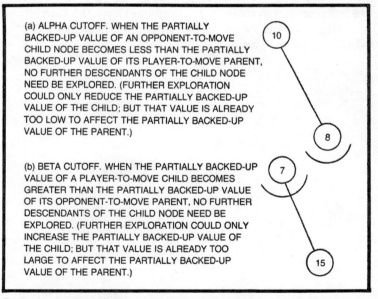

(a) ALPHA CUTOFF. WHEN THE PARTIALLY BACKED-UP VALUE OF AN OPPONENT-TO-MOVE CHILD NODE BECOMES LESS THAN THE PARTIALLY BACKED-UP VALUE OF ITS PLAYER-TO-MOVE PARENT, NO FURTHER DESCENDANTS OF THE CHILD NODE NEED BE EXPLORED. (FURTHER EXPLORATION COULD ONLY REDUCE THE PARTIALLY BACKED-UP VALUE OF THE CHILD; BUT THAT VALUE IS ALREADY TOO LOW TO AFFECT THE PARTIALLY BACKED-UP VALUE OF THE PARENT.)

(b) BETA CUTOFF. WHEN THE PARTIALLY BACKED-UP VALUE OF A PLAYER-TO-MOVE CHILD BECOMES GREATER THAN THE PARTIALLY BACKED-UP VALUE OF ITS OPPONENT-TO-MOVE PARENT, NO FURTHER DESCENDANTS OF THE CHILD NODE NEED BE EXPLORED. (FURTHER EXPLORATION COULD ONLY INCREASE THE PARTIALLY BACKED-UP VALUE OF THE CHILD; BUT THAT VALUE IS ALREADY TOO LARGE TO AFFECT THE PARTIALLY BACKED-UP VALUE OF THE PARENT.)

Fig. 6-10. The alpha-beta procedure detects situations in which further evaluation of a child will have no effect on the value of the parent. No further children of the child node (nor their descendents) need be created or evaluated.

the partially backed-up value of the child node, and the current value is already too small to affect the partially backed-up value of the parent. This situation is known as an *alpha cutoff*.

We can state the principle in general as follows:

*Consider a parent in which the player is to move and a child in which the opponent is to move. If the partially backed-up value for the child is less than or equal to the partially backed-up value for the parent, no further processing need be done on the child and its descendents, and the evaluation procedure can back up to the parent.*

When the parent node is one in which the opponent is to move, the principle is modified accordingly (Fig. 6-10b):

*Consider a parent in which the opponent is to move and a child in which the player is to move. If the partially backed-up value for the child is greater than or equal to the partially backed-up value for the parent, no further processing need be done on the child and its descendents, and the evaluation procedure can back up to the parent.*

This case is known as a *beta cutoff*.

The alpha-beta technique allows us to sometimes ignore some of the children of a node. Since each child that is not terminal is the root of a whole subtree of descendents, we get not only to ignore the child but also all its descendents. Thus the alpha-beta technique can allow vast numbers of nodes to be ignored, hence producing very substantial savings in the time required to explore the tree.

In the next chapter we will see some other heuristics that can reduce exploration time.

# Chapter 7

# Game Playing Programs: Heuristics

The previous chapter described methods for constructing and searching game trees. The enemy of these (and all other) tree searching methods is combinatorial explosion. Unless the size of the tree is strictly controlled, the tree will quickly become too large to be stored in any reasonable amount of memory, or to be searched in any reasonable amount of time.

We can control the size of the search tree by using heuristic methods to limit the width and the depth of the search. The *width* refers to the number of moves that are considered in each position. (If all legal moves are considered, we are conducting a *full-width* search.) The *depth* refers to the number of moves ahead to which a particular line of play is explored.

We must also be able to evaluate the terminal positions, corresponding to the leaf nodes of the game tree. This is a problem in pattern recognition. If an expert in the game were shown a terminal position, he would rate it as being very strong or moderately strong for one side or the other, or as being equally strong for either side. If pressed to explain his rating, the expert would point out certain patterns of playing pieces advantageous for one side or the other. We need for the computer to be able to see the same patterns that the expert sees, and to compute the evaluation function accordingly.

As previously mentioned, one of the most common comments about chess programs is that they show no evidence of long-range planning. Each move the machine makes examined out of context may seem to be quite good. But examining a sequence of such moves reveals no grand plan on the machine's part for bringing about a victory. Unfortunately, very little has actually been done on chess programs using long-range planning. All current programs rely

**Table 7-1. Representation of Chess Pieces**

| Name | Machine Piece | Opponent Piece |
|------|---------------|----------------|
| Pawn | 1 | −1 |
| Knight | 2 | −2 |
| Bishop | 3 | −3 |
| Rook | 4 | −4 |
| Queen | 5 | −5 |
| King | 6 | −6 |

mainly on tree search and evaluation functions. The most that can be done here is to suggest some possible approaches to the problem.

The time and memory required for a tree search will depend on the way in which game positions are represented inside the computer. Let us begin our discussion, then, by looking at some methods for representing game positions.

## REPRESENTING GAME POSITIONS

Most work so far has been done on programs that play board games such as chess or checkers. The discussion will be limited to these, although it can be generalized to other games without too much trouble.

### The Pieces

We need some way of representing the playing pieces in computer memory. Frequently the pieces are simply numbered, with positive numbers being used for the machine's pieces and negative numbers for the opponent's. Table 7-1 is a commonly used representation for chess pieces.

### The Board

The chess- and checker-board is two dimensional with eight rows and eight columns. Because of this our first thought might be to use an 8 × 8 array such as BOARD in Fig. 7-1. Then the value of BOARD (1, 4) would be the code for the piece occupying the square at the intersection of row 1 and column 4. In Fig. 7-1, for instance, BOARD (1, 4) = 5. Using the notation just given for the chess pieces, this says that the square in question is occupied by the machine's queen.

Two-dimensional arrays, however, are not as convenient to manipulate as one-dimensional arrays. There are two subscripts to be manipulated instead of one. And the calculation necessary to find the memory address corresponding to the subscript values is more complicated for two-dimensional than for one-dimensional arrays. For these reasons a one-dimensional array is often used in spite of the two-dimensional structure of the board.

Figure 7-2 shows a one-dimensional array, BRD, for the chessboard. BRD has 64 elements, one for each square of the board. The correspondence between the elements of BRD and the squares of the chessboard is shown by the numbered chessboard in Fig. 7-2. The squares of row 1 correspond to BRD(1) through BRD(8), the squares of row 2 to BRD(9) through BRD(16), and so on. In storing the chessboard in BRD we have dissected it into rows and stored it row by row in BRD. We could have stored it by columns instead of by rows. Storage by rows, though, seems to be the most common.

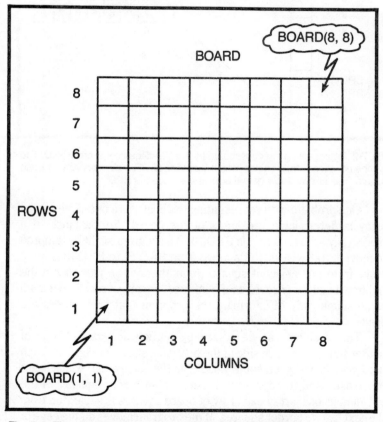

Fig. 7-1. The chessboard can be represented by a two-dimensional array, BOARD. The disadvantage of this representation is that the address calculation necessary to access an element of a two-dimensional array is more complicated than for a one-dimensional array.

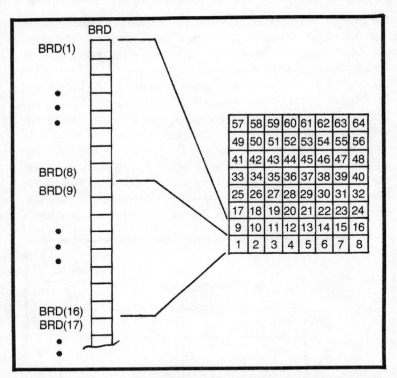

Fig. 7-2. Representing the chessboard by the one-dimensional array BRD. The numbered chessboard shows which element of BRD corresponds to each square. The arrows show how the rows are stored in BRD.

One problem with representing the board as a one-dimensional array is determining the limits of the board. For instance, if a piece—say a king—were on BRD(8), the program might be tempted to move it to BRD(9). But a move from BRD(8) to BRD(9) is not a move from one adjacent square to another, but a move from the rightmost square of row 1 to the leftmost square of row 2. We need some simple way of informing the program that such moves are illegal.

This problem can be solved by putting an extra column of border squares on each side of the board, as shown in Fig. 7-3. Each border square is given some value (7 in the illustration) which is not otherwise used to represent a piece or an empty square. In the one-dimensional array each row of board squares is separated from the next by two border squares. If the program moves off the edge of the board it will land on one of the border squares. The value 7 in the border square will then inform the program that it has moved off of the board.

We can also put two rows of border squares at the bottom of the board and two more at the top. Now the program can detect moves off the top or bottom of the board in the same way that it detects moves off the left or right side. Doing this gives us the array BD in Fig. 7-3. Array BD has 120 elements. We have traded space for time. A program using BD will run faster than one using BRD because of the simple test for the edge of the board that BD provides.

We use *two* rows of border squares at the top and bottom of the board and *two* border squares between each pair of rows in BD because of the knight's move in chess. The knight moves two squares in one direction and one square in the other.

### The Moves

The program must know the legal moves for the pieces. We can provide this information as shown in Fig. 7-4. Each move is represented by a number which when added to the number of the square the piece is on will give the number of the square to which it can move. Thus (using BD to represent the board) adding 1 to the

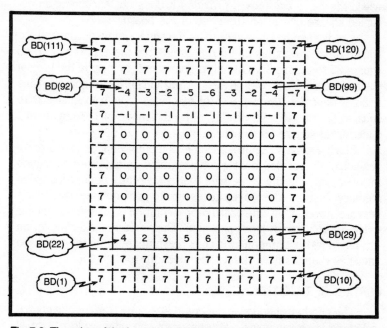

Fig. 7-3. The edge of the board can best be detected by surrounding the actual board by dummy rows and columns having some special value, shown here as 7. The resulting 12 × 10 board can be represented by a linear array, BD, having 120 elements. The diagram shows the contents of BD for the starting position.

square number of a piece moves the piece one square to the right. Adding − 1 moves the piece one square toward the top of the board; adding − 10 moves it one square toward the bottom of the board, and so on.

Each number represents a *move direction*. The number 11, for instance, represents a move along a diagonal in the top-right direction. Adding 11 once to the square number of a piece will move it one square along the diagonal; adding 11 again will move the piece another square along the diagonal, and so on. By repeatedly adding 11, we can move as many squares as we wish along the diagonal until we come to an occupied square or the edge of the board.

These numbers are used in Fig. 7-4 to give the move directions for the chess pieces. Some pieces (such as the king, the knight, and the pawn) can only move one square in a given direction (for the knight the new square is not adjacent to the old one). For these, each move-direction number can only be used once. The other pieces can move any number of squares in a particular direction. For these each move-direction number can be added repeatedly to the number of the original square of the piece, each sum giving a new square to which the piece can move, provided it does not encounter an occupied square or run off the edge of the board.

A move can be represented by the square moved from and the square moved to. Thus 25-35 represents the move of the piece on square 25 to square 35. Often it is convenient to include the type of piece being moved as well as the starting and finishing squares. Thus 6: 26-36 describes the move of the machine's king from square 26 to square 6; and − 5 : 99-55 describes the move of the opponent's queen from square 99 to square 55.

Storing moves requires much less memory space than storing positions. Therefore, most game programs do not store a position for every node in the game tree that is currently being retained in memory. Instead, the moves necessary to get from one node to the next are stored. Only one board representation is stored: the one for the position currently being analyzed. The program makes moves on this board representation as it goes down deeper into the tree, and unmakes them as it works its way back up to the root.

## CONTROL OF TREE SIZE

The number of nodes in the complete game tree for any nontrivial game is astronomical. The program can only explore a small portion of this tree in a reasonable amount of time, using a reasonable amount of memory. Selecting the portion of the tree to be explored is known as *control of tree size*. Naturally, one wants to

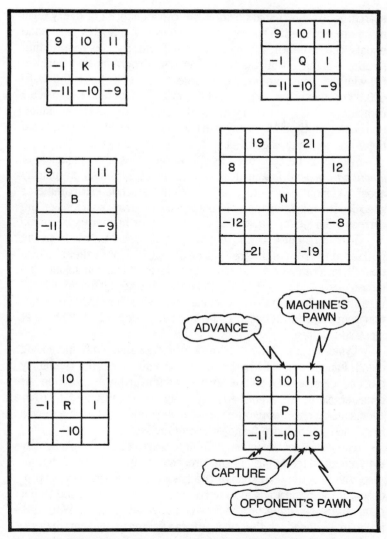

Fig. 7-4. The move directions for each piece are given by the numbers to be added to the current position of the piece to move one square in each direction. The numbers given are for the 120-element array BD. For the pawn, the permissible directions depend on whose pawn it is and whether it is advancing or capturing.

select the part of the tree which contains the most promising lines of play.

Two things must be controlled: the width and the depth.

Some programs—including the highly successful CHESS 4.6—do not attempt to control width at all. They perform a full-width search: in a nonterminal position the consequences of every legal move are explored. The number of children of a nonterminal node equals the number of legal moves from the corresponding position—about 30 in the case of chess. Programs that perform full-width search explore very large trees of from 400,000 to 500,000 nodes. This is only practical on large, fast (and expensive!) computers. And even with a fast computer, there is a strong limitation on the depth to which any one line of play can be followed, since there are so many lines of play that have to be examined.

Width can be controlled by giving the program a sequence of *fanout parameters:* fanout-0, fanout-1, fanout-2, and so on (usually about 10 fanout parameters are sufficient). Each fanout parameter specifies the maximum number of legal moves from positions on the corresponding level that will be earmarked for further exploration.

Thus if fanout-0 = 25, then at most 25 legal moves from the position at the root of the tree will be earmarked for further exploration. (The root can have at most 25 children.) The remaining legal moves are abandoned as being hopeless. Similarly, if fanout-1 = 20 then at most 20 legal moves would be considered for further exploration from positions at depth 1. Every node at depth 1 would have at most 20 children.

Typically, the fanout parameters decrease with increasing depth. Fanout-0 may be in the range 25 to 30: all but the seemingly most hopeless moves will be earmarked for further exploration. At considerable depth, *fanout-10*, say, may be in the range 5 to 10 or even less. At this depth only the seemingly most promising moves from each position are being explored further.

The values for the fanout parameters are usually determined by experiment. This is part of the process of "tuning" the program. Also, the program can change the fanout parameters as play proceeds. If the program is in time trouble, it can decrease the fanout parameters, resulting in a narrower but faster search. When the program is ahead of the clock, it can increase the parameters, resulting in a wider, slower, but more exhaustive search.

In each position, then, we can select only a limited number of moves for further exploration and must abandon the rest. Naturally, we would like to select the most promising moves to explore further and abandon only the less promising ones. How can the program choose the most promising moves?

By using heuristics, the program can assign a plausibility score to each legal move. The list of legal moves is then sorted according to the plausibility scores, with the most plausible move at the beginning of the list and the least plausible move at the end. The moves to be explored further are then selected from the beginning of the list: If the fanout for the position in question was 15, say, then the 15 most plausible moves would be selected for further exploration.

This technique is known as *plausibility ordering*. Plausibility ordering has another advantage. If the selected moves are explored in the order in which they occur on the sorted list, the most plausible move will be explored first, then the next most plausible move, and so on. This improves the effectiveness of the alpha-beta technique described in the last chapter: An alpha or a beta cutoff is most likely when the best moves from a given position are explored first.

The plausibility scores are based on heuristics for the game in question. Each heuristic states some condition that may or may not be true of the move and the number of points that the move will be given or penalized if the condition holds. (If the condition is considered desirable, the move is given points; otherwise it is penalized.) The plausibility score is the sum (taking penalties as negative) of all the points assigned by all the heuristics.

The details of the heuristics depend, of course, on the game in question. Here are some that have been used for chess:

- *Capture*. A move is given points if it captures an opposing piece. The number of points depends on the value of the piece captured.
- *Attack*. A move which increases the number of opposing pieces that the piece being moved attacks is given points.
- *Safety*. A move which places a piece where it will be subject to capture is penalized; a move which takes a piece from a square where it is subject to capture to one where it is safe is given points.
- *Development*. A move which brings a queen, rook, bishop, or knight into play by moving it from its starting square is given points.
- *Advance*. Points may be given for advancing a queen, bishop, or knight toward the opposing side. Alternatively, a penalty can be given any move that retreats one of these pieces.
- *Rules for Particular Pieces*. There are many chess heuristics that apply to particular pieces. For instance, the queen, the bishop, and the knight are considered to be less effective when on the leftmost or rightmost columns of the board. A move which carries one of the pieces to the left or right edge can be penalized. Additional special rules apply to the king, the pawns, and the rook. For instance, castling (the king-

and-rook move that places the king in a protected position) may be given a very high plausibility score. If castling is possible its consequences will always be explored.

Chess abounds in heuristics that can be used for plausibility ordering. But each heuristic requires a certain amount of computation time to determine which legal moves it can be applied to. If too many heuristics are used, the time spent on computation at each node will become too large; this will reduce the number of nodes that can be examined in a reasonable amount of time.

How many points to give or to penalize for each heuristic is usually determined experimentally as the program is tuned.

*Depth control* can be achieved with a series of depth cutoffs. Associated with each depth cutoff is a list of features that might be found on the board. A position at the cutoff depth is terminal *unless* one or more of the features in the associated list is found. If one of the features is found, the line of play will be pursued to greater depths.

For instance, a list with the following form might be stored:

| Depth Cutoffs | Feature Lists |
|---|---|
| depth-1 | feature-list-1 |
| depth-2 | feature-list-2 |
| . | . |
| . | . |
| . | . |
| depth-(n − 1) | feature-list-(n − 1) |
| depth-n | |

If the depth of a node is less than depth-1, the node is nonterminal. If the depth is greater than or equal to depth-n, the node is terminal: no line of play is explored beyond depth-n.

If the depth of a node is in the range depth-1 to depth-n, the feature lists are used to determine whether or not the node is terminal. Suppose, for instance, the depth of a node is greater than or equal to depth-1 but less than depth-2: The position would be examined for the features in feature-list-1. If any are present the node is nonterminal; otherwise, it is terminal. The other cutoffs and feature lists are used in the same way.

The contents of the feature lists are determined by the concept of a dead position, as explained in the previous chapter. The features are things which might cause the nature of the position to change after a move or so, such as the possibility of a capture or an attack. At small depths we can afford to have a large list of such features; at greater depths tree-size control demands that only the features likely to produce the most drastic changes be considered.

Often only a few depth cutoffs, perhaps just 2, are used. The starting values for the depth cutoffs are also determined by experiment during tuning. The program may also vary the depth cutoffs during play, depending on whether it is ahead or behind in time.

## THE EVALUATION FUNCTION

In determining which move to make next, the program uses the backed-up values of the nodes at depth 1 in the search tree. These values result from backing up the values assigned to the terminal nodes by the evaluation function. Thus all the information the program uses in making its next-move decision ultimately originates with the evaluation function. If the program is to make good moves it is essential that the evaluation function be effective in distinguishing favorable terminal positions from unfavorable ones.

On the other hand, the evaluation function must be applied to every terminal node, so the time required to compute it becomes important. Making the evaluation function more complicated may improve its effectiveness, but the increased time required to compute it will mean that fewer terminal nodes can be examined in the time available for a move. Careful tuning of the program is required to obtain a satisfactory tradeoff between the effectiveness of the evaluation function and the time required to compute it.

### Material

In most board games each player starts off with a certain number of each kind of playing piece, his *material*. He may lose material if his pieces are captured by the opponent. He may gain material by changing less valuable pieces into more valuable ones, as when creating kings in checkers or queening pawns in chess.

The material advantage is a component of the evaluation function. For chess, at least, it is the most important component. The side which is ahead in material is ahead in the game. If one side has a substantial material advantage (more than a pawn or two) it may be unnecessary to bother computing the rest of the evaluation function.

(Human players sometimes sacrifice material in return for an improved position—the famous *gambits* of chess. But unless the sacrifice leads to an immediate win, current programs lack the long-range planning ability to follow up on the positional advantage. Hence the rule of thumb that the player who is ahead in material has the best position.)

The material advantage is calculated by assigning values to the different kinds of pieces. For chess the following values are usually used:

| Pawn | 1 |
|------|---|
| Knight | 3 |
| Bishop | 3 |
| Rook | 5 |
| Queen | 9 |
| King | large, often about 200 |

(The king is actually priceless, of course, since he can never be captured; when the king cannot escape the threat of capture the game is lost. Nevertheless, for some calculations it is useful to give the king a value: For instance, the importance of an attack may be judged by the value of the piece being attacked. Also, for the sake of simplicity in calculations one may allow the program to sometimes consider illegal positions in which a king has been captured. In any event, if the king is given a value, it will be large compared to the values of the other pieces.)

The material-advantage calculation for chess is similar to the corresponding calculation for checkers given in the previous chapter. Suppose that $p$, $n$, $b$, $r$, and $q$ are the pawn advantage, knight advantage, bishop advantage, and so on. (If we consider only legal positions, there will be no "king advantage.") That is

$p$ = number of player's pawns − number of opponent's pawns

and similarly for $n$, $b$, $r$, and $q$. Then the material advantage for the position is given by

material advantage = $9q + 5r + 3b + 3n + p$

On this scale the positional advantage seldom exceeds 1.5; no positional advantage is worth more than 1½ pawns. In order to allow a reasonable range of values for the positional component (and to allow those values to be integers, which are easiest for the computer to handle), we can multiply the values of the pieces by some constant, say 100. We will then be working on a scale with pawn = 100 and the positional component will have a range of, say, −150 to +150. The complete evaluation function will be given by

evaluation function
= (material advantage) + (positional advantage)
= $(900q + 500r + 300b + 300n + 100p)$
  + (positional advantage)

The scale "pawn = 100" is, of course, just used as an example; the scale actually used will depend on the method of calculating the positional advantage, and hence on the range of values it can have.

## Position

We can think of the material component of the evaluation function as being a *tactical component*: it is concerned with the immediate gains and losses brought about by each move. The positional component is a *strategic component*: it is concerned with achieving a strong position that will yield advantages in future play. As already mentioned, the importance of the tactical component far outweighs that of the strategical component, since current programs are unable to plan the strategies necessary to take advantage of a superior position.

Nevertheless, the program will often have to evaluate terminal positions in which neither side has a material advantage. In those positions there is nothing left to do but base the evaluation on positional considerations. The positional advantage is computed by giving each side a score obtained by adding points for each desirable feature found on the board and subtracting points for each undesirable feature. The positional advantage is the player's score minus the opponent's score.

Some features commonly used in computing the scores are the following:

- *Attacks.* Points are given for each opponent's piece that is being attacked. The number of points in each case depends on the value of the piece under attack.
- *Defense of King.* The score is penalized if the king is open to attack.
- *Development of Pieces.* The score is penalized if the rooks, knights, bishops, and queen have not moved from their starting positions.
- *Control of the Center.* Points are awarded for controlling the crucial center squares, either by attacking them or occupying them.
- *Mobility.* Points are awarded for each square to which a piece can move without exposing itself to capture.
- *Pawn Structure.* Points are awarded for pawn structures considered to be particularly effective and deducted for those considered to be ineffective.

This is not a complete list, of course; everyone who writes a chess playing program has his own favorite features. No particular list of features has yet to prove itself to be more effective than any other.

Some programs take a different approach to computing the evaluation function than the one outlined above. Two of these approaches are:

- *Table Lookup.* Instead of adding up points for each feature to obtain an overall score, the program can look up the particular combination of features present in a table; the score is then taken from the table. The advantage of *table lookup* is that the table entries can take into account the interactions of the features: For instance, one feature might be worth much more if another feature happened to be present, and perhaps worth much less in the presence of still another feature. Thus one cannot assign points for one feature without taking into account what other features may or may not be present. Arthur Samuels used such a table lookup in one version of his highly successful checkers-playing program.

- *Evaluation Based on Specific Patterns.* Instead of basing the evaluation on the general features of a position, one can look for more detailed and specific patterns; pins and forks as well as the various patterns for forcing checkmate would be examples. As with the general features, points are added to a score for favorable patterns and subtracted for unfavorable ones. The USC chess program uses this approach; a description of it can be found in the June 1973 issue of *Scientific American.* One interesting feature of the USC program is that a language was devised to allow the patterns to be specified by a chess expert with no knowledge of computer programming.

## PLANNING

Successful chess-playing programs such as CHESS 4.6 search trees of from 400,000 to 500,000 nodes for each move they make. A human player, the psychologists tell us, mentally examines about 50 positions for each move he makes. Obviously, much remains to be done in controlling tree size in chess-playing programs. Essentially, new ideas will be needed if the programs are to come anywhere near human performance in this respect.

One of the most attractive and largely untried ideas is to use long-range planning. We have seen in previous chapters how searching within the framework of a plan can greatly reduce the size of the search tree. Again, one of the most common criticisms of current programs by chess players is that the program obviously has no long range plan for winning. Certainly, some kind of planning seems to be necessary if programs are to take advantage of subtle positional features.

Much experimentation will be needed to develop good planning techniques for game playing. A good starting point might be the hierarchical planning techniques discussed in Chapter 5. A plan would be created, refined, modified, and perhaps eventually abandoned as the game progressed. The program would always make a substantial effort to find a good move consistent with the current plan before deciding that the plan should be modified or abandoned. Hierarchical planning would allow the modifications to be made on as low a level as possible.

# Chapter 8
# Pattern Recognition and Perception

When a computer receives information from the outside world, what it usually receives is a mass of unorganized detail. For a picture it will receive a list giving the brightness of each of the hundreds of thousands of individual points that make up the picture. For a sound it will receive a list of thousands of numbers, each one of which gives the amplitude of the sound wave at some instant of time. For a chess position the computer will get a list showing which chess piece (if any) is on each square of the board.

From this mass of unorganized detail the computer must extract the information required to achieve its goals. For a picture the computer will be less interested in the brightness of each point than in recognizing familiar objects, such as doors, windows, tables, and chairs. For a sound it may be interested in identifying spoken words. For a chess position it may want to find pins, forks, X-ray attacks, possibilities for mating in one or two moves, and so on.

When we recognize a pattern, then, we replace a complex, detailed description of an object with a much simpler, less-detailed, but usually more useful, description.

Suppose, for example, we recognize a telephone in a picture. Then we replace the list giving the brightness of each of the thousands of points making up the image of the telephone with the single description "telephone." And this one-word description is far more useful than the original list of brightnesses. First, in our minds we have many useful facts and plans filed under the heading "telephone," how to make a long distance call, for instance. Second, many of our heuristics and plans make reference to telephones; if we need to communicate with our friend who lives on the other side of town, the plan that will immediately come to mind is to see if a telephone is handy and, if so, to call our friend. But before we can carry out this plan, we obviously have to be able to recognize a telephone when we see one.

Just what features we wish to extract from the picture of the telephone will depend on just what we are trying to accomplish. If we only want to call someone, just the word "telephone" might be enough, though we would need to distinguish a pay phone from a private one. An artist painting a telephone, however, would be interested in its orientation with respect to the viewer as well as the way it reflects the light falling on it. A telephone engineer, on the other hand, would be more interested in classifying the instrument as one of the types whose electrical characteristics he is familiar with. And so on.

Humans find pattern recognition easy. Familiar patterns, such as telephones, we learn as children and never give a second thought. Other patterns, such as those on a chessboard or in a musical composition, require training to perceive. But once we have had the training, the patterns seem to "jump out at us," and we need give little thought to finding them. In fact, it is hard to imagine how we could avoid seeing them.

Computers find pattern recognition difficult. Current programs do not recognize patterns nearly as well as we would like. And often large amounts of computation are required to recognize them at all. Pattern recognition is an area in which there is much need for research and much room for bright ideas.

## DEFINITIONS

A *pattern* is simply a collection, or category, of objects. Each of the objects is an example of the pattern and is called a *pattern example*. A rule that determines which objects belong to a pattern and which do not is called a *pattern rule*.

For example, the collection

3, 5, 7, 9, 11

is a pattern, which we will call $P$. (We follow the mathematician's convention of enclosing collections, or *sets*, of objects in braces.) The pattern examples are the five digits 3, 5, 7, 9, and 11. The pattern rule is the following

> An object belongs to the pattern $P$ if it is a whole number greater than or equal to 3 and less than or equal to 11.

Figure 8-1 is another example, a pattern for a printed capital A. The pattern examples are the various printed As shown. The three dots indicate that the list of examples is incomplete: a careful examination of printed works would reveal many other examples differing slightly from the ones shown. Finally, it is very difficult to give a rule for this pattern. We could say something like, "The object must be a printed capital A." But this really sends us back to a list of examples, such as the partial list given in Fig. 8-1 or the more complete list that might be found in a printer's style manual. We could give a long, complicated rule specifying the number of strokes making up an A and the way they must be joined together. Such a rule would include most As but would probably have some exceptions, such as script or old English As. It is often very difficult or impossible to find a simple rule that will cover all examples of a pattern.

In AI literature the word pattern is often used to refer to the pattern rule rather than the collection of examples. In other chapters we will often follow the conventional usage. But the "capital A" example just given shows why the most general definition of a pattern is as a collection of objects rather than as a rule.

The following are some of the specific activities that come under the headings of "pattern recognition" or "perception":

## Pattern Classification

Given a detailed description of an object, we wish to classify it as an example of one or more known patterns. Given the output of an optical scanner when a letter of the alphabet passes under it, for instance, we wish to classify the output as an example of an A, a B, a C, and so on. The classification can be made by using pattern rules or by comparison with pattern examples.

## Pattern Matching

Instead of being given an object and trying to find a pattern that fits, we may be given a pattern to find an object that fits. This technique is often used to extract useful information from a collection of facts, a so-called *data base*.

For instance, suppose our data base contains English sentences that state facts about the real world. A pattern rule could be written as follows:

$x$ AND $y$ ARE BROTHERS.
$x$ IS OLDER THAN $y$.
$y$ MAKES MORE MONEY THAN $x$.

The letters $x$ and $y$ are variables for which English words can be substituted. An example of the pattern is any three sentences that can be obtained from the pattern rule by substituting words for $x$ and $y$.

Fig. 8-1. A pattern for the printed capital A. Each of the different As is a pattern example.

A, *A*, **A**, A ...

We wish to find all pattern examples whose sentences belong to the data base and so are presumably true of the real world. If, for instance, the data base contains the sentences

BOB AND JIM ARE BROTHERS.
BOB IS OLDER THAN JIM.
JIM MAKES MORE MONEY THAN BOB.

then they are a pattern example, since they can be obtained from the pattern rule by substituting BOB for $x$ and JIM for $y$. By searching through the entire data base, we could find all pairs of people—names that could be substituted for $x$ and $y$—for which the statements in the pattern rule hold.

Pattern matching is widely used in AI; we will see further examples of it in connection with natural-language processing, computational logic, production systems, and AI programming languages. The pattern rule is usually simply called the pattern.

### Description

We can use patterns to describe an object. Consider the room you are sitting in. A much-too-detailed description of the room would be a picture of it, given as a list of the brightnesses of the picture points. A less detailed but more useful description would be in terms of tables, chairs, doors, windows, and pictures on the wall. Given a picture of the room, a computer could search for examples of patterns for tables, chairs, and so on, and construct a new description in terms of these patterns. It is this new description which would be appropriate for, say, a robot that had been directed to rearrange the furniture.

### Feature Extraction

Often the original description of an object contains so much extraneous detail that it is impractical to search directly for examples of the patterns we are interested in. Instead we search first for examples of simpler patterns and construct a new description of the object on terms of these simpler patterns. This new, less detailed, description is then analyzed for examples of the patterns of interest.

These simpler patterns are called *features,* and the process of finding examples of them is called *feature extraction*. It is also sometimes called *preprocessing* or *preanalysis*.

Examples of feature extraction are many. In picture analysis, for instance, we must locate the contours that outline objects before we can make a start toward identifying the objects themselves. In analyzing a chess position, we might first systematically search the board for all pins, forks, X-ray attacks, checks, and so on before starting the calculation of the evaluation function.

Often the result of feature extraction is a set of numbers. For instance, given a letter of the alphabet to recognize, the computer might first determine the following:

- Number of straight-line strokes making up the letter
- Number of end points at which lines terminate (E has 3 and C has 2 end points, for instance)
- Number of corners, such as the one at the top of the letter A
- Width of the letter

and so on.

Each number classifies the object as belonging to one of several possible patterns. For instance, the value of "number of straight-line strokes" classified the capital letters as follows:

| Straight-Line Strokes | Pattern |
|---|---|
| 0 | (S, C, 0) |
| 1 | (I, J, G, Q) |
| 2 | (T, X) |
| 3 | (F, H, Z, A) |
| 4 | (E, M, W) |

(we ignore the small strokes placed at the end points of the letters. For instance, I is treated as if it were a single vertical line.)

This suggests that we extend the definition of a feature to include properties such as "number of straight-line strokes." The value of such an extended feature classifies into one of a number of possible patterns. Allowing one feature to correspond many patterns simplifies the description. Also, as we will see in the next section, certain mathematical and statistical operations can be fruitfully applied to the values of the extended features.

We can think of a complicated description, such as a picture, as being worked over by a hierarchy of pattern recognizers. At the lowest level of the hierarchy are the recognizers that process the raw data and extract fairly simple features. These features form a description of the object which is processed by the recognizers on the next highest level. This level extracts features that will be processed on the level above it, and so on. The hierarchy may have as many levels as are needed so that the top level can ultimately recognize the patterns of interest.

## Learning

We wish to teach a computer program to recognize a certain pattern. To do this we first present the computer with objects that are examples of the pattern and objects that are not examples of it, telling the computer which is which. These objects constitute the *training set*. We then present the computer with objects from a *test set* and expect it to tell us which ones are examples of the pattern in question. How many successful identifications it makes tells us how well it learned to recognize the pattern.

For instance, much work has been done on programs that can learn to distinguish printed characters. Such a program could adapt itself to different typefaces with the aid of appropriate training sets. Since there are hundreds of different typefaces this kind of adaptability seems necessary if a character-recognition program is to be generally useful. Another example: Arthur Samuels' checkers program learned to play checkers by modifying its evaluation function. The training set consisted of games taken from checkers textbooks. The moves made by the program were compared with the ones recommended by experts; the program adjusted its evaluation function in an attempt to make its moves agree as much as possible with those of the experts. After playing through large numbers of book games, the program became an excellent checkers player.

In these examples the program *does not* learn what the relevant features are and how to extract them from the raw data. Instead it only learns pattern rules stated in terms of features devised by the programmer. Samuels' checkers program, for instance, did not learn the relevance of material advantage, mobility, control of center, and so on. These features—and the routines for extracting them from the checkers positions—were devised by Samuels. What the program did learn was how to construct an evaluation function of a given form from the features that were provided. Programs that attempt to learn to extract relevent features from raw data have not been nearly so successful.

## Pattern Representation

Another problem is how to represent, or describe, patterns so that they can be communicated to human beings or to computers. That is, can we devise a convenient language for stating pattern rules? No one has yet devised a general purpose pattern language, but several special purpose ones are worth mentioning:

- *Decision Tables*. The condition entries correspond to features that have been extracted from the raw data. Each decision-table rule is a pattern rule. The decision table is usually used to specify (via action entries) actions that are to be taken in response to the patterns that are recognized.
- *Expressions Containing Variables*. These were illustrated in the discussion of pattern matching; there the expressions in question were English sentences. These are widely used in AI languages as well as in the SNOBOL string-processing language. We will return to them several times in the remainder of this book.
- *Subject Matter Oriented Languages.* Such languages are oriented toward the terminology of a particular subject matter so that a subject-matter expert who knows nothing of programming can describe patterns to a program (as well as actions it should take or heuristics it should use in response to the pattern). For example, the authors of the USC chess program devised a language to allow a chess expert to describe important chess patterns and to advise the computer on how to evaluate positions containing examples of the patterns.

If AI programs are to function in specialized subject areas such as chess, chemistry, or medicine, they must be able to acquire knowledge from experts in those areas, experts who know nothing of computer programming. Thus we may expect that easy-to-use languages for describing patterns, heuristics, and plans will become increasingly important.

## FEATURE SPACES, REGIONS, AND PROTOTYPES

The methods described in this section are by no means the final answer to the pattern-recognition problem. But they have been successfully applied to such practical problems as classifying printed characters, blood cells, and chromosomes, as well as to weather prediction. They have also been applied (but with less obvious success) to stock market prediction.

### Feature Spaces

Suppose that feature extraction has been applied to the raw-data description of an object. The feature-extraction process has yielded a description of the object as a set of numbers, as was described in the section on feature extraction. We can think of each set of numbers as being a point in a *feature space*.

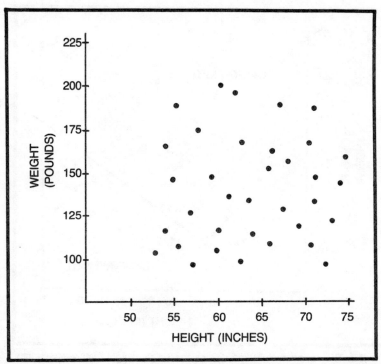

Fig. 8-2. A feature space for the features height and weight. Each person whose height and weight has been measured is represented by a point.

For example, two features that a doctor usually extracts from his patients are their heights and weights. Figure 8-2 shows the corresponding feature space: height and weight form the two axes of a rectangular coordinate system. Each patient is represented by a points whose coordinates are his height and weight.

The feature-extraction process may classify objects in terms of dozens or even hundreds of features. When there are more than two features, we cannot actually plot the points on graph paper. But we can think of the sets of feature values as being points in an abstract multidimensional space. Although we cannot easily visualize such spaces, mathematicians have developed methods for working with them just as easily as we work with ordinary two-dimensional rectangular-coordinate systems.

### Regions

If the features we have extracted are relevant to the patterns we are trying to recognize, we should be able to divide the feature space up into *regions*, each region corresponding to a particular

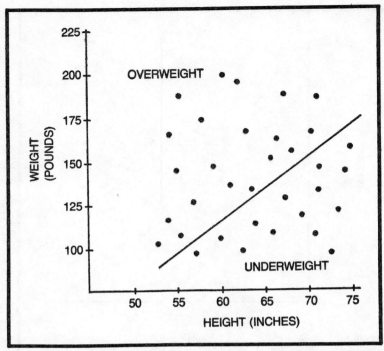

Fig. 8-3. The normal-weight line divides the height-weight feature space into underweight and overweight regions.

pattern. An object will be an example of a pattern only if the point corresponding to the object lies in the region corresponding to the pattern.

For instance, we can divide the height-weight feature space into two regions by drawing the line that represents the normal relationship between height and weight (Fig. 8-3). Persons whose points are above the line are overweight; those whose points lie below the line are underweight. Persons whose points lie exactly on the line are neither overweight nor underweight; here this is a desirable situation but usually it is troublesome: if a point lies exactly on the boundary we cannot tell which region it belongs to and hence which pattern it is an example of.

We like to separate our regions by straight lines whenever possible, since straight lines are easy to handle mathematically. Regions that can be separated by straight lines are said to be *linearly separable*. Some regions are not linearly separable, as is shown in Fig. 8-4. For such regions we must use more complicated curves, such as ellipses, or use a series of line segments instead of a single line.

142

(In multidimensional spaces the analog of a straight line is called a *hyperplane*. Thus, in general, we try to divide the feature space into regions by means of hyperplanes.)

Powerful mathematical techniques have been devised for finding curves and surfaces that divide a feature space into regions. The success or failure of these techniques depend on the features themselves: if the features are really relevant to distinguishing the patterns we are trying to recognize, the techniques will succeed; otherwise, they will fail.

### Prototypes

As an alternative to dividing the feature space into regions, we can plot points corresponding to a typical example—or prototype—of each pattern. Given a point corresponding to an unknown object, we find its distance from each of the prototype points. We then classify the unknown as an example of the pattern to whose prototype it is closest. The distance between two points is given by some formula involving their coordinates; it need not be the usual distance formula used in geometry. Defining a good distance (a measure of the degree of difference between two objects) is one of the challenges of this approach.

### Templates

Another way to use a prototype is as a template. Suppose we are trying to recognize printed characters. We have an example of each character printed on a piece of clear plastic; these prototype

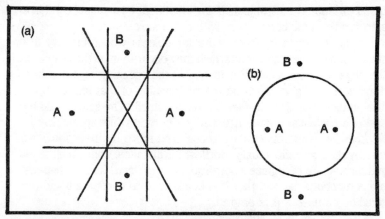

Fig. 8-4. Some regions are not linearly separable. As shown in part (a), no straight line will separate the A-type points from the B-type. But a circle will, as shown in part (b).

characters are the templates. To classify an unknown character, we lay each template over it in turn to see which prototype character most closely matches the unknown.

A computer can make a similar comparison by having the unknown and the templates stored (as lists of brightnesses of points) in different areas of memory. To compare the unknown character with a template, the computer compares the two memory areas, memory location by memory location.

The difficulty with the template approach is that trivial variations in the character being identified will cause the match to fail. If the character is slightly too large or too small, tilted in one direction or the other, or simply not centered in the image, it will probably not match the correct template. In fact, it may well match an incorrect template better than the correct one. Before a character is matched against the templates, it must be preprocessed to give it a standard position, size, and orientation.

## Summary

The methods described in this section have been used successfully in practical applications such as optical character recognition and blood cell identification. On the other hand, they have their limitations and are definitely not the final answer to the pattern-recognition problem.

For the feature-space methods the essential requirement is for a set of easily extractable features whose values really do distinguish the patterns we are trying to recognize so that points corresponding to examples of different patterns will be in different parts of the feature space. For the template method we must be able to eliminate trivial variations in the objects being identified; each must be put in a standard form for comparison with the templates.

None of these methods work for objects whose identity depends more on the context in which they occur than on the details of the objects themselves. For instance, the meaning of a line in a drawing depends as much on the relationship of that line to other lines in the drawing as it does on the line itself. The same could be said of a particular sound uttered by a person while speaking.

Finally, some objects are recognized more by their *functions* than by their specific details. Bottles, for instance, come in all sizes and shapes. We recognize a bottle not so much by its size or shape as by its function: the fact that it is being used to confine a liquid (or could be so used if it is empty).

## IMAGE ANALYSIS

Analyzing images picked up by television cameras is the ultimate challenge of pattern recognition. To date the challenge has not been well met: much work remains to be done. To indicate current thinking on the subject, this section describes the image analysis steps taken by some current experimental systems.

## Image Acquisition

The image from the television camera is sampled at selected points; the brightnesses of those points are converted into numbers which are stored in computer memory. To the computer, then, the image is simply an array of numbers.

## Smoothing

Because of "noise"—errors in the acquistion process—some of the numbers stored in the computer will not correspond to the brightness of the points in the original scene. "Smoothing" refers to mathematical operations designed to eliminate or reduce the effect of such errors. These operations are applied to the picture as it is stored in the computer—that is, to the list of numbers.

For instance, we could search for any point that is brighter than any of the eight points immediately adjacent to it in the picture. Considering that point as likely to be an error, we would change its brightness to that of the brightest of the adjacent points. Alternatively, we could set its brightness to the average of the brightnesses of the adjacent points. A point dimmer than any adjacent point could be treated in a similar way.

Many other smoothing techniques are possible. They must be applied with care, lest the desired image be smoothed out as well as the noise. Such techniques have been used to enhance the images sent back to earth from spacecraft.

## The Primal Sketch

When we sketch a scene, the lines in the sketch correspond to lines separating regions of different brightness in the original scene. A first step in analyzing a scene is to convert it into a sketch—to find the lines that separate regions of differing brightness.

Suppose we move across the image in some straight-line path, as shown in Fig. 8-5. If we write down the brightnesses of the points we encounter, we might get something like this

$$1 \quad 1 \quad 2 \quad 3 \quad 4 \quad 5 \quad 6 \quad 5 \quad 4 \quad 3 \quad 2 \quad 1 \quad 1$$

indicating that as we moved across the image the brightness first increased and then fell off again. When we travel across the image in this way, how can we determine when we cross lines—when we move from one brightness level to another?

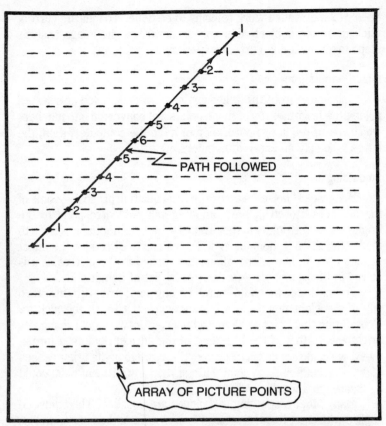

Fig. 8-5. We can move across the array of picture points in a straight-line path and record the brightnesses of the points encountered.

We can apply an operator to the list of numbers to obtain a new list which shows the points at which the brightness level changes. Suppose that the original list is

1 1 1 2 3 4 4 4 4 3 2 1 1 1

We will apply an operator defined by

$$B_{new} = B_{old} - B_{left}$$

which means the value of each new point is calculated by subtracting from the value of the corresponding old point the value of the old point immediately to its left. Here are the old and the new list:

Old:

1 1 1 2 3 4 4 4 4 3 2 1 1 1

New:

0 0 1 1 1 0 0 0 -1 -1 -1 0 0

146

We see that the entries in the new list are different from zero only when the brightness is changing. The points at which the entries in the new list are different from zero correspond to the lines separating regions of different brightness.

(Readers who have studied calculus will recognize that we have just taken the first derivative of the brightness along the line in question. The second derivative is also useful in analyzing brightness variations.)

Now suppose that we set up an array of points in the original image and take lines in different directions through each point, as shown in Fig. 8-6. If we use various operators to analyze the brightness variation along each line, we can locate the lines separating regions of different brightness. A list of such lines, giving properties such as location, length, and orientation for each line, is called a *primal sketch*.

The primal sketch is made up of many short line segments not unlike the pencil strokes that an artist would use in sketching the scene. These short line segments have to be joined together to form the edges that represent the boundaries of objects or parts of objects.

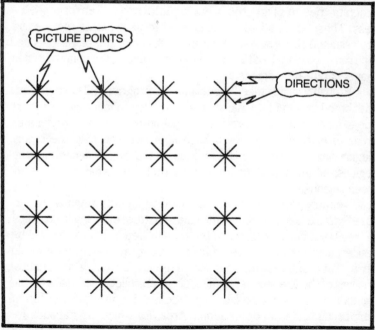

Fig. 8-6. We can analyze the brightness variations along lines going in different directions through each picture point.

Methods of doing this vary, and no procedure that is satisfactory in all circumstances has yet been devised. What the computer has to do is find series of short segments that, taken together, form a straight line or a smooth curve. There is a convenient approach to finding segments that represent a straight line. The program collects the segments into groups that satisfy the following two conditions:

- Each segment in a group is within a few picture points of some other segment in the same group.
- No segment in a group is perpendicular to any other in the same group.

Each group is taken to represent a straight line joining the two segments in the group that are farthest apart.

After edges have been filled in using this or some other rule, the computer can try to fill in gaps by noting that edges should begin and end by forming corners with other edges. If an edge comes to an abrupt halt without joining onto anything else, the program suspects a gap and searches for another edge that the incomplete one could logically be joined to.

Instead of concentrating on the edges separating distinguishable regions, one can concentrate on the regions themselves. The program tries to divide the scene up into areas of uniform brightness. These areas are then considered to be separate regions and are assumed to represent different surfaces in the original scene. One can get a sketch of the scene by constructing the boundary lines that separate the regions.

Probably an advanced scene analysis program will have to work with both lines and regions; that is, it will try to join together short line segments to form regions as well as to recognize regions as areas of uniform brightness. Each approach can help the other. Region analysis can help fill in gaps in the edges separating the regions; edge analysis can help construct the boundary lines between regions.

Texture analysis can also be used to identify regions. A textured surface is one having some kind of pattern on it, such as a piece of wood or a piece of cloth. In the primal sketch the texture will be rendered by many short line segments, again much as an artist would do it. Different textures can be identified by doing a statistical analysis of the line segments. The program collects statistics on the number of line segments having different brightnesses, different lengths, and different orientations. Areas for which the statistics are the same are taken to have the same texture. They may be part of the same region, or at least closely related regions. Areas with substantially different statistics have different textures and almost surely belong to different regions.

We can think of regions as representing surfaces in the original scene—the walls of a room, for instance, or the top of a table. Having identified these surfaces, we are left with the problem of determining the orientation of each surface with respect to the observer. Are we looking straight down on a particular surface, or are we viewing it at an angle?

One approach to this problem is to analyze the illumination of the surfaces. If we know the direction from which light is falling on a scene, the laws of physics tell us how the apparent brightness of the surface will vary with its orientation with respect to the source of light and with respect to the observer. A scene-analysis program can try to find a direction of illumination and a set of surface orientations that are consistent with the observed brightnesses. The mathematical calculations for this kind of analysis can be quite formidable, particularly when the surfaces in question are curved.

With illumination, much information about a scene can be deduced by analyzing shadows. An analysis of both an object and its shadow can give much more information than would an analysis of either one by itself.

Suppose (and at the present state of the art this is a big supposition) that the regions corresponding to different surfaces have been identified and the edges separating them constructed. The problem that remains is to join the regions together to form objects and to identify the objects formed. Specifically, the program wishes to convert lists of regions and edges into a list of meaningful objects, such as tables, chairs, telephones, and so on.

If the scene consists only of blocks, boxes, pyramids, wedges, and other objects consisting of flat surfaces bounded by straight lines, the object-identification problem can be solved fairly straightforwardly.

The idea is this. Edges that are visible in a blocks-world scene can be classified into three types:

1. A convex edge separating two visible surfaces. An example would be the line separating the top and the front face of a block when the block is viewed from the front and slightly from above.
2. A convex edge separating two surfaces, only one of which is visible. An example would be the line separating the back of a block from its top face when the block is viewed from the front and above, so that its back surface is hidden.

3. A concave edge. An example would be a line separating two surfaces of a box when seen from *inside* the box.

Now there are only a limited number of ways in which these three kinds of edges can join together to form corners. The possible corners can be classified according to the kinds of edges that make them up.

For instance, suppose a certain corner is made up of three convex edges coming together at a point. This must be an outside corner of a block. It could not be a corner of a box seen from the inside, since if it were the edges would have to be concave. Suppose that each convex edge is the kind that separates two visible surfaces. Then this must be a corner like one of the top corners of a box, such that all the surfaces making up the corner are visible.

A program applies these ideas by trying to find a consistent labeling of the edges and corners in the scene. Each edge is labeled as one of the three kinds described. Each corner is labeled as one of the permissible kinds. Since each permissible corner can be made up from only certain kinds of permissible edges, the requirement that permissible edges join to form permissible corners constrains the labeling. The program tries different labelings until it finds one that is consistent with all the edges and corners. (If no consistent labeling can be found then the picture is of an "impossible object," something we can draw a picture of but which cannot exist in nature. Such impossible objects were frequently featured in the work of the Dutch artist M.C. Escher.)

Once all of the edges and corners have been classified, it is relatively easy to combine them to form known objects. Using these techniques, programs have been written that analyze quite complicated scenes made up of boxes, blocks, pyramids, wedges, and other plane solids.

Unfortunately, the labeling techniques work only in a "blocks world." They do not work for curved surfaces. A real-world object can be bounded in whole or in part by a curved surface which offers no sharp edges and corners for the labeling program to work on.

Only the first steps have been taken toward the problem of identifying objects in the real world. A few of these steps will be mentioned, but at this point it is not clear whether they are steps in the right direction or not.

A complicated object can be approximated by a simpler geometrical shape. A water glass can be approximated by a cylinder, a telephone by a wedge, a goldfish bowl by a sphere. This is somewhat the reverse of what art books often recommend for beginning artists. The artist is taught to outline a scene by first blocking it out with simple geometrical shapes, such as blocks, spheres, cylinders, and wedges. After the scene is outlined the artist goes back and fills in the details of the objects. The original outlines are eventually erased.

Cylinders are particularly useful for this kind of analysis. This is particularly true if we generalize the cylinder by allowing its diameter to vary as we move from top to bottom. For instance, a Coke bottle can be thought of as a cylinder whose diameter is very narrow at the top, gets larger as one goes down, then gets smaller again, and finally gets larger again at the base.

Many man-made objects have this kind of cylindrical symmetry because of the widespread use of lathes and other rotating devices in manufacturing.

A program using generalized cylinders has been written to identify the different kinds of Greek vases of interest to archeologists.

What has not been used very much to date, but will surely be used extensively in future object identification programs, is the context in which an object occurs. A black, roughly wedge-shaped object sitting on a desk, for instance, is very likely to be a telephone; this would be our tentative identification even if the details were obscure. If the same object was hanging from the ceiling, however, we would look a lot more closely before committing ourselves to an identification. If the details were obscure we might not identify the object at all. Puzzle photographs that challenge us to identify the object depicted are puzzling precisely because they show familiar objects out of context. Making use of our context and our expectations is related to the *frame* idea discussed in Chapters 12 and 13, Representation of Knowledge and Natural Language Processing.

Whatever methods are ultimately developed for scene analysis, it is clear that they will require a tremendous amount of computation. Probably special purpose microprocessors capable of carrying out the same operation on each point in a picture at the same time will be needed. These may be used to build "intelligent" TV cameras, which will deliver to the computer not the raw data of a scene, but lists of surfaces, lines, and perhaps even objects. There is reason to believe that the human optic nerve does a great deal of preprocessing before passing the image on to the brain.

# Chapter 9
# Robots

A *robot* is a machine that functions under its own power and control. Since machines that work under their own power are commonplace these days, what distinguishes a robot is that it also works under its own control. After being assigned a task, a robot should be able to carry out the steps of the task with no further human intervention.

Robots—that is, machines that satisfy the above definition—vary tremendously in their degree of sophistication. At one end of the robot spectrum we have what might be called automatic machines. An automatic machine may be able to carry out a complicated sequence of actions without human intervention. But the sequence of actions will be essentially the same each time the machine is operated. The machine has little or no ability to modify its actions in response to conditions that exist in its environment.

At the other end of the robot spectrum are some of the machines that have been constructed in artificial-intelligence laboratories. These robots use TV cameras or some other means to preceive their surroundings. They can accept and carry out high-level commands for manipulating their environments and will fill in the low-level details themselves.

For instance, a robot told to put the green block in the red box would first locate the green block and the red box in the room. It would then move itself to the vicinity of the green block, going around or removing any obstacles that might stand in its way. The robot might have to remove items sitting on top of the green block before picking up the block and carrying it to the red box. Finally, it may have to remove some of the items that are already in the red box before it has room to put in the green block.

Familiar examples of automatic machines are automatic home appliances such as automatic washers and automatic record changers. Some of these machines can respond to their surroundings in simple ways. A record changer, for instance, detects when the current record is over and initiates the actions to change to a new one. It allows the user to reject a record before it is over. And the changer will detect when all the records have been played and shut itself off automatically. But despite these simple kinds of responsiveness, the record player only plays records; the washing machine only washes clothes. No command we can give either machine will cause it to do the other machine's job.

Such automatic machines have an interesting history, especially since some of the historical examples are a lot closer to what most people would think of as robots than are household appliances.

In the 18th century, Europe was swept by a wave of interest in clockwork automata. These consisted of figures of humans or animals that mimicked familiar activities of those living creatures. One mechanical person played a piece on the harpsichord. Another wrote a legible letter, pausing periodically to dip the quill pen in an ink jar. A mechanical duck would eat, drink, defecate, quack, and splash in the water.

These clockwork robots were usually controlled by pegged drums similar to those found in music boxes. As the drum slowly turned, the pegs on its surface would engage the various mechanisms that caused the figures to perform. The drum, with its pegs, was a kind of Read Only Memory in which was stored the actions the figure was to carry out. To change the figure's actions one would have had to replace the drum with a new one having the pegs in different positions. Usually, there was no provision for such reprogramming: each robot was made to carry out just one sequence of actions. The machines were built for entertainment purposes and seemed new to each audience regardless of how many times they had performed the same routines for other audiences.

Descendents of these early robots can be found today in, of all places, Disneyland. In the "audioanimatronics" exhibits, effigies of Abraham Lincoln and other figures from American history enact scenes for the visitors. The technology has improved considerably—electrical and electronic devices have replaced most of the clockwork—but the idea is the same as that of the 18th century automata.

Incidentally, it was probably the clockwork automata that inspired the first discussions of whether or not machines could think. These imitations of life had a disturbing effect on the people; there were mutterings of witchcraft; and at least one designer of automata was arrested on that charge by the Holy Inquisition!

Also, it was in this historical context that Baron von Kempelen's famous but fraudulent chess-playing machine appeared. The machine, which had a human chess player hidden inside, was represented as a clockwork automaton capable of playing chess. The design of the chess player mimicked that of the other automata: a figure seated before a chess board moved the chess pieces by hand with slightly jerky mechanical motions.

Returning to modern industrial robots, we can go one step beyond the household appliances and the clockwork automata by allowing a robot to be programmed to carry out different sequences of actions. Once programmed, however, these machines will repeat the same sequence of actions over and over, just like the automatic machines already mentioned.

These "pick and place" manipulators are often controlled by plugboards, similar to those found on many pre-computer data-processing machines. The plugboard is organized into rows and columns. Each row represents one possible motion the robot's hand or arm could make. Each column represents one step of the robot's program. A plug at the junction of a row and a column causes the robot to make a particular motion at a particular step in the program. The extent of each motion—how far the hand should move, how tightly it should grasp—is determined by mechanical steps, similar to the margin and tab stops on a typewriter.

The plugs in the plugboard correspond to the pegs on the drums of the clockwork automata. The use of adjustable stops probably never occurred to the 18th century designers; after all, flexibility was not their goal. Once the stops have been positioned and the plugs inserted the robot is programmed, ready to carry out the programmed actions as many times as is required.

Currently used industrial robots display two more jumps in sophistication.

First, the plugboard may be replaced by a potentiometer board. The potentiometers replace the mechanical stops. The setting of each potentiometer determines a particular position to which a part of the robot should be moved.

Without the mechanical stops the robot's manipulators must contain feedback sensors so that the actual position of a part of the robot can be compared with the desired position specified by the setting of a potentiometer on the potentiometer board. Often potentiometers are used for the feedback sensors. At each step of the program, the robot's manipulating parts are adjusted so that the potentiometers mounted on them have the same settings as the corresponding ones in the column of the potentiometer board corresponding to the current program step.

The second step up in sophistication does away with plugboards and potentiometer boards entirely. The robot is guided through the actions desired by a "teacher" using a handheld control box. The robot stores the desired positions in an internal memory as it is guided through them. It can then repeat the motions it has been taught on command as many times as is necessary. In current models a plated wire memory is often used to store the details of the required motions; in the future the plated wire memories will undoubtedly be replaced by something more modern, such as magnetic bubble memory.

These machines often move rather jerkily in going from one remembered position to another (so do the plugboard and potentiometer board machines). For many purposes this does not matter. But if smoothness is essential, as when the robot is spraying paint, large numbers of intermediate positions may have to be stored, usually on magnetic tape. The robot moves from one position to another in very small steps, simulating a continuous motion.

So far none of the industrial robots that have been described used computers; plugboard, potentiometer boards, and plated wire memories have sufficed for control. Until recently computers were too expensive to dedicate to controlling robots; only robots in research laboratories were controlled by computers. Microprocessors have changed all that, of course, and we may now expect to see more and more robots controlled by built-in microprocessors. What additional capabilities can we expect from these computer-controlled robots?

One of the most important jobs that a computer can do is transform between internal and external coordinates. Let us see what this means.

When a robot is programmed by, say, a potentiometer board, the settings of the potentiometers do not directly specify the positions of the robot's manipulators in space. That is, they do not directly specify that, say, the robot's hand should move to a position that is 6 inches above the surface of a table, 20 inches from one edge of the table, and 30 inches from another edge. Instead the potentiometer settings specify the positions of the various joints in the robot's arm and hand. It is up to the person programming the robot to make sure that the programmed joint positions will bring the robot's hand to the desired position in relation to the table.

The positions of the robot's joints and other parts are known as *internal coordinates.* The numbers which give the position of, say, a robot's hand in relation to other objects in a room are called *external coordinates,* or *workspace coordinates.* Obviously it is workspace coordinates that we are really interested in; our interest focuses on how the robot is moving with respect to other objects in its environment and not with the number of degrees through which each joint is turning.

A computer can convert between external and internal coordinates. It can convert a command to, say, move the robot's hand up 6 inches and 4 inches to the left into whatever joint movements are required in order to bring about the desired displacement.

With computer control we can obtain continuous motion without having to store so many positions in memory. Suppose we wish the robot's hand to move smoothly between two positions given in workspace coordinates. Only the initial and the final position need be stored. Using elementary analytic geometry, the computer can calculate the workspace coordinates for a large number of intermediate positions lying along a straight line joining the initial and the final position. After it has converted the intermediate positions from workspace to internal coordinates, the computer can send the control signals to the motors controlling the various joints in the robot's hand and arm.

The computer can carry out many other useful calculations as well. For instance, to move a heavy object from one place to another, the robot must apply a relatively large force to get the object moving, a smaller force to keep it moving at a constant speed in spite of friction, and a force in opposite direction to bring the object to rest in the desired position. (Compare with the manipulations of accelerator and brakes required to maneuver a car in crowded traffic.) The computer can calculate what forces should be applied to the object at each point on its trajectory in order to move it from one position to another as quickly as possible.

With computer control the door is open to far more sophisticated robots than have ever been possible before. Included are the kinds now found only in research laboratories, which interact with their environments in complicated ways to carry out high level commands.

What are the considerations involved in designing a sophisticated robot? We can divide them into three areas:

1. *Effectors or Manipulators.* These are the mechanical components with which the robot manipulates the real world.

2. *Sensors.* These are the devices that transmit information about the real world to the robot. The more sophisticated the robot, the more important the role that sensors will play.
3. *Control.* This is the computer program which accepts commands for the robot to carry out and (based on information obtained from the sensors) causes the effectors to move in the appropriate ways.

## EFFECTORS

*Effectors* include the robot's hands and arms as well as the means for moving the robot from one place to another. Also, at least some of the robot's sensors will need to be movable. If the robot uses a TV camera, for instance, it should be able to point the camera in any direction without having to turn its entire body to face in the direction it wishes to look. And it should be able to look up and down as well as straight ahead.

Industrial robots are usually fixed at their stations along the production line. Research robots can usually move about the room under their own power, and they almost invariably use wheels to do so. The wheels are driven by electric motors; for lightweight robots, stepping motors are useful for this purpose; each step turns the wheels through a known angle. Some science-fiction-movie robots use tracks (like on a bulldozer) instead of wheels, but these do not seem to offer any advantage over wheels. Until there is a real need for robots to walk up and down stairs or to walk over irregular surfaces, probably no one will bother to build a robot with humanlike legs. Wheels are so much simpler.

Most research on effectors centers on robot hands and arms. Early workers in this area tried to adapt the remote manipulators that are used in laboratories to handle radioactive substances. These adaptations were not very successful. The positions of the remote manipulators could not be controlled very precisely. These devices depended very heavily on the human operator watching what the remote manipulators were doing and correcting their positions accordingly. With this visual feedback the operator could do complicated things like screwing the top on a jar, screwing in a light bulb, or striking a match. But with his eyes closed the operator was helpless.

Current experimental robots use hands and arms designed specifically for robot use. The designs emphasize *simplicity* and *precision*. Simplicity means using as simple a scheme of joints as possible. This is to simplify the task of converting between internal

157

and workspace coordinates, to reduce the number of joints that have to be moved simultaneously, and to produce a given motion of the hand. Precision means being able to generate signals to the motors that will move the hand very close to the desired position. This prevents the robot from having to observe the hand as it moves and continuously modify the commands to the motors to correct for errors in the mechanism. (This is what the unsatisfactory remote manipulators required.)

Imitating the human hand and arm is not necessarily the best approach. Continuously rotating wrists are useful for screwing and unscrewing. A telescoping forearm may provide greater simplicity and precision than an imitation of the human elbow.

Current robot arms use either electric motors or pneumatic or hydraulic devices to actuate the hands and arms. The resulting manipulators are quite strong and can handle substantial loads. Under the control of an un-debugged computer program they can also be quite dangerous; at research laboratories robots are often enclosed in cages to prevent bystanders from being hurt by the flailing of powerful but imperfectly controlled arms.

The design of robot hands has become a speciality in itself. For industrial robots the hands are often the tools needed to do the job. The arm of a welding robot would end in a welder; the arm of a painting robot, in a paint sprayer; and so on. These specialized "hands" could be interchangeable; a robot could fit itself in succession with a welder, a screwdriver, a drill, a paint sprayer, a soldering iron, a wrench, and so on, depending on the job to be done.

But even industrial robots require general purpose hands for picking up and positioning the parts being worked on. The simplest general purpose hand consists of parallel jaws, like the jaws of a vise or a pipe wrench. Some experimentation has been done with more complicated hands, but none tested so far come anywhere near to having the versatility of the human hand and fingers. Exactly what design will be best is far from clear; the best design may very well depend on the job for which the robot is intended. And as with arms, imitating the human body slavishly may not be the best way to proceed. When a versatile robot hand is finally designed it may not look very much like a human hand and fingers at all.

## SENSORS

If a robot is to rise above the level of the simple industrial manipulators described earlier, it must be able to sense and respond to its environment.

The most obvious approach is to use a TV-camera eye to let the robot see what is going on around it. Unfortunately, this is not the simplest approach; in fact it is the most complicated. As we saw in the chapter on pattern recognition, image analysis and scene description are still in an imperfect state. At present this kind of analysis can be reliably carried out only on scenes with restricted content, such as those consisting entirely of blocks of various sizes and shapes. And even in these simple situations the programs required for image analysis are long and complex. They must execute on a large, fast computer if they are to yield results quickly enough to be of any use to the robot.

Until the technology of image analysis improves, then, practical robots will probably use simpler sensors than TV cameras.

A robot must be able to locate itself in the room it occupies. If the robot is to follow a fixed path in the room—for example, a delivery robot that must drive down the center of a corridor in going from one room to another—a cable beneath the floor carrying an electric current can be used. Electric sensors mounted on the robot can detect the current and so allow the robot to position itself over the cable.

Sonar, employed by bats, dolphins, and submarines, can be used by robots not only to locate themselves with respect to the walls of the room but also to detect obstacles in their paths as well as the objects they are supposed to manipulate. The robot periodically transmits a pulse of ultrasound; returning echoes indicate the presence of walls and obstacles. The time lag between the transmission of the pulse and the return of the echo gives the distance to the wall or obstacle.

The resolution of sonar—its ability to detect fine details—is limited because of the long wavelength of sound waves. Thus sonar is more useful for detecting obstacles and for locating the robot in a room than for supervising detailed work.

Laser beams have been used in robot sensors in several ways. For instance, the laser can be used like sonar; a burst of light can be transmitted and the time required for the reflected light to return can be measured. Because of the narrowness of the laser beam and the short wavelength of light, the direction of the reflecting obstacle can be located much more precisely than with sonar. On the other hand, because of the very high speed of light, this method only works for obstacles about a meter or more away from the robot. For closer objects the time lag between transmitted pulse and the return is too short to measure.

For closer objects the *intensity* of the reflected laser beam can be used to gauge the distance to the object. At least one robot hand directs light beams from LEDs toward the object the hand is trying to grasp. The intensity of the returning beams is used to position the hand with respect to the object.

Projected light from lasers and other sources can be used to aid scene analysis. For instance, a laser beam can be spread into a thin sheet of light using a cylindrical lens. When this sheet of light strikes an object, a thin line of light, which reveals the contours of the object, is seen. The sheet of light can be scanned over a scene. A TV camera observes the lines formed where the sheet of light encounters objects; this information is then used for scene analysis. Another approach is to project a checkerboard-like grid over the scene. Observing the distortions of the grid as it falls on various objects aids the scene analysis program in determining the sizes and shapes of the objects.

A robot requires a sense of touch as well as of sight. The simplest touch sensors are simply microswitches that close when the hand or arm on which they are mounted encounters an object. More advanced sensors use strain gauges to measure the force which a hand, say, is exerting on the object it holds.

Force sensors become important when a robot is attempting to assemble parts. Because of slight misalignments the parts will usually not go together smoothly on the first try. By measuring the forces exerted on the robot's hand as it attempts to assemble the parts, the controlling computer can determine the nature of the misalignment. It can then send corrective commands to the robot hand so as to align the parts correctly. The force sensors for this purpose can be mounted on the robot's wrist, where they measure the forces exerted on the entire hand.

## CONTROL

All the other chapters of this book are relevant to the control of robots: A robot-control program must maintain a data base or world model containing a description of the robot's surroundings. Problem solving is required to determine which actions will successfully carry out an assigned task in this environment. Problem solving, in turn, involves state-graph and problem-reduction search, planning, heuristics, and logical reasoning. Even the heuristic techniques discussed in connection with game playing can prove useful. Pattern recognition is needed to extract information from sensor readings. If commands to the robot are given in English, natural-language processing is called for. And finally, many, if not most, experimental robots have been programmed in LISP!

Robot control has a few special features of its own, of course. For one thing, it is usually not practical for high-level problem solving programs to work directly with such low-level details as the positions of an arm or wrist joint. Instead the control program is organized into *layers*, or *levels*. The top layer receives high-level commands from the outside world. The bottom layer sends extremely detailed commands to the mechanisms that actuate the robot's effectors.

The intermediate layers work at intermediate levels of detail. The task of each layer is to receive commands from the layer above it and translate these into commands that can be handled by the layer below. (This translation often requires problem solving.) To each layer the layer below it looks like a machine which can accept a certain set of commands. As one goes through the layers from top to bottom, the commands become less powerful and more detailed. At the top layer we can command the robot to assemble a machine from its parts or to place items in boxes. At the lowest level we can command it to rotate its wrist by 5 degrees say, or close the jaws of its hand by 10 centimeters. Each layer represents a robot that will accept commands at a different level of detail. Notice that these different levels of detail fit in well with the ideas of hierarchical planning, described in Chapter 5.

Actually, each level not only receives commands from above, it receives feedback information from below showing what the robot is actually doing. Each level is responsible not only for issuing commands to the next lower level but also for using the feedback information to monitor the execution of those commands and see that they are carried out correctly. If a command is executed improperly, a level must issue additional commands to correct the situation.

# Chapter 10
# Computational Logic:
# Propositions and Predicates

A robot must often use logical reasoning to deduce facts about its environment. This is particularly true when changing one part of the environment causes some change in another part.

Suppose the robot is in a room with a door and a window. By the door is a table, and on the table is a box. The robot's knowledge of its environment could be expressed in part by the following three statements:

1. The table is by the door.
2. The box is on the table.
3. The box is by the door.

Now suppose the robot moves the table so that it is now by the window. Obviously statement 1 must be changed to read:

1'. The table is by the window.

What should be done about statements 2 and 3 is less obvious, at least to the robot. Is the box still on the table after the move? If it is, then obviously (but not to the robot) statement 3 needs to be changed to read:

3'. The box is by the window.

Let us say that the table is moved "carefully" if items resting on the table are not disturbed. The robot could reason as follows:

- If the box was on the table and I moved the table carefully, then the box is on the table.
- The box was on the table.
- I moved the table carefully.
- Therefore, the box is on the table.

Statement 2, then, can remain unchanged.

For statement 3 the robot can reason:

- If the table is by the window and the box is on the table, then the box is by the window.
- The box is on the table.
- The table is by the window.
- Therefore, the box is by the window.

Statement 3, then, would have to be changed to statement 3′.

You may say that the robot could simply look and see where the box was. But if it were trying to plan a complicated sequence of actions in its "head" before actually carrying them out, it would have to have some way of knowning that moving the table would also move the box.

A robot may have to use logical reasoning to deduce when a goal state has been reached or how to reach it in the first place. Suppose the robot's orders were to move the table so that the box would be by the window. It would have to deduce that when the table is by the window, the box is also by the window, and so its goal has been achieved.

Two other areas in which logical reasoning is important are:

1. Proving mathematical theorems.
2. Proving computer programs to be correct. That is, proving a computer program will in fact solve the problem it was designed to solve, and thus is free from "bugs."

Finally, the formalism developed for logical reasoning provides one possible framework for representing knowledge about the outside world inside the computer.

Computational logic—doing logical reasoning with a computer—is based on what is traditionally known as *symbolic logic*, or *mathematical logic*. This, in turn, is divided into two parts, the simpler *propositional logic* and the more complex *predicate logic*.

(The terms *propositional calculus* and *predicate calculus* are often used. The term *calculus* here just means a system for calculating. It has nothing to do with the more familiar differential and integral calculus.)

## PROPOSITIONAL LOGIC

In logic a proposition is simply a statement that can be either true or false. Some examples of propositions are:

"The box is on the table."
"The robot is by the window."
"The sun will rise tomorrow morning."

A proposition is *true* if it is in accord with the facts of the real world. (Or the facts that are being supposed for some particular purpose, as when we contemplate an imaginary world, either for amusement or because of the light it sheds on the real world.) If the proposition is not in accord with the actual or supposed facts, it is *false*. In symbolic logic we often abbreviate true to T and false to F.

Prospositions are usually represented by single letters, much as letters are used to represent numerical quantities in algebra. The letters most commonly used for propositions are *p*, *q*, *r*, and *s*. For example, we might let

> *p* stand for "The box is on the table."
> *q* stand for "The robot is by the window."
> *r* stand for "The sun will rise tomorrow morning."

Then everytime I use *p*, *q*, or *r*, it is as if I used the corresponding proposition. If I make the statement

$$p$$

for instance I am saying

> The box is on the table.

If I say

$$p \text{ or } q$$

I am saying

> The box is on the table or the robot is by the window.

Of course, the correspondence between letters and propositions is not permanent. In algebra we may let *a* stand for 5 and *b* stand for 10 in one problem, and *a* stand for 20 and *b* stand for −100 in another. In the same way, *p* can stand for

> "The box is on the table"

in one problem and

> "It rained yesterday."

in another.

In algebra we often use *a*, *b*, *c*, *d*, and so on to discuss principles and relationships that must hold regardless of what values are eventually substituted for *a*, *b*, *c*, and *d*. In the same way we will often use *p*, *q*, *r*, and *s* in discussions that will hold regardless of what propositions are substituted for the letters. Such discussions are often introduced with statements such as, "let *p* and *q* be any propositions."

## Connectives

There is not much we can do with a single proposition. Logic only starts to get interesting and useful when we join propositions together with connectives such as *or, and, not,* and *implies* to make new propositions.

As Table 10-1 shows, the mathematicians use a variety of exotic symbols to represent these connectives. To make our logical expressions easier to read (and easier to type and print as well) we will follow the lead of some programming languages and use **or, and, not,** and **implies** to represent the connectives. These are set in boldface type to remind us that they are special symbols, not just English words that have somehow found their way into our logical expressions.

When two propositions are joined by a connective, the resulting expression stands for another proposition whose meaning is specified by the original propositions and the connective.

For example, if *p, q,* and *r* stand for the propositions given in the last section, then the expression

**not** *p*

stands for

"The box is not on the table."

and

*p* **or** *q*

stands for

"The box is on the table or the robot is by the window."

## Truth Tables

Suppose we are given some expression involving propositions and logical connectives. Suppose further that we know whether each individual proposition in the expression is true or false. We would like to be able to calculate whether or not the proposition represented by the entire expression is true or false.

**Table 10-1. Typical Mathematical Logic Symbols**

| | Connective | Symbols |
|---|---|---|
| | **and** | ∧ & • |
| | **or** | ∨ \| |
| | **not** | ~ ⌐ |
| | **implies** | ⊃ → |

We can do this in two steps. First we assign each proposition in the expression a *truth value* of either T or F. True propositions get the value T and false ones get the value F.

Second, we treat the connectives **and, or, not,** and **implies** as operators operating on T and F, just like the $+$, $-$, X, and $/$ in an algebraic expression operate on numbers. In other words, we do "logical arithmetic" to calculate the truth value of the entire expression.

Now to do ordinary arithmetic we need addition and multiplication tables for determining the sum or the product of two numbers. In the same way we need **or, and, not,** and **implies** tables to do logical arithmetic. Each table allows us to calculate the effect of the corresponding operator on the values T and F. Such tables are called *truth tables*.

The simplest logic connective is **not.** If $p$ is any proposition, then $p$ will be true if **not** $p$ is false, and vice versa. We can represent this fact with the following truth table:

| $p$ | **not** $p$ |
|-----|-------------|
| T   | F           |
| F   | T           |

Thus if we do not know what proposition $p$ stands for, we do know that if $p$ has the truth value T, then **not** $p$ will have the value F, and vice versa.

The proposition

$$p \text{ or } q$$

is true if $p$ is ture, if $q$ is true, or if both are true. This gives us the following truth table for **or:**

| $p$ | $q$ | $p$ **or** $q$ |
|-----|-----|----------------|
| T   | T   | T              |
| T   | F   | T              |
| F   | T   | T              |
| F   | F   | F              |

The fact that $p$ **or** $q$ is true when both $p$ is true and $q$ is true identifies the **or** of symbolic logic as the *inclusive* **or.** Care must be taken when translating statements into symbolic form, since in English we sometimes use *or* in the *exclusive* sense, meaning that one thing or another is true, but not both.

The proposition

$$p \text{ and } q$$

is true only if both $p$ is true and $q$ is true. This gives us the following truth table for **and:**

166

| $p$ | $q$ | $p$ and $q$ |
|---|---|---|
| T | T | T |
| T | F | F |
| F | T | F |
| F | F | F |

The connective **implies** is slightly tricky. The proposition

$$p \text{ implies } q$$

corresponds to the English statement

"If $p$ then $q$."

That is, we are saying that if the proposition $p$ is true then the proposition $q$ is also true. On the other hand, if $p$ is false, we are saying nothing about the truth or falsity of $q$.

Thus the only way in which $p$ **implies** $q$ can be false is if $p$ is true and $q$ is false. This gives the following truth table:

| $p$ | $q$ | $p$ implies $q$ |
|---|---|---|
| T | T | T |
| T | F | F |
| F | T | T |
| F | F | T |

Let us dwell for a moment longer on the peculiarities of **implies**. In the first place, one proposition can imply another even though they seem to have nothing to do with one another.

Suppose, for instance, that

$p$ stands for "The earth moves around the sun."
$q$ stands for "The speed of light is 186,000 miles/second."

Then

$$p \text{ implies } q$$

is true since both statements are true (the first row of the truth table). This is in spite of the fact the earth moving around the sun and the speed of light have nothing whatever to do with one another.

Even more curious is that a *false proposition implies any proposition*. Suppose

$p$ stands for "The earth moves around the sun."
$q$ stands for "I have a pet unicorn."
$r$ stands for "I have a pet roc."

Again $p$ is true, but $q$ and $r$ must be false, since the unicorn and the roc are mythical beasts. But

$$r \text{ implies } p$$

and

$$r \text{ implies } q$$

are both true, according to the last two lines of the truth table.

Thus the truth of

$$p \text{ implies } q$$

says that when $p$ is true, $q$ will be true, and *nothing more*. It does not say that $p$ and $q$ have any cause-and-effect relationship to one another. And if $p$ is false, then nothing whatever is asserted about $q$.

## Arguments

Given that certain propositions are true, we wish to deduce that others are true in consequence. One way to do this would be to assign truth values of T or F to propositions whose truth or falsity are known and then try to calculate the truth values of the propositions of interest. But often a more direct approach is to devise rules that will allow new true propositions to be deduced from those known to be true. We then use those rules to deduce the propositions of interest from those we know to be true.

Such rules are called *argument forms*. They specify forms of argument which can be shown to be valid. If we argue for the truth of a proposition using only these valid forms, we can rest assured that the conclusion we reach does indeed follow from the premises we assumed.

For example, here is an argument form which in traditional logic is called conjunction.

| | |
|---|---|
| p | (Premise) |
| q | (Premise) |
| p **and** q | (Conclusion) |

The propositions above the horizontal line are the *premises*, which are assumed to be true. The proposition below the line is the *conclusion*. The truth of the conclusion is guaranteed if the premises are true.

The conjunction argument form assures us that if two propositions are known to be true, then the proposition that results from joining the two by **and** is also true. The following is an example of an argument of this form:

| | |
|---|---|
| The book is on the table. | (Premise) |
| The table is by the window. | (Premise) |
| The book is on the table and the table is by the window. | (Conclusion) |

An agument form can be shown to be valid by constructing a truth table for the premises and the conclusion. We then examine every row in the truth table for which the premises are all true—have T entires. If for every one of those rows the conclusion also has a T entry, the argument form is valid. For in that case, whenever the premises are true, the truth table assures us that the conclusion will be true also.

We can validate conjunction using the truth table for **and**, which contains both the premises and the conclusion. There is only one row, the first one, for which both premises are true. In that row the conclusion is also true, and so conjunction is validated.

Here is another argument form, called *Modus Ponens* (MP):

| | |
|---|---|
| $p$ | (Premises) |
| $p$ **implies** $q$ | (Premises) |
| $q$ | (Conclusion) |

MP informs us that if a proposition is true, and that proposition implies another proposition, then the other proposition is also true. An example of an MP argument is the following:

| | |
|---|---|
| It is raining. | (Premise) |
| If it is raining, I must take my umbrella. | (Premise) |
| I must take my umbrella. | (Conclusion) |

We can verify the validity of MP by consulting the truth table for **implies**. Again we find only one row in which both the premises are true, and in that row the conclusion is also true.

Note that the $p$, $q$, and so on that appear in argument forms stand for any propositions. In particular, they can stand for propositions that are themselves given by expressions involving connectives. Thus

| | |
|---|---|
| $p$ **and** $q$ | (Premise) |
| ($p$ **and** $q$) **implies** $r$ | (Premise) |
| $r$ | (Conclusion) |

is also an example of Modus Ponens. Note that when an expression is substituted for a letter in another expression, the substituted expression is enclosed in parentheses.

Now let us use conjunction and Modus Ponens to formalize the robot's argument, given earlier, that the box is by the window when it is on the table and the table is by the window. Let

| | | |
|---|---|---|
| $p$ | stand for | "The table is by the window. |
| $q$ | stand for | "The box is on the table." |
| $r$ | stand for | "The box is by the window." |

The premises for the argument are:

$p$

$q$

($p$ and $q$) implies $r$

The argument itself is written as a series of numbered steps starting with the premises and ending with the conclusion. To the right of each step is a comment showing from which previous steps the current one was derived, and what argument form was used (C stands for conjunction and MP for Modus Ponens):

| | |
|---|---|
| 1. $p$ | (Premise) |
| 2. $q$ | (Premise) |
| 3. ($p$ and $q$) implies $r$ | (Premise) |
| 4. $p$ and $q$ | (1, 2, C) |
| 5. $r$ | (3, 4, MP) |

Steps 1 through 3 are the premises. Step 4 is obtained by applying C to steps 1 and 2. Step 5, the conclusion, results from applying MP to steps 3 and 4. (Note: it does not matter in what order the premises of an argument form occur.)

Finally, it is worth looking at an *invalid* argument form. The following is sometimes known facetiously as *Modus Moron:*

$q$

$p$ implies $q$

$p$

Advertising and politics abound with examples of Modus Moron:

Jones favors closer ties with Cuba.

If Jones were a communist, he would favor closer ties with Cuba.

___

Jones is a communist.

To see that Modus Moron is invalid, we return to the truth table for **implies**. In the third row we see that both of the premises of Modus Moron are true, but its conclusion is false. Since the truth of the premises does not guarantee the truth of the conclusion, Modus Moron is an invalid argument form.

Traditional logic features a large number of argument forms, all of which can be easily verified using simple truth tables. In the next chapter we will see how all the traditional forms can be replaced by a single deductive principle. Therefore, we will not pursue the traditional argument forms any further.

## PREDICATE LOGIC

### Individuals and Predicates

Propositional logic is limited in that it deals only with complete statements. It provides no way to break a statement down into the things about which something is being asserted and the assertion that is being made about them. Predicate logic remedies this limitation.

Consider the proposition

The box is on the table.

This proposition deals with two items from the real world:

the box
the table

A relationship between the box and the table is specified by the words

is on

In predicate logic the items about which a proposition makes an assertion are called *individuals*. For convenience in writing expressions, individuals are given one-word names. Let us name the individuals in the above proposition as follows:

| Individual | One-Word Name |
|---|---|
| the box | BOX |
| the table | TABLE |

The part of the proposition which makes an assertion about the individuals is called the *predicate*. We also give each predicate a one-word name:

| Predicate | One-Word Name |
|---|---|
| is on | ON |

Finally, the original proposition can be written in terms of the predicate and the individuals:

ON(BOX, TABLE)

The predicate is given first, with the individuals following in parentheses. Since this is not the order used in English, it will seem a little strange at first. But one quickly gets used to it.

The individuals that are placed in parentheses following a predicate are called its *arguments*. This is a special use of the word argument, which has nothing to do with the use introduced in the section on propositional logic.

A predicate, together with its arguments, is a proposition. Any of the operations of propositional logic may be applied to it.

For example, let us again go through the robot's reasoning about the table, the box, and the window, but this time using predicates and individuals instead of representing each proposition by a single letter.

We need one more individual

| Individual | One-Word Name |
|------------|---------------|
| the window | WINDOW |

and one more predicate

| Predicate | One-Word Name |
|-----------|---------------|
| is by | BY |

The premises of the robot's argument are

BY(TABLE, WINDOW)
ON(BOX, TABLE)
BY(TABLE, WINDOW) **and** ON(BOX, TABLE)) **implies** BY(BOX, WINDOW)

The argument itself proceeds as before:

1. BY(TABLE, WINDOW)                 (Premise)
2. ON(BOX, TABLE)                   (Premise)
3. (BY(TABLE, WINDOW) **and** ON(BOX, TABLE)) **implies** BY(BOX, WINDOW)       (Premise)
4. BY(TABLE, WINDOW) **and** ON(BOX, TABLE) (1, 2, C)
5. BY(BOX, WINDOW)                 (3, 4, MP)

Note that since a predicate plus its arguments is a proposition, it can be substituted for $p$, $q$, and so on in any of the argument forms of propositional logic. Thus

BY(TABLE, WINDOW)               (Premise)
ON(BOX, TABLE)                 (Premise)

---

BY(TABLE, WINDOW) **and** ON(BOX, TABLE) (Conclusion)

is an example of conjunction.

## Individual Variables

So far we have merely found another way to write propositions. But in terms of the statements and arguments we can make, we have not yet gone beyond propositional logic.

*Individual variables* (or just *variables*) allow us to make statements that would be impossible in propositional logic.

A variable stands for *any* individual. For a proposition containing variables to be true, it must be true regardless on what individual names are substituted for the variables.

We will use the letters $x$, $y$, and $z$ for variables.

Now consider the following proposition:

(BY(TABLE, WINDOW) **and** ON($x$, TABLE)) **implies** BY($x$, WINDOW)

translated into English this reads:

*If the table is by the window and something is on the table, then that thing is by the window.*

Notice the slightly clumsy use of "something" and "that thing." English does not have anything directly equivalent to a variable.

If we assert the above proposition to be true, we are asserting its truth for any individual whose name is substituted for $x$. Thus at one stroke we are asserting

(BY(TABLE, WINDOW) **and** ON(BOOK, TABLE)) **implies**
        BY(BOOK, WINDOW)
(BY(TABLE, WINDOW) **and** ON(BALL, TABLE)) **implies**
        BY(BALL, WINDOW)
(BY(TABLE, WINDOW) **and** ON(VASE, TABLE)) **implies**
        BY(VASE, WINDOW)
(BY(TABLE, WINDOW) **and** ON(PEN, TABLE)) **implies**
        BY(PEN, WINDOW)

and so on for all the other objects whose names could be substituted for $x$.

We could make our statement even more general by using two variables:

(BY(TABLE, $x$) **and** ON($y$, TABLE)) **implies** BY($y$, $x$)

Translated into English this says

*If the table is by something, then anything on the table is also by that thing.*

Again the English version is clumsy.

A few of the many statements incorporated in the above are:

(BY(TABLE, DOOR) **and** ON(GLASS, TABLE)) **implies**
        BY(GLASS, DOOR)
(BY(TABLE, CHAIR) **and** ON(BOOK, TABLE)) **implies**
        BY(BOOK, CHAIR)
(BY(TABLE, ROBOT) **and** ON(VASE, TABLE)) **implies**
        BY(VASE, ROBOT)

For the most general possible version of our proposition we would use three variables:

(BY($x$, $y$) **and** ON($z$, $x$)) **implies** BY($z$, $y$)

The only practical way to translate this into English is to use variables in the English sentence:

*If x is by y and z is on x, then z is also by y.*

Even though some expressions of predicate logic are difficult to represent in English, others can provide very effective representations of English sentences. This is particularly true when the sentence contains "all" or "no" (the latter in the sense of "none").

For instance, the English sentence

*All men are mortal.*

can be expressed as

MAN($x$) **implies** MORTAL ($x$)

which literally says

*If anything is a man, then it is mortal.*

The sentence

*No animals are unicorns.*

can be expressed as

ANIMAL($x$) **implies** (**not** UNICORN($x$))

which reads literally

*If anything is an animal, it is not a unicorn.*


## Instantiation

Substituting the name of a particular individual for a variable is known as *instantiation*. The individual is a particular "instance" of the variable, and hence the name "instantiation." In formal arguments we will abbreviate instantiation to IS.

For example, here is a traditional argument whose subject matter indicates its age:

*All men are mortal.*
*Socrates is a man.*
*Therefore, Socrates is mortal.*

In predicate logic this becomes

1. MAN($x$) **implies** MORTAL($x$)          (Premise)
2. MAN(SOCRATES)                              (Premise)
3. MAN(SOCRATES) **implies** MORTAL(SOCRATES)(1, IS)
4. MORTAL(SOCRATES)                           (2, 3, MP)

Step 3 was obtained by substituting SOCRATES for $x$ in step 1.

As another example of instantiation, let us do the robot's argument using the following premises:

BY(TABLE, WINDOW)

ON(BOX, TABLE)

$\qquad$ (BY($x$, $y$) **and** ON($z$, $x$)) **implies** BY($z$, $y$)

The argument goes as follows:

1. BY(TABLE, WINDOW) $\hfill$ (Premise)
2. ON(BOX, TABLE) $\hfill$ (Premise)
3. (BY($x$, $y$) **and** ON($z$, $x$)) **implies** BY($z$, $y$) $\hfill$ (Premise)
4. (BY(TABLE, WINDOW) **and** ON(BOX, TABLE)) **implies** BY(BOX, WINDOW) $\hfill$ (3, IS)
5. BY(TABLE, WINDOW) **and** ON(BOX, TABLE) $\hfill$ (1, 2, C)
6. BY(BOX, WINDOW) $\hfill$ (4, 5, C)

Step 4 results from step 3 by substituting TABLE for $x$, WINDOW for $y$, and BOX for $z$.

### Existence and Functions

Sometimes we need to assert merely that something exists without further specifying it. For instance, we may wish to say that

$\qquad$ There is a box on the table.

without further specifying the box.

We assert that something exists by making up a name for it and using that name in our expressions. We will use letters $a$, $b$, $c$, and $d$ for these made up names. These letters are called *individual constants*.

We could assert that there is a box on the table, then, by writing

$\qquad$ BOX($a$) **and** ON($a$, TABLE)

The individual constant $a$ is the made-up name for the box that happens to be on the table. The only things we know about $a$ are those implied by the above proposition: (1) $a$ is a box, and (2) $a$ is on the table.

Sometimes the individual whose existence we wish to assert will depend on some other individual. For instance, we might like to say

$\qquad$ Every person has a mother.

But obviously we cannot use the same individual constant for the mother of everybody! We need a way of saying that every person has some mother, but the mothers of different persons are (usually) different.

We do this with *functions*. In mathematics and computer programming a function is something that when applied to a value yields another value. The square root function in BASIC, for instance, always yields the square root of its argument:

$$SQR(4) = 2$$
$$SQR(9) = 3$$
$$SQR(16) = 4$$
$$SQR(25) = 5$$

and so on.

When SQR is applied to a number it yields the square root of that number. Now imagine a function, say $f$, that when applied to an individual yields the mother of that individual. Thus we may have

$$f(JOHN) = SUE$$
$$f(JACK) = JANE$$
$$f(JANE) = MARY$$
$$f(JOE) = HELEN$$

and so on.

This function is what we need to assert that every person has a mother. We write

PERSON($x$) **implies** MOTHER ($f(x)$, $x$)

This says that for any individual whose name might be substituted for $x$, if that individual is a person, then that individual has a mother, denoted by $f(x)$. The fact that the mother of $x$, $f(x)$, depends on $x$ shows that different individuals generally have different mothers.

As with individual constants, the only things we know about a function are those implied by the propositions in which it appears. Thus all we know about $f$ is:

- $f(x)$ is defined only when $x$ is a person.
- $f(x)$ is the mother of $x$.

We will use the letters $f$, $g$, and $h$ for functions.

In mathematical logic two kinds of variables are used. The *universal variables*, like the variables we have been using all along, specify that a proposition will be true for any individuals whose names are substituted for the variables. The *existential variables* specify that certain individuals exist. Each proposition is given a special prefix that specifies which variables are used universally and which are used existentially. In computational logic, however, it usually turns out to be more convenient to just use universal variables, and to use individual constants and functions to indicate existence.

# Chapter 11
# Computational
# Logic: Resolution

Almost without exception modern computational logic programs use a technique known as *resolution*. Resolution is a method of deduction which replaces all the many argument forms of traditional logic. Although many aspects of resolution are quite technical, and hence beyond the scope of this introductory book, we can without too much trouble understand the basic principles on which resolution-based computational-logic programs operate.

## THE RESOLUTION PRINCIPLE

Computational logic has a vocabulary of its own. While we will try to avoid introducing too much technical jargon here, a few technical terms will prove useful.

An *atom* is a proposition that cannot be broken down into other propositions. A proposition represented by a single letter, such as $p$, is an atom, as is a predicate together with its arguments, such as ON(BOX, TABLE). On the other hand,

$$p \text{ and } q$$
BY (TABLE, WINDOW) **and** ON(BOX, TABLE)

are not atoms.

A *literal* is either an atom, or an atom preceded by **not**. Thus

**p**        ON(BOX, TABLE)
**not** $p$    **not** ON(BOX, TABLE)

are all literals. A literal is *positive* if it is not preceded by **not** and *negative* if it is:

| Positive Literals | Negative Literals |
|---|---|
| $p$ | **not** $p$ |
| ON(BOX, TABLE) | **not** ON(BOX, TABLE) |

A *clause* is a series of literals joined by **or**. Thus

$$p \text{ or } q$$
$$(\text{not } p) \text{ or } q$$
$$p \text{ or } (\text{not } q)$$
$$(\text{not } p) \text{ or } (\text{not } q)$$
$$\text{ON(BOX, TABLE) or ON(BOX, DESK)}$$

are all clauses.

The connective **or** can be generalized to connect more than two propositions. We define

$$p \text{ or } q \text{ or } r \text{ or } s \text{ or...}$$

to be true if *at least one* of the propositions $p$, $q$, $r$, $s$, ... is true, and to be false if $p$, $q$, $r$, $s$, ... are all false.

If a proposition occurs more than once in a sequence of propositions, the duplicate occurrences can be eliminated. Thus

$$p \text{ or } q \text{ or } r \text{ or } q \text{ and } p \text{ or } q \text{ or } r$$

are equivalent propositions. That we can eliminate duplicates follows from the phrase *at least one* in the definition of **or**. If $q$ is true, then one occurrence of $q$ is enough to make the entire proposition true; additional occurrences will not make it any truer. And if $q$ is false it will not influence the truth of the entire proposition no matter how many times it occurs.

The order in which $p$, $q$, $r$, $s$, ... occur is also immaterial, since this order plays no role in the definition of **or**.

Using this generalized definition of **or**, then, we can say that a clause has the form

$$l \text{ or } m \text{ or } n \text{ or } o \text{ or } ...$$

where $l$, $m$, $n$, $o$, ... are all literals, propositions that are atoms or negated atoms.

The resolution principle is an argument form that applies to clauses. Consider the two clauses

$$p \text{ or } l \text{ or } m \text{ or } ...$$
$$(\text{not } p) \text{ or } n \text{ or } o \text{ or } ...$$

where $p$ is a proposition and $l$, $m$, $n$, $o$, ... are arbitrarily literals. The resolution principle assures that if both of these propositions are true, then the proposition $l$ or $m$ or $n$ or $o$ ... is also true. Formally, we define the argument form Resolution (R):

| | |
|---|---|
| $p$ or $l$ or $m$ or ... | (Premise) |
| $(\text{not } p)$ or $n$ or $o$ or ... | (Premise) |
| $l$ or $m$ or $n$ or $o$ ... | (Conclusion) |

The positive and negative literals *p* and **not** *p* "cancel out," and all the remaining literals are combined into a single clause.

We can easily argue for the validity of resolution. Suppose that *p* is false. If *p* **or** *l* **or** *m* **or** ... is true, then one of the propositions *p*, *l*, *m*, ... must be true. Since *p* is false, one of the literals *l*, *m*, ... must be true.

What if *p* is true? Then **not** *p* is false. If (**not** *p*) **or** *n* **or** *o* **or** ... is true then one of the propositions (**not** *p*), *n*, *o*, ... must be true.

Thus, regardless of whether *p* is true or false, one of the literals *l*, *m*, *n*, *o*, ... must be true. Hence, by the definition of **or**, *l* **or** *m* **or** *n* **or** *o* **or** ... must be true.

If we limit the number of propositions involved, we can validate resolution using a truth table. Table 11-1 shows the truth table for the following special case of resolution:

$$p \text{ or } l$$
$$\underline{(\text{not } p) \text{ or } m}$$
$$l \text{ or } m$$

If the same literal occurs in both the premises of a resolution, it will occur in duplicate in the conclusion. But duplicate literals in clauses can be eliminated, and we always will eliminate them without specific mention.

Here are some examples of resolutions:

(a)
$$p \text{ or } (\text{not } q)$$
$$\underline{(\text{not } p) \text{ or } r}$$
$$(\text{not } q) \text{ or } r$$

(b)

$$(\text{not MAN(SOCRATES)}) \text{ or MORTAL(SOCRATES)}$$
$$\underline{\text{MAN(SOCRATES)}}$$
$$\text{MORTAL(SOCRATES)}$$

**Table 11-1. Truth Table Verifying A Special Case of Resolution**

| *p* | *l* | *m* | not *p* | *p* or *l* | (not *p*) or *m* | *m* or *l* |
|---|---|---|---|---|---|---|
| T | T | T | F | T | T | T* |
| T | T | F | F | T | F | T |
| T | F | T | F | T | T | T* |
| T | F | F | F | T | F | F |
| F | T | T | T | T | T | T* |
| F | T | F | T | T | T | T* |
| F | F | T | T | F | T | T |
| F | F | F | T | F | T | F |

*denotes both premises true; in each one, conclusion also true

(c)

> The sun is shining or I will take my umbrella.
> The sun is not shining.
> _____
> I will take my umbrella

Now consider the following resolution:

$$p$$
$$\underline{(\textbf{not } p)}$$

The literals $p$ and **not** $p$ cancel each other out, and we are left with the *empty clause*, which contains no literals at all. It is customary to denote the empty clause with the square.

Another way of looking at the empty clause is as representing a *contradiction*. In the above resolution $p$ and ($\textbf{not } p$) are the premises. That means we are asserting both $p$ and **not** $p$ to be true. But this is impossible—if $p$ is true, then **not** $p$ is false, and vice versa. We have contradicted ourselves, and as a result our premises cancel out, and we are left with the empty clause.

This turns out to be true in general. We can only derive the empty clause by resolving a single proposition agains the negation of the same proposition. Therefore, if an argument ends with the empty clause, the premises contained a contradiction that allowed both a proposition and its negation to be derived.

A contradiction may seem to be something to be avoided, but instead it turns out to be the key to the resolution principle. We derive a conclusion from a set of premises by resolution as follows:

- Take the given premises and *the negation of the desired conclusion* as a new set of premises.
- From this new set of premises derive the empty clause.
- Since assuming the original premises to be true and the desired conclusion to be false leads to a contradiction, the desired conclusion must be true whenever the premises are true. Or, in other words, the desired conclusion follows from the premises.

This is the method of reasoning that mathematicians call *reductio ad absurdum*—reduction to absurdity. One assumes that what one is trying to prove is false and shows that this leads to an "absurdity"—a contradiction.

Here are two simple examples of proof by resolution:

(a) Original Premises:
   (**not** MAN(SOCRATES)) **or** MORTAL(SOCRATES)
   MAN(SOCRATES)

Desired Conclusion:

MORTAL(SOCRATES)

Proof:

1. **(not** MAN(SOCRATES)) **or** MORTAL(SOCRATE-
   S)                                             (Premise)
2. MAN(SOCRATES)                                 (Premise)
3. **not** MORTAL(SOCRATES)          (Negated Conclusion)
4. MORTAL(SOCRATES)                          (1, 2, R)
5. □                                         (3, 4, R)

(b) Original Premises:

(**not** ANIMAL(ROVER)) **or** (not UNICORN(ROVER))
ANIMAL(ROVER)

Desired Conclusion:

**not** UNICORN(ROVER)

Proof:

1. **(not** ANIMAL(ROVER)) **or** (**not** UNICORN(ROVE-
   R))                                          (Premise)
2. ANIMAL(ROVER)                                 (Premise)
3. UNICORN(ROVER)                    (Negated Conclusion)
4. **not** UNICORN(ROVER)                     (1, 2, R)
5. □                                          3, 4, R)

As to step 3, note that not (not p) is equivalent to p, as can easily be
verified with a truth table, as is shown in the next section.

## TRANSFORMATION TO CLAUSE FORM

The resolution principle applies only to propositions that are
clauses. If the premises and negated conclusion of a resolution proof
are not in clause form, they must be converted into clauses before
the proof can be carried through.

This conversion is not easy to make intuitively, even for simple
propositions. For instance, it is apt to take some head scratching to
see that

(**not** ANIMAL(ROVER)) **or** (not UNICORN(ROVER))

is equivalent to

ANIMAL(ROVER) **implies** (**not** UNICORN(ROVER))

Fortunately we can prove a set of *identities* that will allow us to
transform propositions from one form into another much as we use
algebraic identities to manipulate algebraic equations.

Two propositions are *equivalent* if they always have the same truth value. We will use the equal sign to indicate equivalence. An identity states that two propositions are equivalent. A proposition can always be replaced by an equivalent one, since the two will always have the same truth value.

An identity is proved using a truth table. For instance, we verify the identify

$$\textbf{not (not } p) = p$$

using this truth table.

| $p$ | not $p$ | not (not $p$) |
|-----|---------|---------------|
| T | F | T |
| F | T | F |

Since the columns for $p$ and **not (not $p$)** are identical, the two will always have the same truth value, and hence are equivalent.

In the same way we can use Table 11-2 to show that

$$p \textbf{ implies } q = (\textbf{not } p) \textbf{ or } q$$

Here is a list of the identities we will need to convert propositions into clause form. All can be verified using truth tables:

    I-1.  **not (not** $p$**)** $= p$
    I-2.  $p$ **implies** $q =$ **(not** $p$**) or** $q$
    I-3.  **not** ($p$ **and** $q$) = **(not** $p$**) or (not** $q$**)**
    I-4.  **not** ($p$ **or** $q$) = **(not** $p$**) and (not** $q$**)**
    I-5.  ($p$ **and** $q$) **or** $r =$ ($p$ **or** $r$) **and** ($q$ **or** $r$)

One more principle that cannot be expressed as an identity is needed. The proposition

$$p \textbf{ and } q$$

asserts that p and q are both true. On the other hand, if we make p and q separate premises

$$p \text{ (Premise)}$$
$$q \text{ (Premise)}$$

**Table 11-2. Truth Table Proof of the Identity p implies q = (not p) or q**

| $p$ | $q$ | not $p$ | $p$ implies $q$ | (not $p$) or $q$ |
|-----|-----|---------|-----------------|------------------|
| T | T | F | T | T |
| T | F | F | F | F |
| F | T | T | T | T |
| F | F | T | T | T |

The columns for the two equivalent propositions are identical

182

then we are also asserting p and q to both be true, since all the premises of an argument are asserted to be true. Therefore

$$p \text{ and } q$$

can always be replaced by the two separate propositions

$$p$$
$$q$$

Let us call this the AND principle.

Now let us convert some propositions into clause form. The parenthesized comments on the right tell which identity or principle is used at each step:

(a) 1. MAN(SOCRATES) **implies** MORTAL(SOCRATES)
    2. (**not** MAN(SOCRATES)) **or** MORTAL(SOCRATES) (I-2)

(b) 1. ANIMAL(x) **implies** (not UNICORN (x))
    2. (**not** ANIMAL(x)) **or** (not UNICORN(x))         (I-2)

(c) 1. (BY(x, y) **and** ON(z, x)) **implies** BY(z, y)
    2. (**not** (BY(x, y) **and** ON(z, x))) **or** BY(z, y)     (I-2)
    3. (**not** BY(x, y)) **or** (**not** ON(z, x)) **or** BY(z, y)     (I-3)

(d) 1. (MAN(x) **or** WOMAN(x)) **implies** MORTAL(x)
    2. (**not** (MAN(x) **or** WOMAN(x))) **or** MORTAL(x)     (I-2)
    3. ((**not** MAN(x)) **and** (**not** WOMAN(x))) **or** MORTAL(x)(I-4)
    4. ((**not** MAN(x)) **or** MORTAL(x))
       **and** ((not WOMAN(x **or** MORTAL(x))     (I-5)
 5  a. (**not** MAN(x)) **or** MORTAL(x         (AND)
 5  b. (**not** WOMAN(x)) **or** MORTAL(x)     (AND)

(e) 1. **not** (not UNICORN(x))
    2. UNICORN(x                      (I-1)

## UNIFICATION

So far none of our example proofs usii. resolution have involved variables. Now let us try a proof where the premises contain variables.

Original Premises:

    (MAN(x) **or** WOMAN(x)) **implies** MORTAL(x)
    WOMAN(JANE)

Desired Conclusion:

    MORTAL(JANE)

Proof: (Premises have been converted to clause form):

  1. (**not** MAN(x)) **or** MORTAL(x)         (Premise)
  2. (**not** WOMAN(x)) **or** MORTAL(x)     (Premise)

3. WOMAN(JANE)                                   (Premise)
4. **not** MORTAL(JANE)                          (Negated Conclusion)
5. (**not** WOMAN(JANE)) **or** MORTAL(JANE)     (2, IS)
6. MORTAL(JANE)                                  (3, 5, R)
7. □                                             (4, 6, R)

We focus our attention on step 4, where

(**not** WOMAN($x$)) **or** MORTAL($x$)

is instantiated to

(**not** WOMAN(JANE)) or MORTAL(JANE)

by substituting JANE for $x$. This was done for the purpose of allowing the resolution

(**not** WOMAN(JANE)) **or** MORTAL(JANE)
WOMAN(JANE)
MORTAL(JANE)

to be performed.

The procedure for carrying out instantiations is known as *unification*. Unification attempts to find substitutions for variables that will make two atoms identical. (Remember that an atom is a predicate together with its arguments, such as WOMAN($x$).) There are two reasons for performing unification:

1. *Resolution*. If the two atoms that were unified (made identical) occur in different clauses and with opposite "signs" (one positive, one negative), then the clauses in which the two occur can be resolved.

2. *Factoring*. If the two atoms that were unified occur in the same clause with the same sign, then the clause contains two identical literals. The duplicate literal can be eliminated. This is called *factoring*, and the clause with the substitutions made and the duplicate literal eliminated is a *factor* of the original clause.

In order to illustrate unification, resolution, and factoring on some moderately complicated clauses, we will need a compact notation for predicates, variables, constants, and functions. Let us assume that:

| | | |
|---|---|---|
| $P, Q, R$ | stand for | Predicates |
| $x, y, z$ | stand for | Variables |
| $a, b, c$ | stand for | Constants (names of individuals) |
| $f, g, h$ | stand for | Functions |

Now consider the two atoms:

$$P(x, f(x), y)$$
$$P(a, z, g(z))$$

The variables in the two predicates are $x$, $y$, and $z$. We wish to find substitutions for these variables, if possible, that will make the two atoms identical.

We examine the two atoms from left to right. We first note that $P$, the predicate name, is the same in both atoms. If this were not true we would have to give up at once, since no substitution for variables could ever made two different predicate names the same.

Now let us look at the first argument in each atom. The arguments in question are $x$ and $a$. These can be made identical if $a$ is substituted for $x$. Making that substitution in the first atom gives:

$$P(a, f(a), y)$$
$$P(a, z, g(z))$$

We move on to the second argument in each atom. The arguments being compared are $f(a)$ and $z$. These can be made identical if we substitute $f(a)$ for $z$. Making that substitution in the second atom gives:

$$P(a, f(a), y)$$
$$P(a, f(a), g(f(a)))$$

There remains only the third argument of each atom. The third arguments are $y$ and $g(f(a))$. Substituting $g(f(a))$ for $y$ gives:

$$P(a, f(a), g(f(a)))$$
$$P(a, f(a), g(f(a)))$$

We have made the two atoms identical by means of the following three substitutions:

$a$ substituted for $x$

$f(a)$ substituted for $z$

$g(f(a))$ substituted for $y$

Now let us see two ways in which the unification just performed can be put to use. Suppose we have the two clauses:

$$P(x, f(x), y) \text{ or } Q(x, y)$$
$$(\text{not } P(a, z, g(z))) \text{ or } R(z)$$

If we make the above substitutions, which unifies the first atom in the first clause and the first atom in the second clause, we get:

$$P(a, f(a), g(f(a))) \text{ or } Q(a, g(f(a)))$$
$$(\text{not } P(a, f(a), g(f(a)))) \text{ or } R(f(a))$$

We can now apply resolution to these clauses, canceling the first literal in each, to obtain

$$Q(a, g(f(a)))\ \textbf{or}\ R(f(a))$$

On the other hand, suppose that the two atoms that were unified occur in the same clause. For example, suppose we have

$$P(x, f(x), y)\ \textbf{or}\ P(a, z, g(z))\ \textbf{or}\ Q(x, y)$$

Making the substitutions that unify the first two atoms gives:

$$P(a, f(a), g(f(a)))\ \textbf{or}\ P(a)\ f(a),\ g(f(a)))\ \textbf{or}\ Q(a, g(f(a))$$

Eliminating the duplicate literal yields:

$$P(a, f(a), g(f(a)))\ \textbf{or}\ Q(a, g(f(a)))$$

This is a factor of the original clause. It turns out that the clause in question has only one factor. But in general, different substitutions can unify different literals in a clause, and so give rise to different factors. Thus a clause may have many factors.

We can now completely describe the process of deriving a conclusion from a set of premises using resolution:

- Start off with clauses corresponding to the premises and the negation of the desired conclusion.
- Derive new clauses using unification followed by resolution or factoring.
- If the empty clause is derived, then the desired conclusion follows from the original premises. If we give up before we have derived the empty clause, however, then *either* the conclusion does not follow from the premises *or* we gave up too soon and with more work the empty clause would have eventually been derived.

As one final example of proof by resolution, Table 11-3 shows the resolution version of the robot's argument that the box is near

**Table 11-3. A Typical Proof by Resolution**

| | |
|---|---|
| 1. BY (TABLE, WINDOW) | (Premise) |
| 2. ON(BOX, TABLE) | (Premise) |
| 3. (**not** BY $(x, y)$) **or** (**not** ON $(z, x)$) **or** BY $(z, y)$ | (Premise) |
| 4. **not** BY (BOX, WINDOW) | (Negated Conclusion) |
| 5. (**not** BY (TABLE, WINDOW)) **or** (**not** ON $(z,$ TABLE)) **or** BY $(z,$ WINDOW) | (3, IS)[1] |
| 6. (**not** ON $(z,$ TABLE)) **or** BY $(z,$ WINDOW) | (1, 5, R) |
| 7. (**not** ON (BOX, TABLE)) **or** BY (BOX, WINDOW) | (6, IS)[2] |
| 8. BY (BOX, WINDOW) | (2, 7, R) |
| 9. □ | (4, 8, R) |

[1]BY $(x, y)$ and BY (TABLE, WINDOW) are unified by substituting TABLE for $x$ and WINDOW for $y$. This unification permits the resolution of step 6.

[2]ON $(z,$ TABLE) and ON (BOX, TABLE) are unified by substituting BOX for $z$. This unification permits the resolution of step 8.

186

the window when the box is on the table and the table is near the window. The notes show where unification was performed and what substitutions were made. No factoring is involved in this argument, but one resolution requires a unification. The notes show which atoms were unified and what substitutions were made.

Unification is not limited to predicate logic. We will see in later chapters several more cases where expressions must be made identical by substituting for variables.

## EVALUATION

Resolution is *complete* in the sense that if the conclusion does follow from the premises, then repeated unification, resolution, and factoring will eventually derive the empty clause.

Resolution can be more easily programmed on a computer, and the resulting program is more efficient than was the case with any previous computational-logic programs.

Resolution programs can handle premises and conclusions far more complex than those illustrated here. But, at present, they cannot handle such complex tasks as proving deep mathematical theorems verifying complex computer programs, or aiding a robot cope with the complexities of the real world (as opposed to a limited laboratory word). For these tasks the resolution program uses up the available time or memory before deriving the empty clause.

The trouble, as is usual in AI, is a combinatorial explosion. Unification, resolution, and factoring derive many clauses that are not relevant to deriving the empty clause. The program wastes its time following lines of reasoning that come to dead ends.

Because of these difficulties some people have given up the possibility that computational logic can handle complex theorem-proving tasks. Others seek restrictions on the way resolution and factoring are done that will reduce the number of clauses generated without destroying completeness. Still others (including the author) feel that the answer lies in using powerful heuristic and planning techniques to guide the resolution program to its goal of deriving the empty clause.

# Chapter 12
# Representation of Knowledge

An intelligent program must possess an internal model of the world that it is supposed to be thinking about. Some programs—those that merely read in problems and print out solution—will do all their reasoning on the internal model and will not interact with the real world at all. But programs that do interact with the real word, such as robot-control programs, also need internal models. They use the models for anticipating and planning the consequences of actions before actually executing those actions in the real world.

In Chapter 2 we investigated an *attribute-value* representation for simple problems. The problem world was described by a certain set of attributes. Each possible set of values for those attributes characterized one possible state of the world. We will return to a more sophisticated version of the attribute-value representation later in this chapter. But first, let us see how we can use predicate logic to describe with a set of propositions.

## REPRESENTATIONS BASED ON PREDICATE LOGIC

Let us start with an example, which is similar to one we have already looked at in Chapter 4.

Figure 12-1 shows the world we wish to model. We have a room containing an alcove. In the room are two tables, A and B; a box; and a robot. The robot can be at the alcove, at table A, or at table B. The box can be on table A, on table B, or the robot may be holding it in his hands.

We will use the following one-word names for the individuals in this world:

| Name | Individual |
|------|------------|
| ROBOT | the robot |
| ALCOVE | the alcove |

| BOX | the box |
|-----|---------|
| A | table A |
| B | table B |

We will define the needed predicates by giving an example of the use of each one. Of course, the predicates can take arguments other than those shown in the examples.

| Example | Meaning |
|---------|---------|
| TABLE (A) | A is a table. |
| EMPTYHANDED(ROBOT) | The robot has nothing in its hands. |
| AT(ROBOT, A) | The robot is at table A. |
| HOLDS(ROBOT, BOX) | The robot is holding the box. |
| ON(BOX, A) | The box is on table A. |

Note that by using these predicates we can make contradictory statements

EMPTYHANDED(ROBOT **and** HOLDS(ROBOT, BOX)

as well as meaningless ones

EMPTYHANDED(ALCOVE)

Care must be taken to avoid both.

We describe the current state of the robot's world with a data base, which is simply a list of statements (propositions) giving facts about the world.

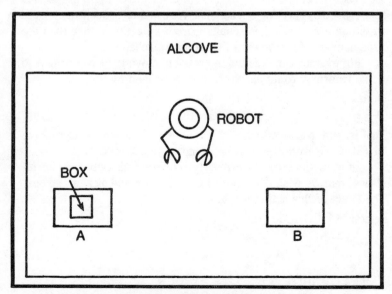

Fig. 12-1. The robot world used in the examples of this chapter.

For instance, suppose we wish to describe the state shown in Fig. 12-1, with the robot standing empty-handed in the alcove and the box on table A. For this state the data base would be:

AT(ROBOT, ALCOVE)
EMPTYHANDED(ROBOT)
ON(BOX, A)
TABLE(A)
TABLE(B)

(We must specify that A and B are tables so we can enforce the condition that the box can only be set on a table.)

Suppose we wished the robot to move the box from table A to table B and then return to its alcove. The final state is:

AT(ROBOT, ALCOVE)
EMPTYHANDED(ROBOT)
ON(BOX, B)
TABLE(A)
TABLE(B)

Notice that most of the statements in the data base remain unchanged. This is typical. Each action we take in a world changes only a few statements in the data base. In a more realistic and complicated world the number of unchanged statements would be far larger than in our simple example.

Therefore, we focus our attention on the *changes* in the data base caused by carrying out actions. We can thus concentrate on the small number of changes resulting from an action rather than the large number of statements that remain unchanged.

For example, the task of the robot in moving the box from A to B and returning to its alcove can be described by

delete: ON(BOX, A)
add: ON(BOX, B)

That is, the overall effect of the robot's actions will be to remove ON(BOX, A) from the data base and add ON(BOX, B).

Other actions can be similarly represented. Suppose, for instance, that we wish the robot to go to table A and pick up the box. The effect of this action would be to

delete: AT(ROBOT, ALCOVE)
EMPTYHANDED(ROBOT)
ON(BOX, A)

add: AT(ROBOT, A)
HOLDS(ROBOT, BOX)

190

Each action we might wish to carry out in the problem world, then, can be represented by an *add list* and a *delete list*. The delete list shows which statements the action will remove from the data base, and the add list shows which ones will be added.

The primitive commands that we can issue to the robot are represented by *operators*. As in Chapter 2, an operator is represented by a *condition* and an *action*. The condition determines whether or not the operator can be applied to a particular state. The action tells how the state will be changed if the operator is applied.

We already know how to represent actions. But what about conditions?

The condition is a proposition that must be true for the state in question if the operator is to be applicable. That is, if by taking the statements in the data base as premises we can derive the condition as a conclusion, then the operator can be applied. Otherwise, it cannot.

Let us see how to represent the operator

PICK UP BOX FROM A

which causes the robot to pick up the box resting on table A. Clearly, the operator can only be applied if the box is on table A, the robot is at table A, and the robot is empty-handed. We represent the operator by the condition together with the add and delete lists for the action:

condition:    ON(BOX, A)
          **and** AT(ROBOT, A)
          **and** EMPTYHANDED(ROBOT)

  delete:  EMPTYHANDED(ROBOT)
         ON(BOX, A)

    add:  HOLDS(ROBOT, BOX)

The condition says that this operator can only be applied if ON(BOX,A), AT(ROBOT, A), and EMPTYHANDED(ROBOT) are all true—that is, all occur in the data base.

(We assume that **and** is generalized to more than two propositions, as was done for **or** in the last chapter. Thus

$$p \text{ \bf and } q \text{ \bf and } r \text{ \bf and } s \text{ \bf and}...$$

is true only if $p, q, r, s, ...$ are all true. Identity I-4 generalizes as well

$$\text{\bf not } (p \text{ \bf and } q \text{ \bf and } r \text{ \bf and } s \text{ \bf and}...)$$

$$= (\text{\bf not } p) \text{ \bf or } (\text{\bf not } q) \text{ \bf or } (\text{\bf not } r) \text{ \bf or } (\text{\bf not } s) \text{ \bf or}...$$

since $p$ **and** $q$ **and** $r$ **and** $s$ **and**...will be false if at least one of $p, q, r, s,$...is false.

Now suppose the current state of the robot's world is

> AT(ROBOT, A)
> EMPTYHANDED(ROBOT)
> ON(BOX, A)
> TABLE(A)
> TABLE(B)

The condition for PICK UP BOX FROM A must follow as a conclusion with the above statements as premises if the operator is to be applicable. Using resolution, we can easily show that the condition does follow from these statements:

| | | |
|---|---|---|
| 1. | AT(ROBOT, A) | (Premise) |
| 2. | EMPTYHANDED(ROBOT) | (Premise) |
| 3. | ON(BOX, A) | (Premise) |
| 4. | TABLE(A) | (Premise) |
| 5. | TABLE(B) | (Premise) |

6.     (not ON(BOX, A))
   or (not AT(ROBOT, A))
   or (not EMPTYHANDED(ROBOT))(Negated Conclusion)

| | | |
|---|---|---|
| 7. | (not AT(ROBOT, A)) | |
| | or (not EMPTYHANDED(ROBOT)) | (3, 6, R) |
| 8. | not EMPTYHANDED(ROBOT) | (1, 7, R |
| 9. | □ | (2, 8, R) |

Step 6, the negated conclusion, was obtained by negating the condition using the generalized version of identity I-4.

When a condition consists only of statements joined by **and**, and each statement may or may not appear in the data base, then we do not really have to resort to resolution. We simply observe that the condition is true if all the statements making it up appear in the data base, and false otherwise. For more complicated conditions, resolution (or some other form of computational logic) will be needed.

It is usually convenient to use variables in conditions as well as individual constants. The resulting conditions are more general. Instead of pinning a particular individual down to, say, ALCOVE, we may use a variable in that position, and allow any individual whose name may be substituted for the variable.

We will be using variables in two different ways in the same operator. In some places we will wish to invite the substitution of a constant for a variable. In other places we will wish to use the constant that has been previously substituted for the variable.

There are a wide variety of notations used to distinguish these two cases. We will employ the following one used by Winston in his textbook on AI:

$>x$  Try to substitute a constant for $x$ so as to make the condition true.

$<x$  Use the constant previously substituted for $x$. *Do not* make a new substitution at this point.

For example, consider the condition

$$\text{ON(BOX, } >x)$$
$$\textbf{and } \text{AT(ROBOT, } <x)$$
$$\textbf{and } \text{EMPTYHANDED(ROBOT)}$$

The $>x$ in ON(BOX, $>x$) instructs us to try to find an individual to substitute for $>x$ such that ON(BOX, $>x$) appears in the data base. Suppose, for instance, the data base contains ON(BOX, A). Then A would be a possible substitution for $>x$.

The occurrence of $<x$ in AT(ROBOT, $<x$) instructs us to see whether this statement is in the data base when $<x$ is replaced by the value previously substituted for $>x$. If A was substituted for $>x$, we must see if AT(ROBOT, A) is in the data base.

Note that we cannot make a new substitution for $<x$. If, for instance, we found AT(ROBOT, B) instead of AT(ROBOT, A), we *could not* substitute B for A. Instead, we could only note that AT(ROBOT, A) is not in the data base, and so the condition is not true with A substituted for $>x$.

As one further example, the above condition would be true for the data base

   AT(ROBOT, B)
   EMPTYHANDED(ROBOT)
   ON(BOX, B)
   TABLE(A)
   TABLE(B)

and B would be substituted for $>x$. On the other hánd, it would not be true for

   AT(ROBOT, ALCOVE)
   EMPTYHANDED(ROBOT)
   ON(BOX, B)
   TABLE(A)
   TABLE(B)

The only possible substituition for $>x$ is B, but AT(ROBOT, B) is not in the data base.

Of course, the condition would not be true for

>    AT(ROBOT, ALCOVE)
>    EMPTYHANDED(ROBOT)
>    TABLE(A)
>    TABLE(B)

since there is no substitution for $>x$ such that ON(BOX, $>x$) is in the data base.

The variable $>x$ can occur only in a condition. But $<x$ can also occur in the add and delete lists. The statements that appear in these lists will depend on which individual constant was substituted for $>x$ to make the condition true.

Consider, for example, the following operator:

> PICK UP BOX

condition:     ON(BOX, $>x$)
    **and** TABLE($<x$)
    **and** AT(ROBOT, $<x$)
    **and** EMPTYHANDED(ROBOT)

delete: EMPTYHANDED(ROBOT)
    ON(BOX, $<x$)

add: HOLDS(ROBOT, BOX)

The condition is true if there is a box resting on something ($>x$), the thing on which the box rests is a table, the robot is at the table, and the robot is empty-handed. The action of the operator is to delete the statements that the robot is empty-handed and the box is on the table, and add the statement that the robot is holding the box.

Thus the condition would be true for the data base

>    AT(ROBOT, A)
>    EMPTYHANDED(ROBOT)
>    ON(BOX, A)
>    TABLE(A)
>    TABLE(B)

and the action taken would be

delete: EMPTYHANDED(ROBOT)
    ON(BOX, A)

add: HOLDS(ROBOT, BOX)

The condition is also true for

>    AT(ROBOT, B)
>    EMPTYHANDED(ROBOT)

ON(BOX, B)
TABLE(A)
TABLE(B)

but since B is substituted for $>x$ instead of A, the action taken is different:

delete: EMPTYHANDED(ROBOT)
ON(BOX, B)

add: HOLDS(ROBOT, BOX)

We recall from Chapter 4 that there were two more operators for controlling the robot: SET DOWN BOX, which caused the robot to set the box down in the table it was next to, and GO TO $a$, which caused the robot to go to place $a$ ($a$ can be A, B, or ALCOVE).

SET DOWN BOX is quite similar to PICK UP BOX:

SET DOWN BOX

condition:     AT(ROBOT, $>x$)
and TABLE($<x$)
and HOLDS(ROBOT, BOX)

delete: HOLDS(ROBOT, BOX)

add: EMPTYHANDED(ROBOT)
ON(BOX, $<x$)

SET DOWN BOX can be applied if the robot is standing next to a table and holding a box. The box is placed on the table and the robot is left empty-handed.

GO TO $a$ moves the robot to place $a$:

GO TO $a$

condition: AT(ROBOT, $>x$)
delete: AT(ROBOT, $<x$)
add: AT(ROBOT, $a$)

The condition here is very general and merely says that the robot has to be somewhere. The real purpose of the condition is to find what constant should be substituted for $>x$ so that AT(ROBOT, $<x$) can be deleted.

## KNOWLEDGE REPRESENTATION AND PLANNING

Facts about the world model are by no means the only knowledge that an intelligent program needs. It also needs *heuristic knowledge*, rules of thumb or hints about how to carry out the tasks requested of it.

Let us see how we might store the knowledge needed to formulate a plan for moving the box from table A to table B.

First let us look at the problem to be solved. We recall that we specify a problem by an *initial state*, a *set of goal states*, and a *set of operators*. We can take the initial state to be

AT(ROBOT, ALCOVE)
EMPTYHANDED(ROBOT)
ON(BOX, A)
TABLE(A)
TABLE(B)

and the operators are those given in the last section.

Usually, we are not interested in every detail of a goal state. We are only interested that some desired condition holds. Therefore, we will specify the goal states by specifying the condition that must hold. Any state for which the condition is true is a goal state.

Thus if we only wanted to assure that the box was placed on table B, the goal would be

goal: ON(BOX, B)

whereas if we wanted to make sure that the robot would return to the alcove after moving the box, we could use

goal:     ON(BOX, B)
     **and** AT(ROBOT, ALCOVE)

and so on.

In working out the steps of a plan, we will concentrate on the goal which each step is to achieve. The initial state for each step will be whatever state the world happens to be in when time comes to carry out that step.

To keep track of the change in the state-of-the-world as each step of a plan is carried out, we provide each step with a delete list and an add list. These lists specify the statements that we know must be deleted or added to achieve the goal specified by the step. Since none of the details of achieving the goal have been specified, these add and delete lists will usually be incomplete. When the step is refined additional statements will be added to the lists. Thus the add and delete lists associated with the steps of a plan let us follow the change in state from step to step *as far as it is known at the current level of planning*. As we refine our plan we will learn more about the change each step causes in the state-of-the-world.

Let us return to the example. The goal we wish to achieve is

goal: ON(BOX, B)

At this point the only change that we know achieving this goal will produce is

add: ON(BOX, B)

These statements constitute the top, least-refined level of our plan, as shown in Fig. 12-2.

To refine a step we need to find a plan that will achieve the goal of that step and is applicable to the current state of the world. Thus, plans are classified in two ways:

1. The goal that carrying out the plan achieves.
2. The condition that must be true of the state-of-the-world in order for this particular plan to be useful.

For instance, consider the plan classified by

goal: ON(BOX, $>x$)
condition: AT(ROBOT, $>y$)
**and** EMPTYHANDED(ROBOT)

This classification states that, (a) this is a plan for placing the box on some object, $>x$, and (b) it is useful when there is a robot present somewhere (at $>y$) and that robot is presently empty-handed. The values substituted for $>x$ and $>y$ can be used in stating the steps of the plan.

We search for a plan that will achieve a particular goal in two steps. First, we try to match the *goal* statement of the plan with the goal to be achieved. In this case the goal to be achieved is

ON(BOX, B)

and ON(BOX, $>x$) matches this, provided that B is substituted for $>x$.

Now we know that the plan will achieve the desired goal, but we do not know if it can be used in the current state of the world. So the second step is to see if the condition is satisfied in the current state. In this case the current state is just the initial state, and the condition will be satisfied provided we substitute ALCOVE for $>y$.

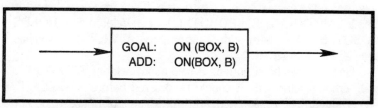

Fig. 12-2. The highest level of the plan for getting the BOX on table B.

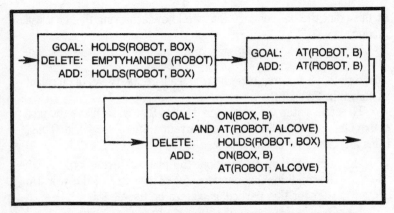

Fig. 12-3. The first refinement of the plan for getting the BOX on table B.

The plan itself consists of three steps:

1. The robot gets the box.
2. The robot carries the box to $< x$, in this case to table B.
3. The robot places the box on $<x$ (table B) and returns to its starting point $<y$ (ALCOVE).

In terms of goals to be achieved and changes produced in the state-of-the-world, we have

1.   goal: HOLDS(ROBOT, BOX)
   delete: EMPTYHANDED(ROBOT)
     add: HOLDS(ROBOT, BOX)
2.   goal: AT(ROBOT, $<x$)
     add: AT(ROBOT, $<x$)
3.   goal: ON(BOX, $<x$)
  **and**    AT(ROBOT, $<y$)
   delete: HOLDS(ROBOT, BOX)
     add: ON(BOX, $<x$)
         AT(ROBOT, $<y$)

Figure 12-3 shows the instantiated version of the plan obtained by substituting B for $<x$ and ALCOVE for $>y$.

The add and delete lists in each step give us some indication of how the state changes from step to step. Thus we know that after step 1, EMPTYHANDED(ROBOT) has been deleted and HOLDS (ROBOT, BOX) has been added; after step 2 AT(ROBOT, $<x$) has been added, and so on.

On the other hand nothing is said about deleting AT(ROBOT, $<y$), although obviously it should be deleted before AT(ROBOT, $<x$) is added. The reason is that at this level of planning we do not

know whether it should be deleted in step 1 or step 2. Can the robot reach the box without moving, or does it have to move somewhere first? Only further refinement of the plan will tell. Thus, as mentioned, the changes in state specified at some high level of the plan are by no means complete.

Each step of the plan can now be further refined. For example, let us see how to refine step 3. The goal we need to achieve in step 3 is

ON(BOX, B) **and** AT(ROBOT, ALCOVE)

Consider the plan classified as follows:

        goal:        ON(BOX, $>x$)
                **and** AT(ROBOT, $>y$)
        condition:   AT(ROBOT, $<x$)
                **and** HOLDS(ROBOT, BOX)
                **and** TABLE($<x$)

The goal part of the classification matches the goal to be achieved provided that B is substituted for $>x$ and ALCOVE is substituted for $>y$.

(Note that the variables $>x$ and $>y$ used in this plan have nothing to do with any variables of the same names used in other plans. It is purely coincidence that the values substituted for $>x$ and $>y$ in this plan are the same as for the one previously considered.)

We must now see if the condition part of the classification holds in the current state-of-the-world. That is, do all three statements in the condition hold at the beginning of the step being expanded? They do, since AT(ROBOT, B) was added in Step 2, HOLDS(ROBOT, BOX) was added in Step 1, and TABLE(B) is true in the initial state. None of three statements have been deleted by later steps.

(Thus we see the usefulness of the add and delete lists, in spite of their incompleteness.)

The steps of the plan are:

    1. operator:   SET DOWN BOX
       delete:     HOLDS(ROBOT, BOX)
       add:        EMPTYHANDED(ROBOT)
                   ON(BOX, $>x$)

    2. operator:   GO TO $>y$
       delete:     AT(ROBOT(, $>x$)
       add:        AT(ROBOT, $>y$)

Figure 12-4 shows the refinement of step 3 in instantiated form.

Note that each step of this plan contains an operator to be applied rather than a goal to be achieved. A step which specifies an

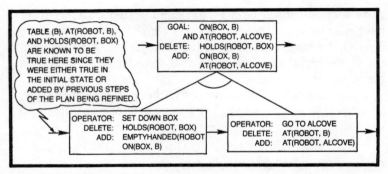

Fig. 12-4. Further refining step 3 of Fig. 12-3. Each step is now an operator—a command that can be issued directly to the robot.

operator rather than a goal is *primitive*; that is, it cannot be refined any further.

Note that the condition for the plan assures that the conditions for applying each individual operator will be met.

To summarize, we can think of each plan as a *hint, proverb, rule of thumb, piece-of-advice,* or *heuristic* for achieving a certain result. The goal part specifies the result to be achieved. The condition part tells when the plan will be useful. In advanced applications we are less concerned with when the steps of the plan can be physically carried out, as with when past experience shows that the plan has a good chance of succeeding. Thus conditions may be based more on the results of experience than upon logical analysis. Consequently, the truth of the condition will not guarantee the success of the plan, but simply designate the plan as something worth trying.

The ideas described here, as well as those found in most current AI literature, are but the first baby steps toward a com-

Table 12-1. Robot Next to Table A and Holding Box in Hands

| ROBOT | | A | |
|---|---|---|---|
| Attribute | Value | Attribute | Value |
| LOCATION | A | IS-A | TABLE |
| HOLDS | BOX | | |
| EMPTYHANDED | FALSE | B | |
| BOX | | Attribute | Value |
| Attribute | Value | IS-A | TABLE |
| SUPPORTED-BY | ROBOT | | |

prehensive technique for creating, storing, recalling, and using plans.

## PROPERTY LISTS

So far we have used statements in predicate logic to represent the facts in our world models. The method that we turn to now is a generalization of the simple *attribute-value* representations for problems discussed in Chapter 2.

We define a *property* as an attribute-value pair. Some examples of properties are:

| Attribute | Value |
|-----------|-------|
| COLOR | RED |
| ENGINE | V8 |
| MODEL | 1978 |
| BODY | SEDAN |
| MAKE | FORD |

These properties are all relevant to discribing an automobile. Clearly many more could be given. Exactly which properties would be needed would depend on the purpose of the description. The properties that would interest the automobile owner, the salesman who sold the car, and the mechanic who has to fix it would not all be the same, though there would be some overlap.

One way to describe the state of a world is to associate with each object in the world a *property list*—a list of all those properties of the object which are relevant to the purpose of the state description.

For instance, let us describe a state of the robot-in-the-room world by giving the property lists of the robot, the two tables, and the box, as in Table 12-1. Obviously this is the situation in which the robot is standing next to table A and holding the box in its hands.

Table 12-2. Robot Next to Table A; Box on Table A

| ROBOT | | A | |
|-------|-------|-------|-------|
| Attribute | Value | Attribute | Value |
| LOCATION<br>EMPTYHANDED | A<br>TRUE | IS-A<br>SUPPORTS | TABLE<br>BOX |
| BOX | | B | |
| Attribute | Value | Attribute | Value |
| SUPPORTED-BY | A | IS-A | TABLE |

Table 12-3. Robot Next to Table B; Box on Table B

| ROBOT | | A | |
|---|---|---|---|
| Attribute | Value | Attribute | Value |
| LOCATION B | | IS-A | TABLE |
| EMPTYHANDED TRUE | | | |
| BOX | | B | |
| | | Attribute | Value |
| Attribute | Value | | |
| | | IS-A | TABLE |
| SUPPORTED-BY B | | SUPPORTS | BOX |

Now suppose the robot sits the box back on table A. The property lists become as shown in Table 12-2. Notice that some properties merely have their value parts changed. For the robot (EMPTYHANDED FALSE) is replaced by (EMPTYHANDED TRUE) and for the box (SUPPORTED-BY ROBOT) changes to (SUPPORTED-BY A). On the other hand, the entire property (HOLDS BOX) was deleted from the property list of the robot, and (SUPPORTS BOX) was added to that of table A in Table 12-2.

As another example, suppose instead of setting the box on table A, the robot carried it to table B and set it down there. The property lists would then become as in Table 12-3. Again the various property lists reflect the situation clearly.

There are two kinds of redundancy in the property lists. First, for the robot's property list we have the attribute EMPTYHANDED and can also have the attribute HOLDS. If (EMPTYHANDED FALSE) is on the property list, then (HOLDS BOX) (or perhaps holds something else) must also be on the property list, whereas if (EMPTYHANDED TRUE) is on the list, then (HOLDS BOX) cannot be on it. In changing the list care must be taken that these two related properties are never in conflict with one another.

The second kind of redundancy is that the property list of the box contains the property (SUPPORTED-BY B), while the property list of table B contains the property (SUPPORTS BOX). This redundancy is not unnatural. When the computer is thinking about the table it needs to know what the table supports, and when it is thinking about the box it needs to know what supports the box. But when the box is moved, care must be taken that both the property lists of the box and the tables are changed accordingly.

One advantage of property lists is that the properties of each object are associated with the object itself. If the program is working with, say, the robot, it does not have to search through a huge data base finding statements that say something about the robot. It has all the properties of the robot collected in a single list.

But perhaps the most important advantage of property lists is that they are already incorporated into the LISP programming language. LISP, discussed further in Chapter 14, is the most widely used programming language in AI. In LISP, symbols such as ROBOT, BOX, A, and B are automatically given property lists. Some of the properties are used by the LISP system for defining constants, assigning values to variables, and naming functions. But the user may also put properties on the property lists, remove them, and change their values. Functions for making these changes are already built into most versions of LISP.

Thus property lists are extremely convenient for the LISP programmer, since the tools for manipulating them are already built into the language and do not have to be created anew for each program.

## SEMANTIC NETS

We can think of objects and their property lists as defining a graph or network. Both the objects and the values are nodes of the graph, while the attributes label arcs. Thus the occurrence of, say, (LOCATION A) on the property list of ROBOT causes the node ROBOT to be joined to the node A by an arc labeled LOCATION.

Such a graph is called a *semantic net*. Figure 12-5 shows the semantic nets corresponding to several states of the robot world.

An interesting feature of semantic nets is that *concepts* as well details of a particular state can be stored. For instance, in Fig. 12-5 two arcs go to a node TABLE. As shown in Fig. 12-6, TABLES can be joined to other nodes in such a way as to represent those features that are common to all tables.

Thus some of the nodes in a semantic net will represent general concepts, such as *chair*, *house*, and *table*. Others will represent specific objects such as *the-chair-I-am sitting-in*, *my-house*, and *the-table-I-am-writing-on*. Still others might represent abstractions such as TRUE and FALSE, or numerical values such as 3.14. The interconnections between all these things are given by the arcs, the label on each arc specifying the intended connection.

In a semantic net the program can start at one node of interest, follow arcs to related nodes, then follow arcs from those to still more distantly related nodes, and so on. This is reminiscent of the human brain's ability to jump from one related idea to another, as in free-association or just everyday thinking. But a network is also a maze,

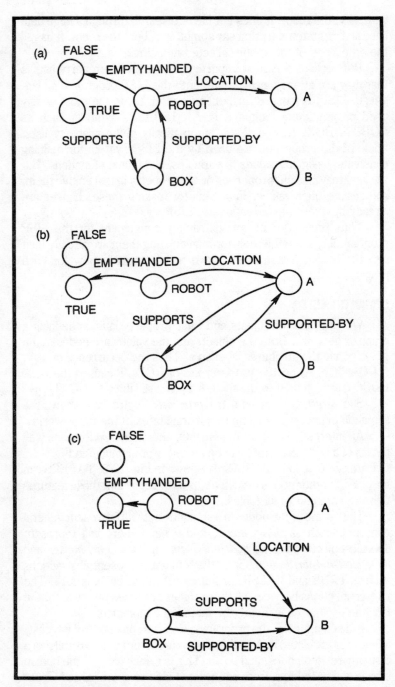

Fig. 12-5. Several states of the robot world represented as semantic nets.

and the computer can get lost in it as easily as it can be guided to the needed information. Some stronger organizing principle may be needed to get the computer quickly to the information it needs.

## FRAMES

The reason human beings are able to get through everyday life without having to reason out every action they take is that everyday life consists largely of a series of *stereotyped situations*. Some examples of such situations are:

- Sitting in one's living room watching TV.
- Driving to work.
- Doing routine work in one's office.
- Attending a college or high-school class
- Eating in a restaurant.
- Cleaning off the table after meal.

People learn how to handle these and many other situations early in life. Thereafter, then can handle the situations without thinking. Or they may concentrate on what is different or interesting, such as what another person present is saying, and carry out with little thought the many other actions the situation may require. What we call common sense is the ability to handle these everyday situations.

For each type of stereotyped situation we expect certain features to be present, even though we have not experienced precisely the present situation before. Before going into a new restaurant, for instance, we expect it to have tables, waiters or waitresses, menus,

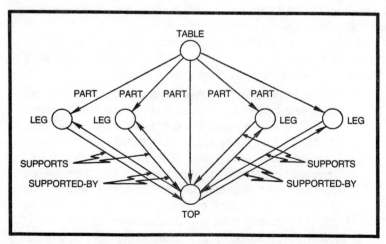

Fig. 12-6. The concept of a table can be represented by a semantic net that shows the parts of a table and how they are related.

a cashier at the door, and so on. Of course, when we actually get in, we may find that some detail is different. Perhaps there are no waiters, but one must carry one's own tray from the serving counter. If so, we will make this minor modification to our expectations but otherwise carry on as before.

A *frame* is a data structure for describing a stereotyped situation. We can think of the frame as having *slots* corresponding to the items we expect to find in the situation. The frame for a living room, for instance, would have slots for the things we would expect to find in a living room, the floor, the walls, the ceiling, the sofa, the armchair, the coffee table, the TV set, and the picture on the wall.

When a frame is first called up it will have *typical*, or *default*, values in most of the slots. For instance, the default value for the TV-set slot in the living-room frame would be a description of a typical color TV set.

Of course, when we go into a particular living room we will find that some of the default values will have to be replaced. Perhaps this living room has a black-and-white TV instead of a color set. Perhaps there is no TV; the TV is kept somewhere else in this house, or possibly the owner is one of those who hates TV and there is no set in the house at all.

These changes are easy to make when they come to our attention. But the important part is the changes we do not have to make, the things we do not have to focus our conscious attention on. We are unlikely to focus much conscious attention on the sofa in a living room, unless perhaps we discovered that there was none! Yet if we should need to imagine a living room we would certainly automatically imagine it to contain a sofa.

A frame, then, summarizes the things we can tentatively assume before we have experienced it or before we have analyzed our experiences. Frames can serve several purposes:

- A program must often reason about situations it is not currently experiencing (unless it controls a robot it never "experiences" the situations it reasons about at all). The frames for those situations will provide the necessary "common sense" assumptions that can be made about them.
- There will be frames for routine tasks, such as moving a box from one table to another. Some of the slots in such a frame will be devoted to plans or heuristics for carrying out the task. A robot will make use of many such frames.
- In analyzing a sentence in a natural language, or a scene picked up by a TV camera, the computer needs to make

certain commonsense assumptions about the outside world. Again frames provide the necessary assumptions. Even if the slots are not filled in with default values, simply knowing what slots have to be filled in is a great help. A scene-analysis program, for instance, instead of searching at random for objects that may or may not be in the scene, can direct its efforts towards filling in the slots in the appropriate frame. A robot in a living room, for instance, could start out by looking for a sofa, then a chair, and so on.

## PRODUCTION SYSTEMS

In connection with planning and computational logic we have already seen several situations in which a *pattern* is matched against items in a data base. Usually the pattern contains variables, and when a match is found the variables will be *instantiated*—particular values will be substituted for them. Matching the pattern will cause a particular plan to be followed or some other action to be taken.

This approach can be used to provide the control mechanism for an intelligent program or for a robot. Control is specified by a list of *productions*. Each production has the following form:

$$pattern \quad -> \quad action$$

Under the direction of a control program the computer searches through the list of productions, trying to match each one against a given data base. When a match is found, the corresponding production "fires," that is, its action is carried out. The item in the data base that fired the production may be marked so that it will not immediately be used again to fire a production. This prevents one production from repeatedly firing on the same data item.

(The control program which matches the patterns and fires the productions can be thought of as an interpreter for a production-system language, just as a BASIC interpreter is an interpreter for the BASIC language. A system for writing productions defines a kind of programming language.)

The form that the data base takes will depend much on the problem at hand. One approach, which attempts to duplicate human behavior, is to let the data base be a *short-term memory* or STM. Like a human being's short-term memory, the STM holds only about seven items of information. When new items enter the memory, old items are displaced from it, that is, forgotten. There is also a long-term memory, and items can be transferred from long-term memory to short-term memory by the action parts of productions. That is, the action part of a certain production may be to "recall" a particular fact, to transfer it to short-term memory. Information picked up by sensors can force their way in to STM: When driving a car we will have to interrupt our thoughts if it becomes apparent we are about to run someone down!

Not all the problems have been worked out of production systems. For instance, it is doubtful that we would always want to consider every possible production that, say, a robot may have as candidate for firing in any situation. Only some subset of productions would be appropriate to a particular situation. Some method is needed to determine which productions should be considered as candidates for firing. An interesting idea is to let the frame for each particular situation have a slot labeled "applicable productions." When a situation is detected, the appropriate frame will be recalled, and the productions it specifies will become current.

# Chapter 13
# Natural Language Processing

One of the first AI projects to receive substantial interest and substantial funding was that of translating from one natural language into another. At the time—in the mid '50s—there was concern that most American scientists and engineers could not read Russian, whereas most Russian scientists and engineers could read English. Since we were then going through somewhat of an inferiority complex with respect to our own technological capabilities, it was natural to worry that our own scientists and engineers were falling behind, since they could not keep up with the brilliant scientific papers that the Russians were presumably turning out like clockwork.

The computer people offered to come to the rescue. They would program computers to translate from Russian into English. The plan was to do about 80 percent of the translation by simple word-for-word substitution. Special fix-up programs would handle the remaining 20 percent of the cases where word-for-word translation proved inadequate. A human editor, who did not have to know Russian, could then polish the English translation. If some awkwardness could be tolerated, the human editing could be omitted.

As expected, about 80 percent of the translation could be done straightforwardly using a dictionary and a modest number of rules concerning grammatical functions and relationships. Unfortunately, the remaiming 20 percent turned out to be very elusive. No one could find a way to translate this 20 percent sufficiently well that minor polishing by a human editor would complete the job. About the best the computer could do was list all possible English translations for the problem words and leave it up to a skilled human translator to select the correct one.

Some of the mistakes these machines made are legendary. "Out of sight, out of mind," was translated into Russian as "blind and insane." "The spirit is willing but the flesh is weak" got translated into the Russian equivalent of "The wine is agreeable but the meat has spoiled."

Eventually, all the translation projects were deemed failures; their funding was withdrawn; and machine translation acquired a bad name that it has yet to live down. Although computers could provide some clerical help to a human translator, they were (with the available technology) just not up to doing the job by themselves.

Yet even though translation has been put on the shelf for the time being, research into natural-language processing goes on. And no wonder. If computers are to be used by the public at large, and not just by a small group of specialists and hobbyists, computers will have to learn to communicate with people in their own language. It seems unlikely that the majority of people will bother to learn to speak the computer's language, nor is there any reason why they should have to.

As with most other areas of artificial intelligence, there are many paths of research being followed. At this point it is completely unclear which approach will be the most successful. The methods described in the remainder of this chapter are typical, and currently seem to be promising, but there is no guarantee that they are the final answer.

## SYNTAX, SEMANTICS, AND TRANSITION NETWORKS

A sentence in a natural (or any other) language can be analyzed from two points of view, *syntax* and *semantics*.

Syntax, or grammar, is concerned with the *form* of the sentence. The sentence

I seen the airplane.

is syntactically incorrect (although perfectly meaningful), since English syntax states that the word "seen" must be preceded by one of the auxiliaries "have," "has," or "had." Note that the syntax says nothing about the meaning of the sentence. It merely says that when one class of word (the past participle of a verb) is used in a correct English sentence, it must be accompanied by another class of word (an auxiliary).

The syntax violation in "I seen the airplane" was sufficiently minor that, although we recognized the sentence was ungrammatical, we had little trouble in guessing what the speaker meant. On the other hand, the "sentence"

Airplane I seen have the

departs so far from correct English syntax that we can make little sense out of it. Its word order is so eccentric that the eye does not find the things it expects in an English sentence, such as a subject, a verb, and predicate noun.

Semantics, on the other hand, is concerned with the *meaning* of a sentence. The sentence

I drank a glass of green kindliness

is meaningless if the words in it are given their usual interpretations, since kindliness neither has color, nor can be drunk from a glass. On the other hand, the sentence is perfectly grammatical, and we can easily analyze it into subject, verb, object, and prepositional phrase.

Ultimately, semantics is everything. We are interested in creating and understanding meaningful sentences. All rules of syntax (except perhaps a few stuck in by pedants while no one was looking) exist to make sure that we will all use words in the same way and so will be able to understand one another. An ordinary person faced with the wildly ungrammatical sentence "Airplane I seen have the" would probably protest not that the sentence is ungrammatical but that "It doesn't make any sense."

Still, most languages do have rules of organization that hold independently of the meanings of the words. These rules can help us identify word patterns without having to worry just yet about the meanings of the words. For instance, both

the large red book on the table

and

a glass of green kindliness

are examples of what linguists call *noun phrases*. The first one is meaningful; the second one is not. But both are noun phrases not because of their meaning or lack of it but because of the way they are constructed from determiners ("a," "the," "this," "that," "these," "those,"), adjectives, nouns, and prepositions. We can identify them as noun phrases without worrying about what they mean.

Syntax, then, allows us to identify word patterns without worrying about their meanings. This is a useful first step in analyzing a sentence.

Let us look at a simple grammar for a small part of English. (It will have to be a small part of English since a grammar for the full English langauge contains thousands of rules.)

We start with the rule that a sentence should have a subject and a predicate. Instead of "subject" and "predicate," however, which describe the functions of the groups of words in the sentence, linguists prefer the terms "noun phrase" and "verb phrase." These simply describe the word patterns without saying anything about their functions.

In writing a grammar, the words "sentence," "noun phrase," and "verb phrase" are abbreviated to S, NP, and VP. To say that a sentence consists of a noun phrase followed by a verb phrase we write:

$$S \rightarrow NP\ VP$$

This rule says that any sentence (in our fragment of English) can be broken down into a noun phrase and a verb phrase. For instance:

|  | NP | VP |
|---|---|---|
| The boys ran home. $\rightarrow$ | The boys | ran home. |

If we are analyzing such a sentence, then, obviously the first thing to do is to look for a noun phrase. After we have found one, the next thing to do is to look for a verb phrase.

But how do we recognize a noun phrase when we see one? The word patterns that make up noun phrases are described by another rule of the grammar:

$$NP \rightarrow (DET)\ (ADJ^*)\ N\ (PP^*)$$

In a rule of grammar, items in parentheses are optional. Therefore, the only thing required in a noun phrase is the noun, N.

On the other hand, the noun can optionally be adorned with a determiner (DET) ("a," "the," and so on), with adjectives (ADJ*), and with prepositional phrases (PP*). The * means that any number of the items in question can occur. Thus can have only one determiner but can have any number of adjectives or prepositional phrases.

The items, if they do occur, must occur in the order specified in the rule. Thus the determiner, if any, must come first, then any adjectives, then the required noun, and finally, any prepositional phrases. The following shows how a noun phrase can be analyzed using this rule:

| NP | DET | ADJ | N | PP |
|---|---|---|---|---|
| The red book on the table $\rightarrow$ | the | red | book | on the table |

If we were analyzing an English noun phrase, then, we should start looking for a determiner. If none is found start looking for adjectives. If none are found, look for a noun. If no noun is found, the group of words in questions is not a noun phrase.

Other groups of words can be defined similarly. For instance,

$$VP \rightarrow VTRAN \; NP$$

says that a verb phrase consists of a transitive verb (VTRAN) followed by a noun phrase (NP). In full English there are several different kinds of verb phrases but this is the only kind we will worry about here.

A prepositional phrase is made up of a preposition PREP) and a noun phrase (NP):

$$PP \rightarrow PREP \; NP$$

Notice that a prepositional phrase has a noun phrase as a constituent, and a noun phrase has a prepositional phrase as a constituent. The prepositional phrase and the noun phrase are defined in terms of one another. This circumstance leads to nested structures such as

the book on the shelf over the door to the kitchen

This is an NP which can be analyzed as:

| DET | N | PP |
|-----|------|----|
| the | book | on the shelf over the door to the kitchen |

The PP can in turn be analyzed as

| PREP | NP |
|------|----|
| on | the shelf over the door to the kitchen |

This new NP can again be broken down into a DET, an N, and a PP:

| DET | N | PP |
|-----|-------|----|
| the | shelf | over the door to the kitchen |

The new PP can be broken down still further, and so on.

This grammatical-analysis method can be carried out by the *transition network* shown in Fig. 13-1. This network describes a series of machines, one machine for each diagram. The states of the machine are the numbered circles. The lines connecting the states show possible transistions from one state to another.

We can think of the machine described by each diagram as being an expert in recognizing a particular word pattern. Thus the S machine is an expert in recognizing sentences, the NP machine an expert in recognizing noun phrases, and so on. Each machine will have to consult one or more of the others to do its job. The NP machine will have to call on the PP machine to recognize prepositional phrases; the PP machine will have to call on the NP machine to recognize noun phrases, and so on.

To recognize a sentence, for instance, we would start the S machine in state 1. In order to get to state 2 it must find a noun

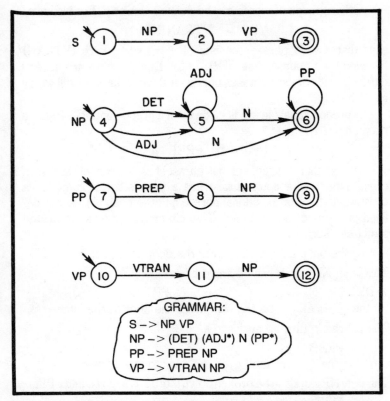

Fig. 13-1. A transistion network for a small subset of English. Each diagram represents a machine for finding the corresponding word pattern. Each machine can call on other machines to find needed patterns.

phrase. The S machine calls on the NP machine to do this job. When the NP machine returns, saying that it found an NP, the S machine goes to state 2. There it finds that a verb phrase is needed. The S machine calls on the VP machine to find a verb phrase. When the VP machine reports success, the S machine can go to state 3. The double circle on state 3 indicates that the S machine's job is finished; it can report back to us that a sentence has been found.

The NP machine is slightly more complicated than the S machine. An NP can begin with a DET, and ADJ, or a N. Therefore there are three transition lines leaving state 4. Which one is followed and what the next state will be depends on whether a DET, ADJ, or N is found.

Since a noun phrase can contain any number of adjectives or prepositional phrases, the NP machine has loops labeled ADJ and PP. The ADJ loop causes the machine to keep returning to state 5 to look for more ADJs until an N is found. It then starts looking for PPs, returning to state 6 after each one to look for another one. When there are no more PPs to be found, the NP machine's job is over, and it returns control to the machine that called on it.

Of course, we do not actually construct a separate machine for each word pattern we wish to recognize. Instead, the machines are represented by tables stored in computer memory. For instance, the following tabulation would represent the NP machine:

| State | Word Pattern | Next State |
|-------|--------------|------------|
| 4 | DET | 5 |
| 4 | ADJ | 5 |
| 4 | N | 6 |
| 5 | ADJ | 5 |
| 5 | N | 6 |
| 6 | PP | 6 |
| 6 | | return |

The last entry is used only if the next-to-last one cannot be—that is, if there are no more PPs to be found.

We can write a computer program that will simualte the behavior of the machines, consulting the tables to find out what each machine would do in each state upon finding a particular word pattern in the sentence being analyzed. As we saw to be the case for the control program for production systems, this program too is a form of interpreter, and the tables which describe the machines are a form of programming language.

As the machines that comprise the transition network work their way through a sentence, they can collect information about the word patterns that they recognize. We can think of a *frame* as being associated with each word pattern. (Frames were described in Chapter 12.) As the machine for that pattern scans though the sentence, it collects information and uses this information to fill in the slots in the frame. For instance, in recognizing a noun phrase the NP machine would fill in slots for the determiner, the adjectives, the noun, and the prepositional phrases. It might also note whether the noun phrase was singular or plural, whether or not it referred to a person and, if so, the gender of the person. Thus a filled in frame for the noun phrase "the tall skinny boy in the yard" might be:

| Slot | Value | Slot | Value |
|------|-------|------|-------|
| DET | the | NUMBER | singular |
| ADJs | tall, skinny | PERSON? | yes |
| N | boy | GENDER | male |
| PPs | in the yard | | |

A simple way to collect this information is to arrange for a particular subroutine to be called for each transition. (Often it is convenient to have one subroutine called before a transition and one afterwards.) The subroutines collect the information and fill in the slots.

The subroutine calling is easy to implement. The addresses of the subroutines are simply added to the tables describing the transition network. (In the form of the tables previously illustrated, each row corresponds to a transition. The addresses of the subroutines to be called before and after each transition, then, are added to the corresponding rows of the tables.) The interpreter is modified to call the subroutines whose addresses are found in the tables at the appropriate times. A transition network with provisions for calling subroutines is called an *augmented transition network*, or ATN.

## CASE GRAMMAR

With ATNs we can recognize word patterns. For each word pattern we can fill in the slots of a frame, giving a fairly complete description of the pattern. The frames describing the various word patterns can be used as a basis for further processing.

Can we do something similar for the sentence as a whole?

One approach to doing this is known as *case grammar*. The word *case* comes from the traditional grammatical cases such as the nominative case and the objective case, which give the function of a word or phrase in a sentence. These traditional cases are called *surface cases*, since they refer to the surface appearance of the sentence and not to the concepts underlying it. The *deep cases* used in case grammar refer to the underlying thought or idea which the sentence communicates.

For instance, consider a sentence describing an action. Some of the deep cases that could be relevant are:

- OBJECT. This is the object that is acted upon.
- AGENT. This is the thing that caused the action to occur.
- CO-AGENT. The agent may have had help in causing the action; the helper is the co-agent.
- INSTRUMENT. Any tool used by the agent or co-agent to carry out the action is an instrument.
- SOURCE.
- DESTINATION. Often an action involves moving an object from one place to another. The source and destination are the place moved from and the place moved to.

- TRAJECTORY. The path taken in going from source to destination.
- CONVEYANCE. The thing in which the object moves from source to destination.

We can associate a frame with each sentence. The slots in the frame correspond to the various deep cases. Analyzing the sentence consists of filling in the slots in the sentence-frame with groups of words. These groups will be the noun phrase found by the ATN. There will also be a slot for the verb, which describes the action.

For instance, the frame for the sentence

John gave the book to Sally

might be as follows:

| | |
|---|---|
| VERB: | gave |
| OBJECT: | the book |
| AGENT: | John |
| SOURCE: | John |
| DESTINATION: | Sally |

Another example:

Bill built the kit using a screwdriver and a soldering iron.

The frame would be:

| | |
|---|---|
| VERB: | built |
| OBJECT: | the kit |
| AGENT: | Bill |
| INSTRUMENT: | screwdriver, soldering iron |

We will not go into the details here of filling in the case slots in the sentence frame. Some of the considerations used, however, are:

- The meaning of a verb may imply the cases of the word groups used with it. "Give," for instance, implies a transfer; we expect, therefore, a SOURCE and a DESTINATION. We further expect that the AGENT will be the same as the SOURCE.
- Prepositions suggest possible cases for the following noun phrases. "With," for instance, often suggests a CO-AGENT is in

John fixed the computer with Jack

or an INSTRUMENT as in

John fixed the computer with a soldering iron.

- The position of a group of words in a sentence can be an important clue to its case; this is particularly true in English, which depends on word order much more than do some other languages. For instance, in the active voice the noun phrase that starts the sentence—the traditional subject—is apt to be the AGENT, as in

The boy hit the ball.

These and other considerations place constraints on the cases of the various noun phrases. Each constraint may be fairly weak—it may imply more than one possible case. But when all the constraints are taken together, they often pin down the case of each noun phrase.

## CONCEPTUAL DEPENDENCY THEORY

*Conceptual dependency* theory carries sentence analysis one more step by analyzing the cause and effect relationships implied by a sentence. In many ways it is similar to case grammar; it fills in slots in frames with values extracted from the sentence under analysis. Many of the slots are familiar from case grammar: OBJECT, SOURCE, DESGINATION, and so on. The AGENT of case grammar is called the ACTOR in conceptual dependency theory.

Conceptual dependency deals not only with actors but also with acts. It attempts to break down a complicated action into one or more primitive acts, such as INGEST, TRANSFER-POSSESSION, EXPEL, MOVE-OBJECT, HEAR, SEE, and so on.

For instance, the sentence

Jack gave the ball to Jane

would be analyzed as

| | |
|---|---|
| ACT: | TRANSFER-POSSESSION |
| ACTOR: | Jack |
| SOURCE: | Jack |
| DESTINATION: | Jane |

whereas

Jack took the ball from Jane

would be analyzed as

| | |
|---|---|
| ACT: | TRANSFER-POSSESSION |
| ACTOR: | Jack |
| SOURCE: | Jane |
| DESTINATION: | Jack |

The meanings of both the verbs *give* and *take* are captured by the primitive act TRANSFER-POSSESSION. But the SOURCE and DESTINATION slots are filled in differently for *give* and *take*.

The next step is to attempt to analyze groups of sentences and extract descriptions of the situations, processes, scenarios, plots, or whatever they may describe. Again a frame approach seems promising. As the program reads through a piece of text sentence by sentence, it will fill in slots in a frame that represents the situation described by the text. The more text that is read, the more slots that can be filled in. The slots already filled in can be used to help analyze the current sentence—by resolving pronoun references for instance, or by helping interpret sentences that are ambiguous out of context. But the details of actually carrying out such an analysis remain to be perfected.

# Chapter 14
# LISP

Artificial-intelligence programs can be written in almost any programming language. All the techniques described in the preceding chapters can be illustrated by programs written in BASIC or FORTRAN. And when fast execution and efficient memory usage are important, as in chess-playing programs, assembly language will probably have to be used.

There are, however, languages specifically designed for AI programming. By far the most widely used of these is LISP, which stands for LISt Processor. LISP has been implemented on many different kinds of computer, including minicomputers, so microcomputer implementations should raise no new problems.

## ATOMS AND LISTS

LISP deals with two kinds of objects, *atoms* and *lists*. (The atoms of LISP have nothing to do with those of predicate logic. In fact, an "atom" in predicate logic is usually represented by a list in LISP.)

### Atoms

Atoms are symbols used to name objects. The objects named can be objects in the program, such as variables and functions, or objects in the world the program is manipulating, such as robots, tables, boxes, rooms, windows, and so on. The following are examples of atoms:

|        |            |
|--------|------------|
| ROBOT  | ALCOVE     |
| BOX    | PLUS       |
| A      | DIFFERENCE |
| B      | SQRT       |

Associated with each atom is a property list, which can be used to describe the named object and specify its relations to other objects.

Numbers are also considered to be atoms in LISP. Thus

|       |        |
|-------|--------|
| 25    | 3.14   |
| $-100$ | $-25$  |
| 2.5   | $-4.5$ |

are all atoms. Numbers are very special cases of atoms, however, since a number cannot name anything or have properties other than its numeric value. As in other programming languages, numbers are used to represent numeric values in arithmetic operations.

## Lists

A list consists of a series of *members* enclosed in parentheses and separated by spaces. The members of a list may be atoms:

(ROBOT BOX A B ALCOVE)
(COLOR RED)
(LENGTH 25)
(A B C D E F G)
(HOLDS ROBOT BOX)

A list can also contain other lists as members:

(A (B C) D (E F G))
((LENGTH 25) (WIDTH 5) (HEIGHT 100))

((AT ROBOT ALCOVE)
(ON BOX A)
(EMPTYHANDED ROBOT)
(TABLE A)
(TABLE B))

(3 (2 5) (3 4 9))

Thus the members of the first example are A, (B C), D, and (E F G). The first and third members are atoms. The second and last ones are lists. As shown in the third example, the members of a list can be written on separate lines. This is often necessary when the elements are themselves lists.

The lists that are members of other lists can, of course, have still other lists as members, and those lists can have other lists as members, and so on:

(((A B C) D) E ((F G) H I))

Such complicated lists are often clearer when the members are written on separate lines:

(((A B C) D)
 E
 ((F G) H I))

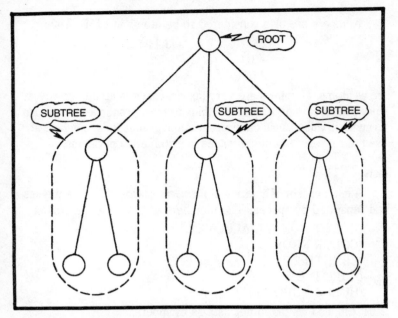

Fig. 14-1. A tree can be thought of as consisting of a root together with one or more subtrees.

## REPRESENTING DATA STRUCTURES WITH LISTS

Let us see how some of the data structures used in the preceding chapters can be represented using lists and atoms.

### Trees

We can think of a tree as consisting of a *root* together with zero or more *subtrees*, as shown in Fig. 14-1. Each subtree is a tree whose root is one of the children of the original tree.

We can represent a tree by a list whose first member is the root of the tree and whose remaining members are its subtrees:

*(root subtree-1 subtree-2 .......................................subtree-n)*

A subtree which consists of a root only, a leaf, is simply represented by the atom which names it.

Thus in Fig. 14-2, the leaf nodes are represented by

E F G H I J K

the subtrees of the root are represented by

(B E F G)     (C H I)     (D J K L)

and the entire tree is represented by

(A (B E F G) (C H I) (D J K L))

222

Each node of the tree is named by an atom. The property list of the atom can contain or refer to all the information that we may wish to associate with the node (a game position, for example).

## Expressions in Predicate Logic

A predicate-logic "atom" is represented by list consisting of the predicate followed by its arguments:

| | | |
|---|---|---|
| (ON BOX A) | represents | ON(BOX, A) |
| (AT ROBOT ALCOVE) | | AT(ROBOT, ALCOVE) |
| (TABLE A) | | TABLE (A) |
| (HOLDS ROBOT BOX) | | HOLDS(ROBOT, BOX) |

Expressions such as

ON(BOX, A) **or** ON(BOX, B)

are represented in *prefix* form. The operator **or** is written first, followed by the subexpressions it joins:

(OR (ON BOX A) (ON BOX B))

In the same way,

(AND (ON BOX A) (AT ROBOT ALCOVE))

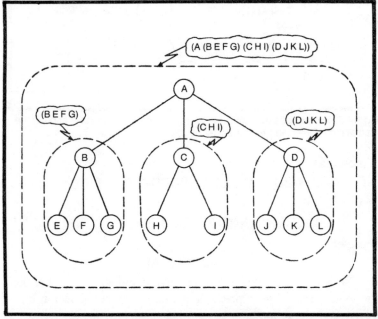

Fig. 14-2. A tree can be represented by a list whose first element represents the root and whose remaining elements represent the subtrees. The subtrees, if not leaves, are represented by lists of the same type.

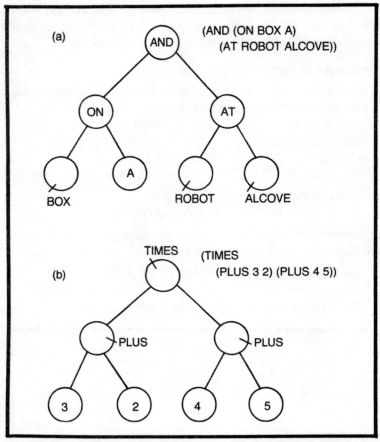

Fig. 14-3. Expressions in logic or arithmetic have a tree structure and can be represented as lists in the same way as trees.

represents

ON(BOX, A) **and** AT(ROBOT, ALCOVE)

and

(NOT (ON BOX A))

represents

**not** ON(BOX, A)

Note that the representation of a predicate-logic expression has the same form as the representation of a tree. As shown in Fig. 14-3a, the expression

(AND (ON BOX A) (AT ROBOT ALCOVE))

is the same as that of a tree whose root is AND. The children of the

224

root are ON and AT. The children of ON are BOX and A, and the children of AT are ROBOT and ALCOVE. Notice that the leaves of the tree are individuals such as BOX, A, ROBOT, and ALCOVE, while the nonleaf nodes are logical operators such as AND, or predicates such as ON and AT.

Arithmetic expressions are also represented in tree form. Thus

$$(3 + 2)*(4 + 5)$$

would be represented as

(TIMES (PLUS 3 2) (PLUS 4 5))

which also corresponds to a tree representation, as shown in Fig. 14-3b.

Since an expression is represented as a tree, programs which manipulate trees can be used to manipulate expressions.

### Graphs

For every node of a graph we must specify what arcs leave that node and what node each arc ends on.

Figure 14-4 shows two ways of representing a graph by lists. The first is a list of triples of the form

*(node arc node)*

each of which indicates that the arc in question joins the first node to

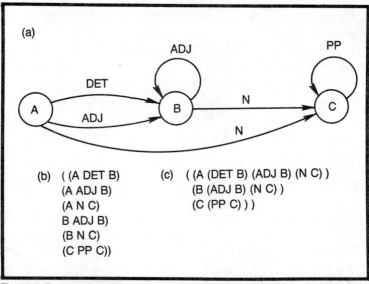

Fig. 14-4. Two ways to represent a graph by lists. The example graph is a slightly simplified version of the state diagram for the "noun .phrase machine" of Chapter 13.

the second one. The second is a list of lists of the form

*(node (arc node) (arc node) (arc node)* ·····················*)*

The first member of this list identifies a node. The remaining members correspond to arcs leaving that node. For each arc the arc label and the node the arc ends on are given.

## Other Methods

The methods described for representing trees, expressions, and graphs are widely used. But there is nothing sacred about them. Other methods are possible and should be used when they are more appropriate for a particular problem.

## ELEMENTS OF LISP PROGRAMMING

### Functions and Arguments

A LISP system is a function-evaluating machine. The user types in a function and its arguments; LISP types back the result of applying the function to the arguments.

The function and its arguments are written in *prefix* form, with the function first followed by the arguments. Thus, PLUS is the addition function in LISP, and

(PLUS 3 5)

denotes the sum of 3 and 5. If we typed in (PLUS 3 5), LISP would respond with 8.

In illustrating user-LISP dialogs, we will show the user's input starting at the left margin and LISP's responses indented two places. Thus the exchange just mentioned would be written:

```
(PLUS 3 5)            user
   8                  LISP
```

The following dialog will introduce some other functions:

```
(DIFFERENCE 9 4)
   5
(MINUS 2)
   -2
(TIMES 4 3)
   12
(QUOTIENT 3 2)
   1.5
(SQRT 9)
   3
```

226

The arguments of a function may themselves be expressions. LISP will evaluate the arguments first before applying the function to them:

(PLUS (TIMES 3 4) (DIFFERENCE 9 5))
   16
(TIMES 3 (PLUS 2 (TIMES 4 5)))
   66

The first expression is equivalent to

$$(3*4) + (9-5)$$

and the second is equivalent to

$$3*(2 + (4*5))$$

## List Functions

The most interesting functions in LISP are, of course, not those which do arithmetic but those which manipulate lists. Before we can illustrate them, however, we must see how LISP solves a problem that arises in most programming languages.

Let us switch from LISP for a moment to BASIC, since everybody knows BASIC. Consider the two BASIC statements

10 PRINT 3+5
20 PRINT "3+5"

In the first statement the computer treats 3+ 5 as an expression to be evaluated and prints 7, the result of the evaluation. But in the second statement the quote marks signal that 3+5 is a string of characters rather than an expression, so the computer simply prints 3+5.

The same problem occurs in LISP. The list

(PLUS 3 5)

can be an expression to be evaluated or it can just be a list whose members are the atoms PLUS, 3, and 5. If the latter interpretation is intended, we must precede the list by a single quote mark:

'(PLUS 3 5)

The following dialog illustrates the distinction:

(PLUS 3 5)
   7
'(PLUS 3 5)
   (PLUS 3 5)
(DIFFERENCE 5 9)
   -4

'(DIFFERENCE 5 9)
   (DIFFERENCE 5 9)
'(A B C)
   (A B C)
(A B C)
   ERROR

The error results because when LISP is given (A B C), it tries to interpret A as a function and B and C as its arguments. It thus searches the property list of A for a function definition. Assuming A has not been defined as a function by the user, no definition will be found, and LISP will indicate an error.

For historical reasons, unfortunately, three of the list-manipulating functions have names that are not meaningful. One simply has to memorize their meanings.

CAR returns the first member of a list:
(CAR '(A B C D))
   A
(CAR '(AT ROBOT ALCOVE))
   AT
(CAR '((A B) (C D) E))
   (A B)

CDR, pronounced *couder*, returns the remainder of a list after the first member has been removed:
(CDR '(A B C D))
   (B D C)
(CDR '(AT ROBOT ALCOVE))
   (ROBOT ALCOVE)
(CDR '((A B) (C D) E))
   ((C D) E)

CONS, pronounced with a soft *s*, adds a new first member to a list:
(CONS 'X '(A B C))
(CONS 'AT' (ROBOT ALCOVE))
   (X A B C)
   (AT ROBOT ALCOVE)
(CONS '(X Y) '(A B))
   ((X Y) A B)

Note that atoms such as X and AT also have to be quoted if they are to stand merely for themselves. We will see presently what unquoted atoms represent.

APPEND, the first list-manipulating function with a decent name, joins two lists together:

(APPEND '(A B) '(X Y))
    (A B X Y)
(APPEND '(1 2 3) '(4 5 6))
    (1 2 3 4 5 6)

Like the arithmetic functions, the list-manipulating functions can be combined to form expressions:

(CONS (CAR '(X Y Z)) (CDR '(A B C)))
    (X B C)
(APPEND (CDR '(X Y Z)) (CDR '(A B C)))
    (Y Z B C)

### Variables

Like most other programming languages, LISP allows values to be assigned to variables. Whenever a variable appears in an expression, it is replaced by its value. LISP uses atoms for variables.

The function SETQ assigns a value to a variable.

(SETQ X 5)
    5
(SETQ Y 10)
    10

Thus X and Y have now been assigned the values 5 and 10. When they appear in an expression their values will be substituted:

X
    5
(PLUS X Y)
    15

When an atom is quoted, it stands for iself; when it is not quoted, it stands for its value.

Y
    10
'Y
    Y

If the atom is part of a list that is quoted, it stands for itself:

(TIMES X Y)
    50
'(TIMES X Y)
    (TIMES X Y)

The value of a variable can be changed as often as is necessary:

```
(SETQ X 25)
    25
X
    25
(SETQ X '(A B C D))
    (A B C D)
X
    (A B C D)
(CAR X)
    A
(CDR X)
    (B C D)
```

The Q in SETQ tells us that the first argument is automatically quoted. Thus in (SETQ X 25), X stands for itself even though we do not (and must not) precede it with a quote mark.

The value returned by SETQ is always the value that was assigned to the variable. But the *side-effect* of assigning the value to the variable is much more important than the value the function returns. Usually, SETQ is executed purely for the side effect, and the value the function returns is ignored.

### Defining New Functions

One programs in LISP by defining new functions. These user-defined functions can then be typed in with their arguments just like the built-in functions we have been discussing.

Suppose we wished to define a function SQUARE, which will yield the square of a number, the number multiplied by itself. We would like SQUARE to behave as follows:

```
(SQUARE 2)
    4
(SQUARE 3)
    9
(SQUARE 4)
    16
```

We would define SQUARE as follows:

```
(DEFINE (SQUARE X) (TIMES X X))
    SQUARE
```

The function definition is a list with three members. They are:

- DEFINE. This is the LISP function which is responsible for accepting definitions and storing them in memory.

- (SQUARE X). The members of this list are the name, SQUARE, of the function being defined, and a dummy variable, X, which stands in place of the argument. When the function is invoked, the value of the argument will be temporarily assigned to X. If the function had more than one argument, then that number of dummy variables would be required.
- (TIMES X X). This expression computes the value the function is to return, using the value of the argument that has been assigned to the dummy variable X.

Thus if we type

(SQUARE 2)

the value of X is set to 2. Then (TIMES X X) is equivalent to (TIMES 2 2), whose value is 4, the value returned by the function. After the function finishes executing, X is reassigned whatever value it had before the function was invoked.

The arguments of DEFINE, (SQUARE X), and (TIME X X), are automatically quoted so that they stand for themselves. No evaluation takes place when the function is defined, but only when it is invoked.

The value returned by DEFINE is the name of the function being defined. This value is of no interest, and we will usually not bother to show it. DEFINE is another LISP function executed for its side effects.

Let us try a few more definitions:

(DEFINE (CUBE X) (TIMES X (TIMES X X)))

The function CUBE returns the cube of its argument:
(CUBE 2)
   8
(CUBE 3)
   27

We can, of course, define new list-manipulating functions too:

(DEFINE (SECOND X) (CAR (CDR X)))

SECOND returns the second member of a list:
(SECOND '(A B C D))
   B
(SECOND '((A B) (C D) E))
   (C D)

Here is a function with two arguments:

(DEFINE (JOIN X Y) (APPEND (CDR X) (CDR Y)))

JOIN removes the first member from each of its two arguments, and then joins the remainders of the two lists together:

(JOIN '(A B C) '(X Y Z))

    (B C Y Z)

(JOIN '(1 2 3 4) '(5 6 7 8))

    (2 3 4 5 6 7 8)

The more complicated function definitions usually have to be written on more than one line:

(DEFINE (JOIN X Y)

(APPEND (CDR X)

(CDR Y)))

We will usually break things up so that the arguments of each function are written one under another, as shown.

### Predicates

Most programming languages have an "IF statement" which allows the execution of a program to be governed by the conditions which do or do not hold for the data. We now wish to see how this end is accomplished in LISP.

To begin, in LISP *true* and *false* are represented by the atoms T and NIL. The fact that NIL represents *false* is another of those little quirks of LISP that we must, with a sigh, memorize.

T and NIL are themselves their own values, and therefore never have to be quoted:

T

    T

NIL

    NIL

A *predicate* is a function whose value is T or NIL. Each predicate corresponds to some condition that may or may not hold for its arguments. If the condition holds for the arguments supplied, the predicate returns T. If the condition does not hold, the predicate returns NIL.

The predicate EQUAL returns T if its arguments are the same:

(EQUAL 5 5)

    T

(EQUAL 5 7)

    NIL

(EQUAL 'A 'B)

    NIL

(EQUAL 'C 'C)

```
         T
(EQUAL '(A B C) '(A B C))
         T
(EQUAL '(A B C) '(A B C D))
      NIL
```

GREATERP and LESSP compare the values of numbers:

```
(GREATERP 5 3)
      T
(GREATERP 3 5)
      NIL
(LESSP 3 5)
      T
(LESSP 5 3)
      NIL
```

ZEROP distinguishes the number 0:

```
(ZEROP 0)
      T
(ZEROP 25)
      NIL
```

ATOM distinguishes atoms and NUMBERP distinguishes numbers.

```
(ATOM 25)
      T
(NUMBERP 25)
      NIL
(ATOM 'A)
      T
(NUMBERP 'A)
      NIL
(ATOM '(A B C))
      NIL
(NUMBERP '(A B C))
      NIL
```

The names of many LISP predicates end in P. But, alas, exceptions such as EQUAL and ATOM limit the usefulness of the convention.

### The COND Function

The COND function is the "IF statement" of LISP. It has the following form:

```
(COND (condition-1 expression-1)
      (condition-2 expression-2)
                   •
                   •
                   •
      (condition-n expression-n))
```

Each condition is an expression that normally will evaluate to T or NIL, although any value other than NIL will be considered "true." COND evaluates each condition in turn. When it finds the first condition whose value is not NIL, it evaluates the corresponding expression and returns that value as the value of the entire COND expression. If all the conditions evaluate to NIL, COND returns the value NIL.

For example, let us define an arithmetic function SGN whose value is 1 if its argument is greater than 0, 0 if its argument equals 0, and $-1$ if its argument is less than 0:

```
(DEFINE (SGN X)
    (COND ((GREATERP X 0) 1)
        ((ZEROP X) 0)
        ((LESSP X 0) -1)))
```

If the value of X is greater than 0, then the value of the first condition, (GREATERP X 0), will be T; and COND will return the value 1. If the value of X is 0, (GREATERP X 0) will be NIL, but (ZEROP X) will be T; COND will return the value 0. If the value of X is less than 0, both (GREATERP X 0) and (ZEROP X) will be NIL. But (LESSP X 0) will be T, and COND will return the value $-1$.

If the value of X is neither greater than 0 nor equal to 0, then it must be less than 0. There is really no need to evaluate (LESSP X 0): IF (GREATERP X 0) and (ZEROP X) are both NIL, then (LESSP X 0) must be T. This observation allows us to simplify slightly the definition of SGN:

```
(DEFINE (SGN X)
    (COND ((GREATERP X 0) 1)
        ((ZEROP X) 0)
        (T -1)))
```

The third condition is just T itself and so is always true. Whenever (GREATERP X 0) and (ZEROP X) are both NIL, the third condition will be T, and so SGN will return the value $-1$. If (GREATERP X 0) or (ZEROP X) happens to be T, however, then (T-1) will have no effect: It is the *first* condition that is T that determines what value COND returns.

This technique of using T for the last condition in COND is widely used in LISP programming.

Regardless of which definition we use, SGN will return the expected values:

(SGN 3)
    1
(SGN 0)
    0
(SGN −25)
    −1

## Recursive Functions

A particularly simple and elegant way to define a function is to define it partially in terms of itself. This is called a *recursive definition*.

For example, let us define a function LENGTH whose value is the number of elements on a list:

(LENGTH '( X Y Z))
    3
(LENGTH '(A B C D E F))
    6
The elements being counted may themselves be lists:
(LENGTH '((A B C) (X Y)))
    2
(LENGTH '((A B) (C D) (E F)))
    3
An atom contains no elements, so its length is 0:
(LENGTH 'A)
    0
(LENGTH 'B)
    0
The length of the empty list, ( ), which has no elements, is of course, 0:
(LENGTH '( ))
    0
Now here is another peculiarity of LISP. The empty list, ( ), is represented inside the computer in the same way as the atom NIL, which we have used to represent "false." As far as the computer is concerned, ( ) and NIL are the same thing:
(EQUAL '( ) NIL)
    T

235

Since NIL is an atom, so is the empty list:
(ATOM '( ))
    T
We obtain the empty list if we take the CDR of a list having only a single element:
(CDR '(A))
    NIL
(EQUAL (CDR '(A)) '( ))
    T
(ATOM (CDR '(A)))
    T

Now we are ready to give the recursive definition for the function LENGTH:
(DEFINE (LENGTH X)
    (COND ((ATOM X) 0)
        (T (PLUS 1 (LENGTH (CDR X)))))))

Looking at the COND, we see that the definition of LENGTH breaks down into two cases. For the first case, (ATOM X) is T; for the second case, (ATOM X) is NIL.

In the first case, LENGTH returns the value 0 whenever (ATOM X) is T. Thus all atoms will be assigned length 0. What's more, since the empty list, ( ), is the atom NIL, the first case assigns the empty list a length of 0.

If (ATOM X) is NIL then the second case, given by the second line of the COND, will apply. To see how this case works, suppose the value of X is the list (A B C). The computer will do the following:

- Compute (CDR X). Since the value of X is (A B C), the value of (CDR X) is (B C).
- Compute (LENGTH (CDR X)). Since the value of (CDR X) is (B C), the value of (LENGTH (CDR X)) is 2.
- Compute (PLUS 1 (LENGTH (CDR X))). Since the value of (LENGTH (CDR X)) is 2, the value of (PLUS 1 (LENGTH (CDR X))) must be 3. The value 3 is returned as the length of the original list (A B C), which is of course correct.

The only question which remains is that we have defined LENGTH in terms of itself. In working out the value of (LENGTH '(A B C)), we have used the fact that (LENGTH '(B C)) has the value 2. How can we get away with that?

Let use see exactly what happens when we request the value of (LENGTH '( A B C)). We go to the definition and give X the value (A B C). Since (A B C) is not an atom, the second case holds, and the value of (LENGTH (CDR X)) is requested. Since the value of (CDR X) is (B C), this is equivalent to requesting the value of (LENGTH '(B C)).

To find the value of (LENGTH '(B C)) we must return to the definition. The value of X is now (B C). (X will have a different value every time we use the definition.) Since (B C) is not an atom the second case applies, and the value of (LENGTH (CDR X)) is again requested. This time the value of (CDR X) is (C), so we are asking for the value of (LENGTH '(C)).

Finding (LENGTH '(C)) takes us back to the definition again. Again (C) is not an atom, the second case applies, and the value of (LENGTH (CDR X)) is required. The value of (CDR '(C)) is the empty list, ( ), so we now need the value of (LENGTH '( )).

The next step is crucial. You may have been wondering what would keep us from repeatedly invoking the function LENGTH forever. What prevents this is that each time we use LENGTH the list we apply it too has one fewer elements than the previous time. Eventually we must apply LENGTH to the empty list ( ). But the empty list is handled by the first case, which does not involve invoking LENGTH again.

Thus when we return to the definition to find (LENGTH '( )), the first case holds, and the value returned is 0.

But now that we know the value of (LENGTH '( ))), we can go back and find the value of (LENGTH '(C)), which is defined to be the value of (PLUS 1 (LENGTH '( ))). This value is 1.

But knowing the value of (LENGTH ' (C)), we can compute the value of (LENGTH ' (B C)). By the definition the value of (LENGTH ' (B C)) equals the value of (PLUS 1 (LENGTH ' (C))), which is 2.

Finally, the value of (LENGTH ' (B C)) is used to calculate the value of (LENGTH ' (A B C)), as has already been illustrated.

To compute the value of (LENGTH ' (A B C)), then, the LENGTH function is invoked 4 times:

| Expression | Value |
|---|---|
| (LENGTH ' (A B C)) | 3 |
| (LENGTH ' (B C)) | 2 |
| (LENGTH ' (C)) | 1 |
| (LENGTH ' ( )) | 0 |

We can think of the computer as working its way down the expression column of this table and then back up the value column. The function LENGTH must be invoked four times before any values can be computed at all. The value of (LENGTH ' ( )) is computed first. This value is then used to compute the value of

(LENGTH '(C)), which is used to compute the value of (LENGTH ' (B C)), and so on.

We can summarize the essential features of a recursive definition as follows:

- The definition must contain a COND with at least two cases (there may be more).
- It must be possible to evaluate at least one of the cases without the use of the function being defined.
- When the function being defined is invoked, its argument must be simplified in such a way that repeated invocations will lead to a case that can be evaluated without invoking the function being defined again. (For instance, each time LENGTH was invoked its argument had one less element. Eventually (LENGTH ' ( )) was invoked, and this could be evaluated without invoking LENGTH again.)

Here is another example of a recursive definition. Suppose we want a function, SUBST, that will substitute a value for a variable in an expression. (Such a function would be useful in doing predicate logic, to name just one application.) The following illustrate SUBST:

    (SUBST 'TABLE 'X '(AT ROBOT X))
      (AT ROBOT TABLE)
    (SUBST 3 'X '(TIMES X X))
      (TIMES 3 3)
    (SUBST 'X (TIMES 5 5) 'Y '(PLUS 10 Y))
      (PLUS 10 (TIMES 5 5))

In general we want to define a function (SUBST X Y Z) that will substitute the value of X for the value of Y in the value of Z. The value of Y is not necessarily an atom, though it usually is in practical applications of the function.

Here is the recursive definition of SUBST:

(DEFINE (SUBST X Y Z)
        (COND ((EQUAL Y Z) X)
              ((ATOM Z) Z)
              (T (CONS (SUBST X Y (CAR Z))
                       (SUBST X Y (CDR Z))))))

SUBST has three cases. The first two do not invoke SUBST again; the third one does.

The first case is when the value being substituted for is the same as the value being substituted into:
(SUBST '(A B) 'U 'U)
  (A B)

In this case the value of X is returned.

The second case is where the value of Z is an atom which is not equal to the value being substituted for:

(SUBST '(A B) 'U 'V)

'V

In this case no substitution is possible, and the value of Z is returned.

The third case is where recursion takes place. We break the value of Z down in to (CAR Z) and (CDR Z). SUBST is then called to do the substitutions in (CAR Z) and (CDR Z). The resulting values are recombined into a single expression using CONS.

For example, suppose we are trying to find the value of (SUBST 'A 'U '((F U) (G U))). The value of Z is ((F U) (G U)); The value of (CAR Z) is (F U), and the value of (CDR Z) is ((G U)). Applying SUBST to (CAR Z) and (CDR Z) gives:

| Expression | Value |
|---|---|
| (SUBST X Y (CAR Z)) | (F A) |
| (SUBST X Y (CDR Z)) | ((G A)) |

(Remember that the value of X is A and the value of Y is U.) The CONS function adds (F A) to the list ((G A)) to obtain ((F A) (G A)), which is the value of (SUBST 'A 'U '((F U) (G U)))

Is the definition of SUBST a valid recursive definition? Or could it go into a loop, invoking SUBST repeatedly without end?.

The definition of SUBST is valid. If we repeatedly take CARs and CDRs of an expression, we will eventually arrive at an atom (possibly NIL). Therefore, eventually SUBST will be called with an atom for its third argument. Then one of the first two cases will apply (if the first case doesn't apply the second surely will). In fact, before the evaluation is complete, SUBST will have been invoked with every atom in the value of Z as its third argument.

### The Program Feature

Although recursive definitions are simple and elegant, they do not always represent the most efficient way to compute the value of a function. Every time a function invokes itself, information describing the invocation has to be stored inside the computer. This information takes up memory space, and time is required to store it. A recursive function may call on itself many times before any results are computed; much space and time can be taken up with the recursive calls before the computation of the desired value even begins.

The program feature of LISP allows one to define functions by means of programs similar to programs in other languages, such as

BASIC or FORTRAN. Many functions can be computed more efficiently by programs than by recursive definitions.

Let us illustrate with a program for LENGTH:

```
(DEFINE (LENGTH X)
        (PROG (N)
                (SETQ N O)
        LOOP
                (COND ((ATOM X) (RETURN N)))
                (SETQ N (PLUS N 1))
                (SETQ X (CDR X))
                (GO LOOP)))
```

PROG is the LISP function which interprets programs. It has the form:

$$(PROG\ \textit{local-variables}$$
$$\textit{program-step-1}$$
$$\bullet$$
$$\bullet$$
$$\bullet$$
$$\textit{program-step-n})$$

Immediately following the atom PROG is a list of local variables. (In LENGTH there is one local variable, N.) The program uses the local variables for "scratch pad" storage: a value that needs to be saved is assigned to a local variable in one part of the program; the assigned value is later used in another part of the program.

The variables are local in the sense that an assignment to one of them will not a affect the value of a variable with the same name outside the program. For instance, an assignment to N in the definiton of LENGTH will only affect the value of N in the definition of LENGTH. It will not affect the value of N elsewhere—in another function definition, for instance.

Following the list of local variables are the steps of the program. There are two kinds of program steps:

1. *Expressions.* These are lists such as:

$$(SETQ\ N\ (PLUS\ N\ 1))$$

These expressions serve the same purpose as "statements" in other languages. Although these expressions have values, their values are ignored; the expressions are evaluated for their "side effects" such as assigning values to variables. The above expression, for instance, increases the value of N by 1.

2. *Labels*. These are atoms; the only label in LENGTH is LOOP. These serve the same purpose as labels in assembly language or statement numbers in BASIC or FORTRAN. One can direct the computer to "go to" them from elsewhere in the program. In LENGTH, evaluating

> (GO LOOP) causes the expression following the atom LOOP to be evaluated next.

The program for LENGTH starts out by setting the value of N to O. It then checks to see if the value of X is an atom. If it is, (RETURN N) will stop the program from executing and return the value of N as the value of PROG and hence as the value of LENGTH. Currently the value of N is 0, so if the value of X is an atom, the value of (LENGTH X) will be 0, which is what is desired.

Assuming the value of X is not an atom, the program repeatedly executes a loop that extends from LOOP through the end of the program. Each time through the loop 1 is added to the value of N by

> (SETQ N (PLUS N 1))

and the first element is removed from the value of X by:

> (SETQ X (CDR X))

As the program goes around the loop it removes the elements from the value of X one-by-one, and uses N to count the number of elements removed. Eventually, all the elements will be removed, and the value of X will be ( ) or NIL. Since NIL is an atom,

> (COND ((ATOM X) (RETURN N)))

will cause the program to return the value of N. Since N counts the number of elements that have been removed, and all the elements have been removed, the value of N is the number of elements on the list that was the original value of X.

Suppose, for instance, we requested the value of (LENGTH '(A B C D E)). The initial value of X would be (A B C D E). The successive values of X and N each time the program reached the label LOOP would be:

| Value of X | Value of N |
|:----------:|:----------:|
| (A B C D E) | 0 |
| (B C D E) | 1 |
| (C D E) | 2 |
| (D E) | 3 |
| (E) | 4 |
| ( ) | 5 |

241

Since ( ) is an atom, (COND ((ATOM X) (RETURN N))) would cause PROG to return the value 5, which is the correct value for (LENGTH '(A B C D E)).

When should we use recursion and when should we use a programmed loop? It is usually not efficient to use recursion when we are merely working through the elements of a list. Thus the recursive definition of LENGTH (which simply counts the elements on a list) is a poor one. The programmed version counts the elements faster and using less memory, since we do not have a new invocation of LENGTH for every element on the list.

Then when is recursion recommended? Many data structures contain parts which have the same form as the structure itself. A list can contain other lists as elements. An expression can contain subexpressions, which are themselves expressions. A tree can contain subtrees. If we are defining a function to process a list, an expression, or a tree, it is natural to call the function being defined to process an element that is a list, a subexpression, or a subtree. The same results can be achieved using the program feature, but the resulting program is usually much more complicated than the recursive function definition.

Another consideration is this. Let us call the depth of nesting the number of times an item contains a similar item as a part. In the list

$$(A \ B \ (C \ (D \ E) \ F) \ G \ H)$$

the depth of nesting for (D E) is 2, since (D E) is an element of (C (D E) F) which is in turn an element of (A B (C (D E) F) G H). Usually this depth of nesting is fairly small—much smaller than the number of elements on a typical list. As a result, the number of recursive calls is minimized, and so is the inefficiency associated with recursion.

In LISP, we use the CAR function to go from a list to its first element, which may also be a list. On the other hand, when we are simply working through the elements of a list, we use CDR to remove the elements one-by-one, thereby exposing succeeding elements on the list. Thus recursions involving the CAR of a list are usually appropriate; but those involving the CDR could usually best be replaced by programmed loops.

For instance, the function SUBST defined in the last section involves two recursive calls:

$$(SUBST \ X \ Y \ (CAR \ Z))$$
$$(SUBST \ X \ Y \ (CDR \ Z))$$

From what has just been said we know we can improve the efficiency of SUBST by retaining the recursion involving CAR but replacing the one involving CDR by a programmed loop. Doing this, we get the following program:

```
(DEFINE (SUBST X Y Z)
        (PROG (U V)
              (COND ((EQUAL Y Z) (RETURN X))
                    ((ATOM Z) (RETURN Z)))
         LOOP
              (COND ((NULL Z) (RETURN U)))
              (SETQ V (SUBST X Y (CAR Z)))
              (SETQ U (APPEND U (LIST V)))
              (SETQ Z (CDR Z))
              (GO LOOP)))
```

The program starts out by checking for the cases (EQUAL Y Z) and (ATOM Z), just as the recursive definition did. If (EQUAL Y Z) is T, the value of X is returned as the value of the function; if (ATOM Z) is T, the value of Z is returned as the value of the function.

Otherwise, the loop beginning at LOOP is executed repeatedly. Each time through the loop (SETQ Z (CDR Z)) removes the current first element of the value of Z. Thus each element on the original value of Z takes its turn as being the first element.

Each time through the loop

(SETQ V (SUBST X Y (CAR Z)))

calls SUBST recursively to perform the substitution on the first element of Z. The result of performing the substitution is assigned to the local variable V. As we repeat the loop, each element of the original list will take its turn as the first element of Z. The successive values of V will be the results of performing the substitution on those elements.

The list which results from performing the substitution on each element of the original value of Z is built up as the value of the local variable U. Local variables always start out with the value NIL; thus the value of U is initially the empty list. Each time through the loop the current value of V is added to the end of that list by

(SETQ U (APPEND U (LIST V)))

The function (LIST V) surrounds the value of V with one set of parentheses, making it into a one-element list: the value of (LIST 'A) is (A). This one-element list is then appended to the value of U; the result is that the value of V is added as an element to the value of U.

Eventually all the elements will be removed from the value of Z, and the value of Z will be ( ). The predicate NULL returns T for the empty list and NIL otherwise. Thus when all the elements of the original value of Z have been processed, and the processed elements have been placed on the list U, then

(COND ((NULL Z) (RETURN U)))

returns the value of U as the value of PROG and hence as the value of SUBST.

Suppose, for instance, the value of this is requested:

(SUBST 'A 'B '((C B) (B D)))

The values of X and Y will be 'A and 'B respectively. The values of Z, U, and V each time the computer reaches the label LOOP are as follows:

| Z | U | V |
|---|---|---|
| ((C B) (B D)) | ( ) | ( ) |
| ((B D)) | ((C A)) | (C A) |
| ( ) | ((C A) (A D)) | (A D) |

Finally, versions of LISP on large computers have a function, MAPCAR, that will apply another function to every element of a list. Using MAPCAR is even more efficient than using a programmed loop. The looping still takes place, but it takes place in the machine-language routine that implements MAPCAR rather than in the LISP program.

### Property Lists

As has been mentioned already, LISP associates a property list with each atom. The property list carries information that we wish to associate with a particular atom. On the proptery list of ROBOT, for instance, we might place everything we need to know about the robot—its location, whether or not it is holding something, and so on.

In LISP the *data base*—the information that the program needs about the world it is manipulating is usually stored on the property lists.

The property list of an atom is not usually manipulated using list-manipulating functions such as CAR, CDR, APPEND, and so on. Instead, special functions are provided for manipulating property lists. The most important of these are GET and PUTPROP.

For instance, suppose that in the robot-in-the-room problem that we have been using as an example, we wished to record that the current location of the robot is the alcove. We could write:

(PUTPROP 'ROBOT 'ALCOVE 'LOCATION)

This gives the property LOCATION the value ALCOVE. If the property LOCATION is not already on the property list of ROBOT, it is placed on that property list, again with the value ALCOVE. To find the location of the robot, we would use the function GET:

> (GET 'ROBOT 'LOCATION)
> ALCOVE

To record a move of the robot to a new location we would change the value of the property location using PUTPTOP:

> (PUTPROP 'ROBOT 'TABLE 'LOCATION)

after which GET would yield:

> (GET 'ROBOT 'LOCATION)
> TABLE

Since each atom has its own property list, we can easily keep track of the locations of as many different robots as we wish:

> (PUTPROP 'ROBOT1 'ALCOVE 'LOCATION)
> ALCOVE
> (PUTPROP 'ROBOT2 'TABLE 'LOCATION)
> TABLE
> (GET 'ROTOT1 'LOCATION)
> ALCOVE
> (GET 'ROBOT2 'LOCATION)
> TABLE

Notice that the value of the PUTPROP function is the value that it places on the property list: the value of (PUTPROP 'ROBOT 'ALCOVE 'LOCATION) is ALCOVE. Despite this, PUTPROP is another function that is executed more for its side effects than for the value it returns. The important thing is the change PUTPROP makes in the property list and not the value of the expression containing it.

### Other Versions of LISP

As is the case with some other languages, different people who have written LISP interpreters have implemented slightly different versions of the language. As is usual in these cases you must consult the language manual for the particular version you are using to see exactly what features are available and how they have been implemented. Here are a few of the major differences between the version of LISP described in this chapter and some other versions:

In some versions of LISP one must use the function QUOTE instead of a single quote mark. One writes (QUOTE A) instead of 'A.

This makes expressions such as

(SUBST 'A 'B '((C B) (B D)))

**much** clumsier:

(SUBST (QUOTE A) (QUOTE B) (QUOTE ((C B) (B D))))

In order that users may retain their sanity, versions of LISP that use the QUOTE function usually provide a way of entering functions and their arguments that does not require quoting all the arguments. Thus instead of typing in

(CONS (QUOTE A) (QUOTE (B C D)))

one can type

CONS (A (B D C))

That is, one types in a *pair* consisting of a function CONS and a list of arguments (A (B C D)). The arguments on the list are automatically quoted, so the use of the clumsy QUOTE function is avoided. As usual, the computer returns the value of the function:

CONS (A (B C D))
(A B C D)

Notice that the simplified version works only when functions and their arguments are typed in for immediate evaluation. When an expression involving functions occurs in another function definition, the long form must be used.

Function definitions involve a function LAMBDA which assigns the values of the arguments of a function to the dummy variables used in the definition. (The name LAMBDA comes from the fact that mathematicians use the Greek letter lambda to stand for this function.) In many older versions of LISP, for instance, the definition of the function SQUARE would be written

DEFINE (((SQUARE (LAMBDA (X) (TIMES X X)))))

instead of the simpler

(DEFINE (SQUARE X) (TIMES X X))

used in most modern versions. (The LAMBDA function is available in modern versions and can be used for special purposes, as when one wants to define a function without giving it a name. But one doesn't have to use LAMBDA in every definition.)

The function SETQ can only be used inside function definitions. To directly enter a request for the computer to assign a particular value to an atom, one uses a function CSETQ instead of SETQ.

## LISP Interpreters

LISP can be implemented on small computers. An implementation for the PDP-8 minicomputers is given in the bibliography. The listing of this interpreter would be well worth studying by anyone who would like to implement LISP on a personal computer. The PDP-8 interpreter occupies about 2K words; this would correspond to about 4K bytes on a microprocessor.

# Bibliography

**GENERAL**

1. Edward Feigenbaum and Julian Feldman, eds., *Computers and Thought,* McGraw-Hill, New York, 1963.
2. Philip Jackson, Jr., *Introduction to Artificial Intelligence,* Petrocelli/Charter, New York, 1974.
3. Nils J. Nilsson, *Problem-Solving Methods in Artificial Intelligence,* McGraw-Hill, New York, 1971.
4. Bertram Raphael, *The Thinking Computer,* W. H. Freeman, San Francisco, 1976.
6. James. R. Slagel, *Artificial Intelligence: The Heuristic Programming Approach,* McGraw-Hill, New York, 1971.
7. Patrick Henry Winston, *Artificial Intelligence,* Addison-Wesley, Reading, Mass., 1977.

**PROBLEM SOLVING TECHNIQUES**

8. Wayne A. Wickelgren, *How to Solve Problems,* W. H. Freeman, San Francisco, 1974.
See also [3] and [6].

**PLANNING**

9. Earl D. Sacerdoti, *A Structure for Plans and Behavior,* Elsevier, New York, 1977.

**CHESS**

10. Peter W. Frey, ed., *Chess Skill in Man and Machine,* Springer-Verlag, New York, 1977.
11. Edward W. Kozdrowicki and Dennis W. Cooper, "COKO III: The Cooper-Koz Chess Program," *Communications of the ACM,* July, 1973, p. 411.

12. Monroe Newborn, *Computer Chess*, Academic Press, New York, 1975.
13. Herbert A. Simon and William G. Chase, "Skill in Chess," *American Scientist*, July-August, 1973, p. 394.
14. Albert L. Zobrist and Frederic R. Carlson, Jr., "An Advice-Taking Chess Computer,"*Scientific American*, June, 1973, p. 92.

## PATTERN RECOGNITION AND PERCEPTION

15. Partrick Henry Winston, ed., *The Psychology of Computer Vision*, McGraw-Hill, New York, 1975.
See also [2] and [7].

## ROBOTS

16. James S. Albus and John M. Evans, Jr., "Robot Systems," *Scientific American*, February, 1976, p. 76.
17. David Heisman, *Building Your Own Working Robot*, TAB Boos, Blue Ridge Summit, Pa., 1976.
18. Ralph Hollis, "Newt: A Mobile, Cognitive Robot," *Byte*, June, 1977, p. 30.
19. James L. Nevins and Daniel E. Whitney, "Computer-Controlled Assembly," *Scientific American*, February, 1978, p. 62.

## COMPUTATIONAL LOGIC

See [3] and [6].

## NATURAL LANGUAGE PROCESSING

21. Roger C. Schank, *et. al.*, "Inference and Paraphrase by Computer," *Journal of the Association for Computing Machinery*, July, 1975, 309.
22. R. Simmons and J. Slocum, "Generating English Discourse from Sematic Networks," *Communications of the ACM*, October, 1972, p. 891.
See also [7].
20. Neil M. Goldman, "Sentence Paraphrasing from a Conceptual Base," *Communications of the ACM*, February, 1975, p. 96.

## LISP

23. G. van der Mey and W. L. van der Poel, *A Lisp Interpreter for the PDP-8*, DECUS (Digital Equipment Corporation User's Society), Maynard, Mass., 1968, DECUS No. 8-102a. Program writeup, program listing, and paper tape are available.
See also [7].

# Index